VOLUME 558

THE ANNALS

of The American Academy *of* Political
and Social Science

ALAN W. HESTON, *Editor*
NEIL A. WEINER, *Assistant Editor*

AMERICANS AND RELIGIONS
IN THE TWENTY-FIRST CENTURY

Special Editor of this Volume

WADE CLARK ROOF
University of California
Santa Barbara

 SAGE Periodicals Press *THOUSAND OAKS LONDON NEW DELHI*

The American Academy of Political and Social Science

3937 Chestnut Street   Philadelphia, Pennsylvania 19104

Board of Directors

ELIJAH ANDERSON
LYNN A. CURTIS
LANI GUINIER
FREDERICK HELDRING
KATHLEEN HALL JAMIESON
RICHARD D. LAMBERT

IRA A. LIPMAN
SARA MILLER McCUNE
MARY ANN MEYERS
HENRY W. SAWYER, III
ANTHONY J. SCIRICA

Officers

President

Vice President
KATHLEEN HALL JAMIESON, *First Vice President*

Secretary
ANTHONY J. SCIRICA

Treasurer
MARY ANN MEYERS

Counsel
HENRY W. SAWYER, III

Business Manager
MARY E. PARKER

Editors, THE ANNALS

ALAN W. HESTON, *Editor*
ERICA GINSBURG, *Managing Editor*

RICHARD D. LAMBERT, *Editor Emeritus*
NEIL A. WEINER, *Assistant Editor*

Origin and Purpose. The Academy was organized December 14, 1889, to promote the progress of political and social science, especially through publications and meetings. The Academy does not take sides in controverted questions, but seeks to gather and present reliable information to assist the public in forming an intelligent and accurate judgment.

Meetings. The Academy occasionally holds a meeting in the spring extending over two days.

Publications. THE ANNALS of the American Academy of Political and Social Science is the bimonthly publication of The Academy. Each issue contains articles on some prominent social or political problem, written at the invitation of the editors. Also, monographs are published from time to time, numbers of which are distributed to pertinent professional organizations. These volumes constitute important reference works on the topics with which they deal, and they are extensively cited by authorities throughout the United States and abroad. The papers presented at the meetings of The Academy are included in THE ANNALS.

Membership. Each member of The Academy receives THE ANNALS and may attend the meetings of The Academy. Membership is open only to individuals. Annual dues: $51.00 for the regular paperbound edition (clothbound, $74.00). Add $12.00 per year for membership outside the U.S.A. Members may also purchase single issues of THE ANNALS for $15.00 each (clothbound, $19.00). Add $2.00 for shipping and handling on all pre-paid orders.

Subscriptions. THE ANNALS of the American Academy of Political and Social Science (ISSN 0002-7162) is published six times annually—in January, March, May, July, September, and November. Institutions may subscribe to THE ANNALS at the annual rate: $220.00 (clothbound, $260.00). Add $12.00 per year for subscriptions outside the U.S.A. Institutional rates for single issues: $39.00 each (clothbound, $45.00).

Periodical postage paid at Thousand Oaks, California, and additional offices.

Single issues of THE ANNALS may be obtained by individuals who are not members of The Academy for $19.00 each (clothbound, $29.00). Add $2.00 for shipping and handling on all prepaid orders. Single issues of THE ANNALS have proven to be excellent supplementary texts for classroom use. Direct inquiries regarding adoptions to THE ANNALS c/o Sage Publications (address below).

All correspondence concerning membership in The Academy, dues renewals, inquiries about membership status, and/or purchase of single issues of THE ANNALS should be sent to THE ANNALS c/o Sage Publications, Inc., 2455 Teller Road, Thousand Oaks, CA 91320. Telephone: (805) 499-0721; FAX/Order line: (805) 499-0871. *Please note that orders under $30 must be prepaid.* Sage affiliates in London and India will assist institutional subscribers abroad with regard to orders, claims, and inquiries for both subscriptions and single issues.

Postmaster: Send address changes to the Annals of the American Academy of Political and Social Science c/o Sage Publications, Inc., 2455 Teller Road, Thousand Oaks, CA 91320.

Printed on recycled, acid-free paper

THE ANNALS

© 1998 *by* The American Academy *of* Political *and* Social Science

Editorial Office: 3937 Chestnut Street, Philadelphia, PA 19104.

For information about membership* (individuals only) and subscriptions (institutions), address:

SAGE PUBLICATIONS, INC.
2455 Teller Road
Thousand Oaks, CA 91320

From India and South Asia,		*From the UK, Europe, the Middle*
write to:		*East and Africa, write to:*
SAGE PUBLICATIONS INDIA Pvt. Ltd		SAGE PUBLICATIONS LTD
P.O. Box 4215		6 Bonhill Street
New Delhi 110 048		London EC2A 4PU
INDIA		UNITED KINGDOM

SAGE Production Staff: KELLY GUNTHER, ERIC LAW, DORIS HUS, and JOHN SHAW
*Please note that members of The Academy receive THE ANNALS with their membership.
Library of Congress Catalog Card Number 96-67081
International Standard Serial Number ISSN 0002-7162
International Standard Book Number ISBN 0-7619-1310-6 (Vol. 558, 1998 paper)
International Standard Book Number ISBN 0-7619-1309-2 (Vol. 558, 1998 cloth)
Manufactured in the United States of America. First printing, July 1998.

The articles appearing in THE ANNALS are indexed in *Academic Index, Book Review Index, Combined Retrospective Index Sets, Current Contents, General Periodicals Index, Public Affairs Information Service Bulletin, Pro-Views,* and *Social Sciences Index.* They are also abstracted and indexed in *ABC Pol Sci, America: History and Life, Automatic Subject Citation Alert, Book Review Digest, Family Resources Database, Higher Education Abstracts, Historical Abstracts, Human Resources Abstracts, International Political Science Abstracts, Managing Abstracts, Periodica Islamica, Sage Urban Studies Abstracts, Social Planning/Policy & Development Abstracts, Social Sciences Citation Index, Social Work Research & Abstracts, Sociological Abstracts, United States Political Science Documents,* and/or *Work Related Abstracts, Westlaw,* and are available on microfilm from University Microfilms, Ann Arbor, Michigan.

Information about membership rates, institutional subscriptions, and back issue prices may be found on the facing page.

Advertising. Current rates and specifications may be obtained by writing to THE ANNALS Advertising and Promotion Manager at the Thousand Oaks office (address above).

Claims. Claims for undelivered copies must be made no later than twelve months following month of publication. The publisher will supply missing copies when losses have been sustained in transit and when the reserve stock will permit.

Change of Address. Six weeks' advance notice must be given when notifying of change of address to ensure proper identification. Please specify name of journal. Send address changes to: THE ANNALS of the American Academy of Political and Social Science, c/o Sage Publications, Inc., 2455 Teller Road, Thousand Oaks, CA 91320.

THE ANNALS

of The American Academy *of* Political *and* Social Science

ALAN W. HESTON, *Editor*
NEIL A. WEINER, *Assistant Editor*

─────────────── **FORTHCOMING** ───────────────

THE CHANGING EDUCATIONAL
QUALITY OF THE WORKFORCE
Special Editors: Robert Zemsky and Peter Cappelli
Volume 559   September 1998

THE FUTURE OF FACT
Special Editors: Elihu Katz and Jeffrey J. Strange
Volume 560   November 1998

EMOTIONAL LABOR IN THE SERVICE ECONOMY
Special Editors: Ronnie J. Steinberg and Deborah M. Figart
Volume 561   January 1999

───

See page 2 for information on Academy membership and
purchase of single volumes of **The Annals.**

CONTENTS

BOOK DEPARTMENT CONTENTS

INTERNATIONAL RELATIONS AND POLITICS

AFRICA, ASIA, AND LATIN AMERICA

EUROPE

UNITED STATES

SOCIOLOGY

ECONOMICS

IN MEMORIAM

It is with great sadness and regret that the American Academy takes note of the death of its president, Marvin E. Wolfgang. Dr. Wolfgang served as president of the Academy from 1972 until his untimely death at age 73 in April of this year.

Dr. Wolfgang was director of the Sellin Center for Studies in Criminology and Criminal Law of the University of Pennsylvania, where he continued a long and extremely influential tradition of quantitative and theoretical studies in the sociology of crime. His early study in 1958, *Patterns of Criminal Homicide*, began a lifelong practice of grounding criminology in a strong empirical base that was to shape research in the field and forever change our understanding of murderers and their victims. Another of his early studies, *The Measurement of Delinquency* (1964), jointly authored with Thorsten Sellin, his mentor and the longtime editor of *The Annals*, set a standard for judging the seriousness of delinquent behavior.

Delinquency in a Birth Cohort, with T. Sellin and R. Figlio, published in 1972, became a model for quantitative studies combining longitudinal and cross-sectional data aimed at understanding the relationship of society, delinquency, and criminal behavior. For the last 10 years, Dr. Wolfgang carried on a collaborative study of a delinquency cohort in China modeled on this and other studies.

Among his many honors, Dr. Wolfgang received two Guggenheim Fellowships, a Fulbright Scholarship, the Dennis Carrol Prize from the International Society of Criminology, the very prestigious August Vollmer Research Award from the American Society of Criminology, the Beccaria Gold Medal for outstanding contribution to criminology from the German, Austrian and Swiss Society of Criminology, and honorary doctor of law degrees from the City University of New York and the Academia Mexicana de Derecho Internacional. He was the first recipient of an award established in his name by Guardsmark, Inc., for distinguished achievement in criminology. His contributions to criminology were perhaps best summarized in 1994 by the *British Journal of Criminology*, which called him "the most influential criminologist in the English-speaking world." This influence was extended through his scholarship, his very active involvement in public policy including service on many national commissions, his strong opposition to the death penalty, and a large number of students who have carried on his tradition of quantitative criminology and involvement in public policy.

As president of the Academy, Dr. Wolfgang organized many outstanding Annual Meetings on a variety of national and international subjects, including a major meeting celebrating the U.S. bicentennial. During a period of increasing academic specialization, Dr. Wolfgang helped guide the Academy toward maintaining the unique position of *The Annals*, a position that was facilitated by moving the publication of the journal from the Academy to Sage Publications. At the time of his death, Dr. Wolfgang was working with the Board of the Academy to introduce a number of changes in the Academy, which are likely to be implemented in the near future.

A salute to the long and distinguished career of Dr. Wolfgang and his dedicated service to the Academy.

PREFACE

As a new century approaches, we have the opportunity to reflect on the role and significance of religion in the United States. From one perspective, a new century is no more than an imposed ordering of time bearing little intrinsic meaning; yet from another, it is a marker of some consequence regarding the future of institutions and traditions that have for so long played a part in shaping American society. For a country where religion is so voluntaristic, and hence always in some degree of flux, it is an occasion for mapping where we are in relation to the past and for speculating about where we might be going. Religion is particularly well suited as a basis for such critical reflection since its themes reach so deeply into American public life and widely influence our notions of national identity and experience.

Martin E. Marty sets the tone for this exercise in reflection in the lead article, "Revising the Map of American Religion." In it, he forces us to confront the discontinuities, innovations, and other evidence of religious fluidity that cannot be contained by neat boundaries and categorical styles of thinking. Marty is concerned with conceptual maps and suggests that we must increasingly draw from both ways of conceiving American religion—as bounded and less bounded, if not unbounded. Examples of the first are distinct institutions and traditions, long privileged in social analysis of religion; examples of the second are the fluid religious and spiritual identities that have characterized the scene especially in recent decades. While the latter hardly replace the former, the former without the latter are incomplete. As we shall see, boundary themes of the sort Marty describes surface in one way or another in the articles that follow.

In another general article, N. J. Demerath III examines what amounts to a long-standing shibboleth of American life: the notion that ours is an exceptionally religious society. Because religion is so closely linked with our national identity and ideology, it lends itself to self-congratulatory embellishment and notions of a distinct, tightly bound religious culture. Looking at the United States in comparison with a dozen or so other countries, Demerath considers three major religious aspects: civil religion, religious organizations and congregations, and individual belief and behavior. In each instance, he exposes the misguided assumptions and faulty religious and cultural comparisons lying behind American claims of exceptionalism and offers a more balanced perspective of America's uniqueness, concluding that we should think of it more as a matter of kind than degree.

Juan Eduardo Campo looks at pilgrimage centers generally in the United States. Often neglected in analysis of American religion, these centers reflect a popular, diverse style of religious life, tapping emotions and undergirding experiences that cannot be contained by conventional religious structures. Campo looks at three types of pilgrimage centers: those of civil religion, organized religion, and cultural religion. His interpretation suggests that, while they are all obviously different, Catholic pilgrimage centers and places like Gettysburg and Disneyland function very much alike in sustaining popular religious culture. Modernity, he suggests, is resulting in the globalizing of pilgrimages and is restructuring them by means of expert systems and the use of contemporary technologies, which make it increasingly possible for Americans (and others) to "cross large time-space distances" in imagery and experience and to re-create a sense of place.

Many of the articles focus upon the historical religious traditions so identified with American culture. William McKinney comments upon what has come to be called mainline Protestantism: once a well-established religious culture and set of institutions with considerable public influence but, in this century, without their privileged role and status. McKinney points to this tradition's historical function of bridging conflicting ideas and movements and ponders the future of its liberal ethos and value system, precisely at a time when a mediating voice is needed in the public square. Despite diminished influence, he points to some positive developments: the rediscovery of a social ministry; greater opportunities for women; racial, ethnic, and gay and lesbian inclusiveness; expanded lay ministries; interfaith dialogue; a reclaiming of hymnody and worship; and the birth of new institutions devoted to specialized and cooperative ministries.

The situation for evangelical Protestantism is vastly different, given decades of membership growth and an increasing commitment to engaging the culture. But that engagement varies in what appears to be a growing split within the more conservative Protestant sector. Mark A. Shibley looks at the world-affirming version of evangelicalism, emphasizing seeker-friendly megachurches, widespread acceptance of popular culture, adaptable organizational forms, and a prosperity ethic congenial with middle-class values. Shibley underscores the point that we should not confound born-again Christianity and the cultural politics of the Christian Right. While there is overlap, resurgent popular evangelicalism is not to be understood as a reactionary social movement; neither is this style of evangelicalism to be explained necessarily by strict moral and doctrinal boundaries distinguishing it from the wider society. Looking at the more marginalized and reactionary religious constituencies, Mark Juergensmeyer focuses upon the wave of antimodernism that has brought violence to many parts of the world and now to the United States. Militia movements and attacks on abortion clinics, fueled in part by reconstruction theology and Christian Identity thinking, remind us that the legitimacy of modern, egalitarian society is in question for those who see themselves as threatened by social and cultural change, both real and perceived. Moreover, we are made aware that struggles over religiously based conceptions of America and its values remain just beneath the surface and, indeed, often erupt into the public domain.

For African Americans, the role of the church has always had its distinctive features, combining black consciousness and religious ethics. But as Cheryl

Townsend Gilkes points out, the contemporary black church is a remarkably adaptive institution. Increasingly, she argues, it is being transformed by the expansion of a black middle class, professionalization of its services, new styles of worship, and changing gender relations, including growing numbers of women clergy. In some ways, the new urban, middle-class black church resembles the popular evangelicalism of white America, yet, in other ways, it remains distinctive in its tradition of adaptation to changing historical circumstances. As Gilkes says, the "mighty causes" of civil justice and socio-economic equality continue to call.

American Catholicism since the period of Vatican Council II has been in a state of accelerated change. Two commentators offer their interpretations. Michele Dillon considers the paradox arising out of the simultaneous rejection of papal teaching and an enduring commitment to Rome on the part of many Catholics. Rather than leaving the church, these Catholics claim the author-ity to interpret doctrine and draw off their own "lived" faith and knowledge; empowered by the heritage to critique those aspects of doctrine and practice they cannot accept, independently minded believers revamp their religious styles yet hold on to their Catholic identities. Mary Johnson recognizes a disjuncture between institution and spirit and speculates about the emer-gence of a "spiritual-institutional" church that "weaves spiritualities through institutions in new, and old, ways." She discusses what she calls "spiritual capital" within the Catholic tradition and is optimistic about the changes that should come with younger generations, changes she thinks will reshape Catholic narratives and spiritual styles. In both articles, we see the working out within America's largest religious community of Marty's more unbounded, fluid religious and spiritual themes.

Roger Friedland and Richard Hecht look at Jerusalem as symbol and stone, at the religious and political aspects of this important city on the global stage. They sort out the intricacies of the city's sacrality and sovereignty with particular attention to how it functions for Israeli and Palestinian politics and the growing symbolic importance of Jerusalem for American evangelical Christians. The complex linkages between this city and religious communi-ties in the United States are discussed in some detail, underscoring that Jerusalem is a global symbol not just for Jews but also for Christians and Muslims.

Few developments have had more long-term impact upon American reli-gion in this past half-century than the shift in immigration patterns. This demographic shift is a subject for discussion in two articles. Anthony M. Stevens-Arroyo looks at the increase in Latino populations and changing ethnic and religious styles. Cultural and institutional changes flowing from this expanded stream of immigration are, however gradually, bringing about recognition and acceptance of the experiences of Latinos and Latinas as part of the American mosaic and as altering both the Protestant and Catholic landscapes. Ideological as well as analytic considerations are discussed in some detail. Raymond Brady Williams gives attention to immigrants from

India and Pakistan, immigrants who are bringing Hindu, Sikh, Jain, Muslim, and Christian traditions to the United States. Williams observes how these groups, like many other immigrant groups before them, are often more religiously active in this country than they were in their homelands. With the changing demographics and rapid movement of these constituencies into the American mainstream, it is also obvious that an older Judeo-Christian tradition fashioned in earlier decades of this century is now losing its hold upon the culture and that, in its place, is emerging, as Williams says, "a reformulation, a revision, or perhaps a negotiation of a new synthesis" of American public religious values.

The two final articles in the collection address more generally the future, one article focusing upon emergent religious forms and the other upon generational shifts in religious views. Donald E. Miller discusses "new-paradigm" churches which, as he says, are "appropriating stylistic and organizational elements" of a changing culture. Miller raises the possibility of a postdenominational Christianity with substantial changes in worship and music, a restructuring of religious organizations, and further democratization in access to the sacred—changes that, as he says, stem from a challenge not of the message but of the medium through which the message is presented. In my own article, I single out the widespread interest in spirituality by the post–World War II generations as a marker of unease with conventional religious belief and practice and of a corresponding quest for a more experiential, deeply meaningful lived faith. What this might mean for American religious life, and for organized religion in particular, is discussed along with several possible scenarios of the future.

WADE CLARK ROOF

ANNALS, *AAPSS*, **558**, July 1998

Revising the Map of American Religion

By MARTIN E. MARTY

ABSTRACT: The concept of mapping religion and then acting on the basis of that concept necessarily involves discussion of another concept, that of boundaries. The notion of discerning neat boundaries serves well for assessing the inherited institutions of religion in America; assessments of trends within them reveal impressive continuities in organization and structures of meaning. Many of the most important religious developments in the last third of the century, however, appear to be less bounded—or even unbounded—and on the blurry landscape of boundarylessness there are more evident discontinuities, innovations, and evidence of fluidity. An analysis of several trends on the unbounded landscape suggests that, in the new century, there will be a great deal of interchange and conflict between these two ways of conceiving American religious dynamics.

Martin E. Marty, the Fairfax M. Cone Distinguished Service Professor Emeritus at the University of Chicago, directs the Public Religion Project. A fellow of the American Academy of Political and Social Science, he has most recently published The One and the Many: America's Struggle for the Common Good.

THE concept of boundaries has become central in much social scientific and political discourse. The acts of defining boundaries, transgressing them, and being limited by them enter into discussions of power and other elements in human relations. In the simplest physical as well as metaphorical sense, mapmakers serve geographers and citizens by drawing boundaries. The cartographers follow upon the work of surveyors, who measure the landscape and determine, for example, where the lines between states should fall.

When a coastline or a river provides a natural barrier and matches the line between political jurisdictions, it is easy for mapmakers to provide a line of demarcation that will be both visible and credible to all who use the map. When their drawn lines cross and interrupt undifferentiated prairie or desert landscapes, however, they will be indiscernible to people on the landscape and credible only for limited purposes. The rendered boundary lines announce, for example, that here Arizona ends; here New Mexico begins. So it is and shall be, we shall see, with what is natural and what seems arbitrary in the situation of religion and matters of the spirit on the American landscape today.

The eyes of children or naive adults can help the literal-minded to see what they had earlier missed on the landscape and to become suspicious of the all-purpose serviceability of the lines cartographers draw on the maps that are designed to represent the reality of physical sites. In *Strange Dreams* (1996), Brian Andreas gives voice to the vision of the child and the unsophisticated in books that listen to unnamed "StoryPeople," who express themselves through hand-stamped print, as if epigrammatically. One of these "tweaks," as the author calls them, quotes an anonymous, folkloric "he" who says, "I like Geography best, he said, because your mountains & rivers know the secret. Pay no attention to boundaries."

Whoever would assess American religious phenomena at this century's end will and must "pay attention to boundaries" that have been drawn over the spiritual landscape. But it has become more and more apparent that scholars must also be attentive to what secrets the figurative "mountains and rivers" know and what they reveal about religious circumstances and movements.

THE LIMITED LEGITIMACY OF BOUNDARIES

"Pay no attention to boundaries," yet boundaries are there. Whoever enters a small city will notice that at once. At the edge of town, a sign erected by the local service club will list a number of separate bounded entities, thus: "The churches of —— welcome you." Similarly, in a city of any size, the Yellow Pages of the telephone book, in its always extensive entry "Churches and Synagogues" (a section bounded alphabetically by "Chiropractors" and "Cigars"), will list hundreds of institutional embodiments of what the people in them—which means in denominations and then congregations—would argue are essentially expressions of boundless spiritual realities.

A reader of this section of the phone book will find in the alphabetized sequence of denominations and congregations a list of institutions that are very vivid to those who belong to them. For many adherents, these organizations simply represent religion for them. Thus religion equals church or synagogue participation. But the alphabetical and institutional approach is at the same time confusing and arbitrary. The boundaries between the entities that fall under the letter U, for example, are thick and well defined. Here are Ukrainian Orthodox, Unitarian Universalist, United Church of Christ, United Holy Church of America, United Methodist, United Pentecostal, United Protestant, Unity School of Christianity, Universal Fellowship of Metropolitan Community Churches, and Unification Church. Transgress any boundary and you will be aware of the reality of the different worlds that these various U denominations represent.

Some observers, noting the erosion of authority and the apparent increase of religion not tied to institutions, speak of this as a postdenominational age, or at least a time when denominational life has become especially problematic.[1] Observing adherents close to the figurative landscape, as they interview people and watch them in action, the reporters and scholars emerge with very different agents' descriptions from the descriptions offered by agents bounded by denominations and similar inherited institutions. The mountains and rivers of the spirit lay bare their secrets. In such cases, the "pay no attention to boundaries" dictum makes sense. We are shortly to pursue some of the kinds of boundaryless distinctions that Brian Andreas tweaks in his apt and provocative word about landscapes and boundaries.

AMBIGUITY OVER
BOUNDARIES

Boundaries are helpful for describing the contours of American religion in two prominent ways. Both of them suggest relative continuity and even changelessness in the religious scene. The first, as noted, demarcates denominations and congregations. The second represents the lines social scientists apply after engaging in survey research, especially by polling the public.

Concerning the former, little need be said here since there is little news on the boundary front. Whoever consults the *Yearbook of the American and Canadian Churches 1997* will find that for all the changes of the half-century—sexual revolutions, the invention of the Internet, radical theological experiments, ecumenical endeavors, and the like—the yearbook for 1997 will not look much different from that of 1947 (Bedell 1997). There were and are over 200 church bodies, their changed names reflecting chiefly mergers within denominational families, not across boundaries between them. Therefore, there are subtle redrawings of the denominational family trees as various subgroups of Presbyterians, Lutherans, and the like find others of their subgroup kin, and link with them. When the Evangelical and Reformed merged with the Congregational Christian body in 1957 to form the United Church of Christ, they manifested an impressive exception more than they set a trend.

In respect to morale and prosperity, of course, these denominations have enjoyed or suffered very differing and sometimes surprising fates. Together, the leaders of all of them know there has been a general subversion of authority as the laity and local clergy have questioned the hierarchies or the church convention rulings and then generally gone their own ways whenever they found denominational stipulations to be inconvenient or uncongenial.

The boundary line has tended to hold with respect to the issue of who gets to enter the clergy—do women? Homosexuals? This was in most cases the question that represented the first and last line of meaningful denominational authority. It has become increasingly difficult to excommunicate those who were perceived to have become errant and wayward, or even to picture leadership or the community as a whole trying to exercise rights to excommunicate or to claim such rights.

Consequently, many of the old purposes of denominations have eroded or disappeared, making it less valid or valuable than before to "pay attention" to denominational boundaries. They now served less well than they had been devised and intended to serve, for instance, as signalers or definers of the actual beliefs of members. For one thing, most denominations or movements could not always contain the polarized parties within them. One had to ask what kind of Catholic or Presbyterian it was who encountered you, so vastly did they differ from each other. Using a doctrinal textbook or a manual of discipline would as likely miscue or mislead an interviewer of many typical Lutherans or Methodists, so vaguely would their belief and behavior match the boundaries on the printed page.[2]

As with their intentions, so with their realities: fates among them differed. Those called "mainstream" in Protestantism, and, with them, many in Roman Catholicism, continued to relate to population cohorts of those who told poll-takers they preferred or found their identity in Catholicism, Episcopalianism, and the like. But declines in mass attendance and the drastic decline in clerical ranks suggest that "the mountains and rivers" of Catholic spirituality do not match the boundaries on the pages of the *Yearbook of the American and Canadian Churches 1997*. Similarly, the very significant declines in the measurable and active membership of those who prefer mainstream Protestantism—United Methodism, United Church of Christ, Presbyterian Church (U.S.A.), and more— made up some of the major news of the half-century. And controversies, putatively and in part over doctrine in the conservative bodies such as the Southern Baptist Convention and the Lutheran Church–Missouri Synod, were as much expressions of culture wars as they were comprehensible (to the laity and most clergy) battles over centuries-old statements of doctrine.

At the same time, one notes that through all these changes and assaults on denominations and denominationalism, the very impulse to keep measuring and the intensity of the conflicts showed how much denominations, now altered in character, continued to mean in the age that was supposed to be postdenominational. Denominations survive. Boundaries between them mean something, even if it is something different from their meaning a half-century ago.

As with the boundaries in the *Yearbook of the American and Canadian Churches 1997*, so with the public opinion polls. There has been surprising continuity in what can be measured and thus boundaries there. One may take only the most regular, constant, publicized, and even eponymic polling agency for the example. What the public knows as the Gallup Poll, at the Princeton Religious Research Center, is a dramatic illustration of religious continuities. In the report *Religion in America 1996*, the Gallup people turned in a near end-of-century assessment.

Despite . . . ebbs and flows, one of the most remarkable aspects of America's faith is its durability. In the face of all the dramatic social changes of the past half century—depression, war, the civil rights movement, social unrest, technological change—the religious beliefs and practices of Americans today look very much like those of the 1930s and 1940s. (Gallup 1996, 8)

I cannot resist noting a continuity in continuities of judgment on this matter, by reference to an assessment made by an interfaith triad of scholars in 1968. They wrote in the peak year of social change and unrest in America, at a time when it was more natural to remark on the possibility or actuality of revolutionary change than to note continuities. Yet

while the authors spoke of such "revolution" and reported on its dimensions, all three found reason to note how little any of this would show up in opinion polls taken in, say, 1952 and 1968. Their observations may be idiosyncratic, or a reflection on the hermeneutics of opinion polling, but whoever revisits the statistics of survey research in 1952 and 1968 and 1996 is likely to agree with the Gallup judgment just quoted (Greeley, Marty, and Rosenberg 1968).

Back to Gallup, who compared the 1940s and 1990s in the recent work. In 1944, 96 percent of those polled said they believed in God; in 1994, 96 percent said the same. In 1950, 39 percent of the people said they "happened to attend church or synagogue" that week; after a high of 49 percent in 1955 and 1958 and lows of 40 percent in 1970 and 1990, 43 percent made the claim about attendance in 1995. In 1940, 72 percent claimed church or synagogue membership; after a high of 76 percent in the 1940s and lows of 65 percent in 1988 and 1990, 69 percent avowed membership in 1995.

Of course, there was change within the patterns of continuity revealed on the pollsters' maps. At mid-century, the Princeton people would not even have asked whether someone was "born again"—the term was then culturally confined to the old Bible Belt. Now, extended, thinned out, vague as a boundary setter, the term "born again" was credibly self-descriptive for 41 percent of the people surveyed in 1995.

Perhaps more significant as an alert to the presence of "mountains and rivers" that do not match map boundaries were Gallup findings that 69 percent of the people thought religion was an "increasing influence" in American life in 1957; only 14 percent thought so in 1970; 37 percent thought it was increasing in 1995 (Gallup 1996, 20, 29, 41, 43). Of all the Gallup measurements, this one wavers most and may be the least reliable. Responses may reflect historical naïveté, reaction to significant events on the religious scene or the absence of them, cultural distractions, and the like. Yet its presence among the questions and responses serves to alert the public to the subtleties and high drama of cultural shifts in the eyes of citizens, whether church members or not.

THE MAPMAKERS AND
THE PHOTOGRAPHERS:
CHANGES IN PERCEPTION

Denominations and congregations survive and evidently hold what we might call the active loyalty of about 40 percent of the American people and the passive loyalty of about 60 percent, year in, year out. Historian Brooks Holifield reported on assessments of church attendance estimates that about 35 percent attended regularly in late colonial America, and 36 percent in the middle of the nineteenth century. By 1887, the figure may have been 35-40 percent, and, in 1906, 40 percent claimed to attend regularly—as is the case today—"though the claims might be exaggerations" in every case (Holifield 1994, 26-28). That is, about two out of five Americans can be counted on to support the inherited if innovative and adaptive institutions of religion

week in, week out. About three out of five think of themselves as "on the rolls" and are evidently summonable for special occasions, causes, and expressions of fidelity. Yet the task of chronicling their vagaries and vicissitudes in the course of the past half-century presented challenges to the chroniclers and mapmakers of religion, who on the bases of autobiography, perception, and other kinds of measurements aside from writing denominational history or taking institutionally focused polls, knew that they also needed to draw maps or take photographs that did more justice to the secrets of the figurative religious "mountains and rivers" as they paid less attention to drawn boundaries.

At the time of the nation's bicentennial, I was asked to take a stab at redrawing the map paying no attention to denominational boundaries. Already then—some, with benefit of hindsight, today might say "tardily"—my map took notice of the fact that the observing and writing about denominations provided insufficient, inaccurate, and even distorting of visions of American religion (Marty 1976, 4-5). With a different set of questions or surveying tools, one could come up with different answers and measures. To "pay no attention to boundaries" then meant, as it usually does, paying attention to different, and different kinds of, boundaries, just as the photographer notes the boundaries created against plains and sky by mountains or those created by the banks of rivers.

In 1976, six elements seemed to be able to contain nondenominationalized perceptions of religion in America: mainline, evangelicalism and fundamentalism, Pentecostal-charismatic, the new religions, ethnic religion, and civil religion. Keeping an eye on these only informally bounded expressions, I rather boldly and perhaps a bit foolishly wrote that "if there are spaces between these clusters, spheres of belonging that are not species of these genera, voids or unmapped areas, they have escaped me entirely." But I hedged this with the avowal that if this was what I thought was a "plausible fourth [the denominational map having been second in a discernible sequence of four to that date] map of religious America, some day there will be fifth or sixth maps" (Marty 1976, 17, 204).

For instance, the Church of Jesus Christ of Latter-day Saints, or Mormons—who are 5 million strong and rapidly growing—represented a subculture or culture that shared some elements (such as moral claims matching evangelicalism's) with others, but was also very distinctive. Mormons were a church, but they were also a people, just as Jews are a people whether individual Jews are observant or not. One could find other such examples, even if less statistically prominent than the Mormon exception or addition to the map.

INDIVIDUALIZED,
INVISIBLE, PROTEAN,
POSTMODERN RELIGION

What the tools of measurement, cartographic instead of photographic, institutional instead of spiritual, failed to suggest were presences and changes that more obviously "[paid] no attention to boundaries." These have become sufficiently significant, and, for some of the population, so determinative and so nearly normative that it would not be misleading to institutionalize them and begin to draw boundaries around them. This expression deserves separate treatment in any accounting of American religion.

Noninstitutional religion

Only historians captive of the denominational vision at midcentury would have insisted that they had covered the subject by noting the career of church bodies or synagogue life, in either particularized or open, ecumenical, and interfaith or interactive ways. They were alert to the ways in which citizens of many faiths came together under what Peter Berger called the "sacred canopy" (1967) of shared religious expressions—for example, in civil or public religion (Bellah 1967). Such expressions overarched the faith groups, as in religious support for a so-called American way of life that attracted people of most faiths—just as it was potentially subversive of their integrities. The civil religion could command loyalties or appeal to some elements in religious response that the particular bodies could not summon, for example, in wartime. The boundaries between religious institutions remained through it all but were less decisive than one might have imagined in determining the outlook of people who chose to identify with them. This indeterminable character took numerous forms.

Invisible religion

What Emile Durkheim called "collective representations" (Pickering 1984, 283-90, 371-73) of a public or a nation in religion, or what Berger called the "sacred canopy" (Berger 1967), also did not attract and express all the religious energies in the United States or in any late-modern, industrialized, free society. Beyond a canopy and a great relativizer of institutions ("pay no attention to boundaries"), there existed what Thomas Luckmann, in one of the more decisive labelings of the period, called "invisible religion" (Luckmann 1967). It was not truly invisible, if by that one meant disembodied, meaning that there were no people in whom its expressions could be observed. Rather, these expressions simply did not form conventional, palpable, measurable, or traditional institutions.

Loss of boundaries
within the self

Psychologist Robert Jay Lifton, in a book significantly titled *Boundaries* (1969), won concurrence among many readers with his observation that there was emergent a "protean" sort of individual, named after the god Proteus, who could take an infinite number of forms or guises. Lifton posed over against this a reactionary emergent that he called "constrictive," one who, fearing that he or she might be overwhelmed by change and that his or her commitments and persona would be dissolved, built up strong psychic defenses and ruled out

signals that were in any way uncongenial—a sort of fundamentalist-prone individual.

The boundaryless individual was free to pick and choose among sets of religious symbols, to be eclectic, to live with apparent contradictions in attachments, to make fleeting commitments, and to refuse to be loyal to defined dogmatic or traditional systems. Boundaries between sacred and secular, religion and nonreligion, inherited religion and innovative impulses, assent to authority and radical claims for autonomy, characterized the protean person in matters of faith. Such a type developed partly in response to the market situation— so many options were available and bid for attention—as well as because of an increase in mobility, plus the appeals of mass communication, the contacts made with "others" in mass higher education, intermarriage, and the like (Lifton 1969).

Individualized religion

Robert Bellah most notably pointed to recent trends that saw the individual in isolation from community and collectives in matters religious. Now the figures that suggest retention of the loyalty of believers to religious institutions, expressions that are manifest in survey research, were shown to be partly illusory. The spiritual scene had become increasingly a buyer's market. This was not an entirely new situation. Immigrants had had the choice of whether to affiliate with the transported religious communities from "the old country," to go shopping for new expressions, or not to practice at all. In all cases, there were agents ready to market what might appeal to the seeker (Bellah et al. 1985).

Next, the revivalist, evangelist, and conversionist approaches in new cities and on the frontier were developed in evangelical Protestantism but were also prominent in Catholicism (Dolan 1978) and led to denominationalism in Judaism (Raphael 1984). But the revived, evangelized, and converted people, in those earlier terms, characteristically took their responsive impulses to communities: the Catholic parish, the Reform or Conservative synagogue, Methodist or other Protestant collectives, and the like.

The choice
to be spiritual

In Bellah's reporting and in the eyes of the many observers who agreed with him, the demand was that the subject make a choice. Peter Berger, reflecting the etymology of the word "choice" in the Greek word *haeresis*, called this "the heretical imperative" (1979). In making a choice, the agent might well find a way to remain, as it were, in control of the sacred. This meant that he or she might live largely independently of religious collectives, indifferent to organized religion or even hostile to it. In the course of the last quarter-century, many rejected the very word "religious" and chose to claim that they were "spiritual." They might remain nominal or marginal members of theistic religious groups, but they turned their attention to the idea of connecting to spiritual "energies" that they thought were pulsing

through the cosmos. Literary critic Harold Bloom called these expressions "the American religion" (Bloom 1992).

In all these cases, too much could be made of novelty. Martin Luther spoke for the central religious traditions of the West when he stressed personal appropriation and commitment: just as one must die by oneself, one must believe by and for oneself. But in those traditions, the collective (for example, "the congregation of Yahweh," "the Body of Christ," "the people of God," "the Church Catholic") always had priority, and from the symbolic pool of each collective one drew for one's own sustenance. In late-twentieth-century times, it is the individual who sets the terms; to the degree that he or she found an institution that matched the chosen spiritual trajectory, that institution would be put to work and would attract measures of loyalty that could easily be later abandoned.

The erosion of
public-private boundaries

While the line between private and public religion had not been completely eroded—citizens still usually spoke of religion as a private affair— it became ever more clear that religion, far from disappearing or being marginalized, had remained and had to be acknowledged in the public spheres of life. This was evident in the controversies over U.S. Supreme Court decisions. It was apparent in the addition of new groups to the political (which is a species of the genus public) realm. The various movements on the religious Right such as the Moral Majority or the Christian Coalition had to be reckoned with by major political parties, just as the voice of Catholic bishops, of Jewish and African American religious leaders, and, of course, mainstream Protestant interventions in politics had long been apparent and heeded. When religion went public, new coalescences appeared, ad hoc alliances prospered, and boundary meant less and less.

In local communities, the various boards—school, clinic, zoning, town, hospital, library, and the like—were sounding boards and battlefields, as religious individuals and collectives vied for their place in the public sector. Meanwhile, signals from the public, especially through mass communications, meant that the private could not be kept private and preserved. Another boundary deserved and attracted less devotion than before.

Clerical or professional leadership and lay participation

One of the major differentiations in the realm of the spirit through the modern centuries had been between clergy and laity, between religious authority imposed from above and the religion of the folk that endured and prospered subversively, as it were. The religious market situation, the claims for autonomy in matters of personal import, the availability of higher education, and the increasing awareness among publics of the competition of claims between religious authorities were factors that led to what Mark Chaves documented as a "crisis of religious authority" (Chaves 1991). He saw this trend, not secularization, representing one of the great changes of the time; or, rather, he thought this authority crisis was itself the mark of secularization.

For example, before midcentury, most communicants in the one-fourth of the American citizenry that was Roman Catholic rarely had opportunity to pursue higher education. In what was called ghetto Catholicism, bright young men might be plucked from obscurity, sent to seminary, indoctrinated and equipped, and then ordained to be transmitters of authority unquestioned to a putatively passive laity. Catholicism prospered through doctrinal proclamation, canonical imposition, and priestly enforcement. "What the pope says, what the archbishop claims, what my priest insists upon goes" would have been a characteristic expression. The laity might drag their feet, be selective about following clergy, express quiet dissent, or leave the fold, but assent to ascribed and official authority was still a mark of Catholicism.

After World War II, the GI bill made the college and university experience available to millions. Catholics became among the most highly educated among American religious cohorts. As the number of priests declined after the Second Vatican Council (1962-65), there were new openings for positive lay expression. The enlarged opportunity for women to assume all but ordained leadership (women were not allowed to be ordained) demonstrated that traditional lines of authority meant less than before. On the other hand, many women leaders—pastoral associates and the like—often attracted more response than did ordained male clerics.

With the new learning and increased awareness of issues, the Catholic laity became better equipped to do its own appraising of priestly, or what Catholics called magisterial, claims and often neglected or even rejected these. Thus the papal proclamation *Humanae Vitae*, condemning "artificial" birth control in 1968, did not match the experience of or ring true to the understanding of huge Catholic majorities, and they were ready to convey as much with their actions. This did not mean that Catholics no longer wanted to be led. It did mean that leadership had to win support through charisma, rhetoric, or example and not merely to assert it. Needless to say, a similar situation prevailed pretty well across the board in religion. Professional and ordained clergy remained in place and often won impressive support, but an expressive laity altered the concepts of authority and its realizations.

Ad hoc and crisscrossing
ecumenical patterns

Concurrent with all the other changes occurring in the religious situation was an erosion of boundaries between the institutions or communities. Many of these resulted from positive impulses. Thus the Christian ecumenical movement received encouragement from leaders throughout mainstream Protestantism and Catholicism. But from the beginnings of the movement in Prot-

estantism and Orthodoxy in 1910 and through the midcentury realization of the World Council of Churches and the modern National Council of Churches in 1948 and 1951, ecumenism meant ordered, negotiated ententes between religious bodies, each of which remained intact, bounded, and autonomous (Neill and Rouse 1967).

By century's end, while the ordered forms persisted, what we might call ad hoc ecumenism had challenged the traditional forms. Christians and Jews kept up their official guards, especially as Jews, fearing intermarriage, conversions to Christianity by marital partners, or ceased observances, tightened regulations about marriage, although to little avail. Yet Jews and Christians both rather unguardedly crossed many boundaries. Many evangelical Protestants, historically standoffish in interfaith affairs, came into close relations with Jews, thanks to their common commitment—though for vastly different reasons—to Israel. The same evangelicals and Pentecostals often found ad hoc but not superficial common cause with many Catholics on issues such as opposition to abortion or acceptance of charismatic expression. They then forgot old hostilities and demarcations. Many individuals in mainstream Protestantism were self-declared evangelicals. Many evangelicals moved into the mainstream along with leaders like Billy Graham, who had more access to power than did those Protestants who at midcentury had tried to hold on to a monopoly on mainstream religious expression and authority.

A kind of crisscrossing or crazy-quilt pattern of interfaith and ecumenical relations developed. All of it was erosive of confessional and denominational boundaries. Certain Methodists therefore found more in common with certain Catholics on social issues than they did with other sorts of fellow Methodists or Catholics "back home." The same Methodists might make common cause with Jews or Lutherans on another set of themes, while the same Catholics might oppose all of them on still others, making their common cause then with conservative evangelical Protestants. Jews who welcomed evangelical support for Israel resisted evangelical efforts to convert Jews.

No central authority in Rome, Geneva, Wittenberg, Canterbury, Jerusalem, or New York could issue effective and enforceable guidelines on the ecumenical front. Of course, there could be reactionary countertrends, and these developed among Southern Baptists and Missouri Lutherans in the 1970s. Members of these denominations were successful at raising denominational boundary lines but at fearful expense to the integrity of their organizations. Ironically, the victors in conflicts within such bodies were often seen by outsiders not as defenders of their particular Baptist or Lutheran heritages. Instead, they appeared to be generic Protestant fundamentalists or, for another example, devotees of new church-growth movements that often contradicted central theological themes of such traditions.

It was sometimes said that the ecumenical movement had become comatose by century's end. Instead, it could be argued that the ecumenical spirit thrived but now found forms that did not match old boundaries and disciplines.

*Unbounded pluralism
    turned multicultural
    turned postmodern*

At midcentury, for various reasons, American religionists began to seek new models for national life. Leaders within the old mainstream Protestant hegemony were having to yield their hold on power in what Harvard historian William Hutchison (1989) called "the second disestablishment" of such religious elements. Coalitions and common endeavors during World War II led many under the "sacred canopy" to seek ways to recognize diversity in American religious life. Newly assertive Catholics, Jews, and, eventually, African American Protestants did not want to be perceived as marginal.

As a result, new inventions such as the Judeo-Christian tradition were coming to maturity around midcentury (Silk 1988). By 1955, Will Herberg and other sociologists could take for granted that, under the American sun, Protestant, Catholic, and Jew formed a triad (Herberg 1960), and Father John Courtney Murray, S. J., in *We Hold These Truths* (1964), effectively made the claim that there were four parties, secularism or secular humanism being the fourth. In *The Religious Factor* (1961), sociologist Gerhard Lenski, while concentrating on one metropolis, Detroit, showed that black Protestantism was its own self-dependent religious entity. Now observers had noticed five cohorts in what, it was agreed upon, would be called American religious pluralism.

No sooner was the ink dry on these sociological and theological treatises than many new voices were heard. In the 1960s and 1970s, these challenged the old and neatly bounded forms for comprehending pluralism. Gender was an issue: women, gay, and lesbian leaders asserted that they represented different voices that had to be reckoned with independently. "Others" came to be a prosperous category, as Orthodox Christians, Mormons, Muslims, new religions, and Native American spiritualities all came into the spotlight and found a voice and a home. The particularities of pluralism were chopped ever finer in the category of multiculturalism. Under its canopy were to be found groups within which people gained political power and pursued political identities. Others challenged old dominant groups, spoke up for their ancestors as victims, and made positive, enriching contributions.

While the multicultural impulse was often salutary for the people within the groups involved, claims for multicultural integrity often, ironically, relativized the situation. The groups sounded more and more like each other even as they claimed difference (Menand 1992). As many of them challenged national religious metahistories and canons, they also often helped produce predictable countercanons and new components in the stories of ways to be American and religious (Marty 1996). This is not the place to question the integrity of these groups or to enlarge upon the double effect through which they both particularized and relativized religious expression. The only point to be made here is that, taken together, their efforts led to a further erosion of boundaries by their very multiplicity and often mutually exclusive claims.

The American pilgrim on a sacred journey therefore was free to be ever more eclectic. High-church Anglicans in Episcopal cathedrals came to sing the evangelical "Amazing Grace." In mainstream Protestantism, God could be addressed as he or she or both or neither. White evangelicals sang black spirituals. Catholics on spiritual retreat might read Zen texts or Hasidic stories. Jews, often uncomfortable with kin Christianity, reached for more distant, Asian spiritual expressions to enhance their own. One might stay within a camp and thus be aware of boundaries, but the camp boundaries did not any longer hold captive or define the people within them. The people could reach across the old lines for whatever pleased or helped or challenged them in their spiritual journeys. The result was a kind of pastiche spirituality, made up of montages and collages of spiritual signals and symbols: it came to be called postmodernity.

Where boundaries survive

It would be misleading to claim that all American religion at century's end could be captured with one metaphor. From the beginning, we have argued that the lines drawn on the religious maps remain and have certain kinds of significance. But the metaphorical mountains and rivers have their own secrets, which are now being laid bare. All too visible are those features of the landscape and climate that do not show up on the maps where political and organizational lines have been drawn.

New line-drawing also goes on, among people like Robert J. Lifton's "constrictive" types as well as among people of open outlook. These latter seekers pursue integral and organic outlooks and ways of life through what has been called *ressourcement*, a return to sources. Extreme forms of this retrieval occur in fundamentalist efforts to draw boundaries and hold adherents with them while they promote negative views of the "other." Moderate forms of this also take the form of patterns of resistance against the erosive and dissolving elements in American life, its spiritual marketplaces and cafeteria lines.

In the new century, one may expect a continued drama among those who, like so many around the world, have at least three choices. Some turn tribal and exclusive within their boundaries. Others seek to choose communal life of a more open character but still respectful of boundaries. Still others heed the call to "pay no attention to boundaries" and then invent new kinds of responses.

Notes

1. Pioneers in formulating this literature are Robert Wuthnow, who, in *The Restructuring of American Religion*, saw "parachurch" or "Special Purpose Groups" as a challenge (Wuthnow 1988, 100-32), and Wade Clark Roof and William McKinney, who, in *American Mainline Religion*, regarded "individualism" as a threat to the vitality of denominations and

congregations (Roof and McKinney 1987, 244-51).

2. Among the first to note this erosion of distinctives, or ignorance about it, was Gerhard Lenski in *The Religious Factor* (Lenski 1961). Several years before Lenski published, John A. Hardon, S. J., illustrated how relatively useless it was to follow the lines of dogmatic book boundaries to describe denominations such as the Methodists, Baptists, and the like; too few clergy and lay members were aware of, moved by, or content with the founding doctrines, and many had determined other ways to relate to the denominational traditions (Hardon 1956). But see works like *Reimagining Denominationalism* (1994), by Robert Bruce Mullin and Russell E. Richey, for illustrations in which denominational vitalities can be discerned and reconceived.

References

Andreas, Brian. 1996. *Strange Dreams.* Vol. 4, *Collected Stories and Drawings of Brian Andreas.* Decorah, IA: StoryPeople.

Bedell, Kenneth B. 1997. *Yearbook of the American and Canadian Churches 1997.* Nashville, TN: Abingdon Press.

Bellah, Robert N. 1967. Civil Religion in America. *Daedalus* 96(Winter):1-21.

Bellah, Robert N., Richard Madsen, William M. Sullivan, Ann Swidler, and Steven M. Tipton. 1985. *Habits of the Heart: Individualism and Commitment in American Life.* Berkeley: University of California Press.

Berger, Peter L. 1967. *The Sacred Canopy: Elements of a Sociological Theory of Religion.* Garden City, NY: Doubleday.

————. 1979. *The Heretical Imperative: Contemporary Possibilities of Religious Affirmation.* Garden City, NY: Anchor Books.

Bloom, Harold. 1992. *The American Religion: The Emergence of the Post-Christian Nation.* New York: Simon & Schuster.

Chaves, Mark Alan. 1991. Secularization in the Twentieth-Century United States. Ph.D. diss., Harvard University.

Dolan, Jay P. 1978. *Catholic Revivalism: The American Experience, 1830-1900.* Notre Dame, IN: University of Notre Dame Press.

Gallup, George H., Jr. 1996. *Religion in America 1996.* Princeton, NJ: Princeton Religion Research Center.

Greeley, Andrew M., Martin E. Marty, and Stuart E. Rosenberg. 1968. *What Do We Believe? The Stance of Religion in America.* New York: Meredith Press.

Hardon, John A. 1956. *The Protestant Churches of America.* Westminster, MD: Newman Press.

Herberg, Will. 1960. *Protestant, Catholic, Jew: An Essay in American Religious Sociology.* Garden City, NY: Anchor Books.

Holifield, E. Brooks. 1994. Toward a History of American Congregations. In *American Congregations.* Vol. 2, *New Perspectives in the Study of Congregations,* ed. James W. Lewis and James P. Wind. Chicago: University of Chicago Press.

Hutchison, William R., ed. 1989. *Between the Times: The Travail of the Protestant Establishment in America, 1900-1960.* New York: Cambridge University Press.

Lenski, Gerhard. 1961. *The Religious Factor: A Sociological Study of Religion's Impact on Politics, Economics, and Family Life.* Garden City, NY: Doubleday.

Lifton, Robert Jay. 1969. *Boundaries: Psychological Man in Revolution.* New York: Vintage Books.

Luckmann, Thomas. 1967. *The Invisible Religion: The Problem of Religion in Modern Society.* New York: Macmillan.

Marty, Martin E. 1976. *A Nation of Behavers.* Chicago: University of Chicago Press.

———. 1996. *The One and the Many: America's Struggle for the Common Good.* Cambridge, MA: Harvard University Press.

Menand, Louis. 1992. Being an American. *Times Literary Supplement,* 30 Oct., 3-4.

Mullin, Robert Bruce and Russell E. Richey. 1994. *Reimagining Denominationalism.* New York: Oxford University Press.

Murray, John Courtney. 1964. *We Hold These Truths: Catholic Reflections on the American Proposition.* New York: Sheed & Ward.

Neill, Stephen C. and Ruth Rouse, eds. 1967. *A History of the Ecumenical Movement.* 2d ed. Philadelphia: Westminster Press.

Pickering, W.S.F. 1984. *Durkheim's Sociology of Religion: Themes and Theories.* London: Routledge & Kegan Paul.

Raphael, Marc Lee. 1984. *Profiles in American Judaism: The Reform, Conservative, Orthodox, and Reconstructionist Traditions in Historical Perspective.* San Francisco: Harper & Row.

Roof, Wade Clark and William McKinney. 1987. *American Mainline Religion: Its Changing Shape and Future.* New Brunswick, NJ: Rutgers University Press.

Silk, Mark. 1988. *Spiritual Politics: Religion and America Since World War II.* New York: Simon & Schuster.

Wuthnow, Robert. 1988. *The Restructuring of American Religion: Society and Faith Since World War II.* Princeton, NJ: Princeton University Press.

Excepting Exceptionalism:
American Religion in Comparative Relief

By N. J. DEMERATH III

ABSTRACT: American religion is a major component of the triumphal exceptionalism that has long set the United States apart from other nations. Our frequent label as the world's most religious advanced nation has given pride to many citizens, if not to all. This article offers a reassessment of the claim in the context of a larger cross-national investigation of religion, politics, and the state in some 14 countries around the globe. With this as a comparative backdrop, the article examines three putative sources of uniqueness: our civil religion (versus our separation of church and state); our religious organizations and congregational style; and our high levels of individual religious belief and behavior. The article concludes that America's uniqueness is overstated and constitutes more a matter of kind than degree.

Jay Demerath is professor of sociology at the University of Massachusetts, Amherst. A longtime student of American religion's relation to politics and the state, he has recently shifted from the local to the global in examining the same issues cross-nationally.

EVERY nation that endures and flourishes requires at least some belief in its own uniqueness. In the United States, this belief has long had the quality of fanaticism. To be an American is to be told repeatedly that one's country represents the best, the most, the highest, the purest, and so forth. This is certainly true of American religion. The United States has long been touted as the most religious of all the world's advanced nations, and the notion of a divinely favored "city upon a hill" lies at the core of our national convictions.

Recently, S. M. Lipset has noted the "double-edged" quality of this "American exceptionalism" (1996). He argues that we do, indeed, have a distinctive concoction of values and institutions, but that it accounts for some of our faults as well as our virtues. Both individualistic values and a democratic polity have costs as well as benefits. This is not the time to rehearse these arguments. Instead, I want to reassess exceptionalism's special premise regarding American religion.

Over the past five years and more, I have made research visits to some 14 countries around the world as part of a cross-national study of religion, violence, politics, and the state. The countries range from Brazil and Guatemala in our own hemisphere to Northern Ireland, Sweden, and Poland in Europe; Egypt, Israel, and Turkey in the Middle East; Pakistan, India, Thailand, and Indonesia in South Asia; and China and Japan in the Far East. They represent not only a wide variety of world religions but a multitude of political differences.

The sometimes hidden agenda of any comparative study is comparison with one's own lot. Here I want to make that agenda explicit. If one compares U.S. religion to religion in these and other countries around the globe, just how exceptional are we? Specifically, I want to consider three levels of American religion from this cross-cultural perspective. The first takes up the religion of society as a whole—its culture and its politics. The second concerns the organized religion of congregations, churches, and denominations. Finally, the third involves levels and styles of individual religious involvement.

AMERICAN CIVIL RELIGION: IS IT HOLDING AND IS IT UNIQUE?

One of the strongest identifiers of America as a religious society is the way its religion is publicly invoked and symbolically brandished. Our most important national holidays, such as July Fourth and Memorial Day, are religiously consecrated. Virtually every session of the nation's daily legislative business is prefaced by prayer. Both our coins and our politicians proclaim religious mottos. Our rites of passage—whether weddings, funerals, or presidential inaugurations—are marked with religious observance. Religious solace and supplication accompany every national crisis.

All of this is part of what Robert Bellah (1967) first termed America's "civil religion." In Bellah's view, this "Judeo-Christian" common denominator is a rich residue of a historical experience that has become a binding cultural force. The country is irretrievably religious at its roots and in its most luxuriant foliage. This is an important part of America's distinctiveness, since few other societies can boast such a natural melding of religion and nationhood.

Yet there are reasons to pause before accepting this portrayal. It is not clear whether this is an analysis of America's mythology or a contribution to it. On the one hand, our civil religion may not function quite the way it is depicted. On the other hand, other societies have their own versions of a civil religion, though some stretch the concept and its possibilities rather than merely illustrating it. Let me consider both complications in turn.

Some 13 years ago, *The Annals* published another collection on American religion, which included an article by Rhys Williams and me entitled "Civil Religion in an Uncivil Society" (1985). Our basic thrust was to question whether a society that had grown so raucously complex could any longer sustain or be sustained by civil religion and whether its manifestations had not become more form than function—more icing than cake. Since then, other reasons for doubt have emerged.

Williams and I (1991) have also explored the paradoxical tension between our heralded civil religion and our no less legendary "separation of church and state." Actually, these two seemingly inconsistent syndromes are strangely symbiotic. Each is a guard against the other's excesses, and each provides a countervailing assurance as a boost to the other's legitimacy. That is, we can indulge a symbolic civil religion precisely because there is a substantive separation of church and state in important matters of government policy; at the same time, our separation is never a total rupture because of the presence of overarching civil religious ceremonials.

It should be noted that some foreign observers see our church-state separation as the basis of a very different version of American exceptionalism, one that singles us out more for secularism than religiosity. However, our separation is not only far from complete or consistent; it is also far from unique. Virtually all national constitutions offer some guarantee of free religious exercise. While our initial First Amendment provision against a religious "establishment" is much more distinctive, even this occurs de facto, if not de jure, in most other countries. Governments everywhere are eager to preserve their own autonomy, especially for participating in the international political economy. Strains toward such separation even occur in a theocracy such as the 1979-89 Iranian Republic (cf. Demerath 1991).

Meanwhile, America's civil religion has been pressured by more than its church-state separation. Our burgeoning pluralism includes increasing numbers of Muslims, Hindus, and Buddhists outside the Judeo-Christian tradition. Moreover, Richard Neuhaus (1984) has argued that religion has become conspicuously absent from our "naked public square," and Steven L. Carter (1992) has termed ours a "culture of disbelief"—

though both are really lamenting the absence of more conservative religion in the national arena. In fact, Robert Wuthnow (1988) suggests that America now hosts not one but two civil religions—one liberal and one conservative—and this may vitiate the very point of civil religion as something both unitary and unifying.

James D. Hunter (1991) insists that religious cohesion has given way to "culture wars," although I have argued that this phrase is more incendiary than accurate given an American public huddled in the middle on key issues (Demerath and Yang 1997) and when one compares these expected abrasions of a democratic polity to the far more bloody conflicts of countries such as Guatemala, Northern Ireland, Israel, and India (Demerath and Straight 1997).

Civil religion remains alive in the United States, though perhaps not well. But what about other countries around the world? It is true that media depictions of religion abroad often make it seem a far more likely source of national violence than cohesion—and many countries could be added to the conflicted four mentioned previously. Yet there are also abundant cases like the United States where civil-religious traditions are straining to hold the center despite centrifugal pressures.

Virtually every Latin American country has a dominant Catholic legacy, albeit one in increasing competition with surging conservative Protestant movements and resurgent indigenous religion, such as Afro-spiritualism in Brazil and Mayan practices in Guatemala. Poland would seem to illustrate Catholic civil religion at its apogee, though in fact the Catholic church has experienced declining influence since the Communists were overthrown in 1989 and the church's ties to the winning Solidarity labor movement were cut. Poland now seems on course with the rest of Western Europe, where Catholicism is increasingly marginalized. Ironically, this is even true of France, where the basic notion of a civil religion was given impetus by two scholars working more than a century apart, Jean-Jacques Rousseau (1770) and Emile Durkheim (1912).

Meanwhile, Sweden illustrates a related pattern of formal religious disestablishment. It has recently decided to end its long-standing officially Lutheran status at the turn of the century, and some suggest that Anglican England could follow soon thereafter. Many British now regard the Anglican church and monarchy as alternately charming and charmless artifacts of the past that are merely symbolic. But as scholars of culture and increasing numbers of British Catholics and especially Muslims can attest, symbols can be very powerful indeed and are often anything but "merely." Much of British law remains anchored in Anglican custom.

The Middle East and the so-called Qur'an belt present a different civil religious scenario. Islamic countries such as Egypt, Turkey, Pakistan, and Indonesia share a theme with important variations. The theme involves the establishment problem first confronted by the United States some 200 years ago, namely, how can a struggling secular state keep a strong religious culture from becoming too dominant as a civil-religious force? The political elites in all of these countries are terrified by the example of Iran under the Ayatollah Khomeini and Afghanistan under the Taliban. Some have dealt with the problem more successfully than others.

In Egypt—as in neighboring Algeria—a protracted armed conflict has resulted. In Turkey, the great Kemal Attaturk established the norm of state secularism in the 1920s, and his heirs are defending it against a newly mobilized Muslim movement that some call "fundamentalism light." Pakistan now publicly describes itself as a country undergoing Islamization, but many of its leaders privately seek separation from its influence in order to operate successfully in a secular international political economy. Somewhat the same pattern has occurred in Indonesia, though with the help of a state-promoted civil religion called "pancasila" that was strategically devised following World War II to embrace the nation's vast religious diversity.

Meanwhile, Thailand's Buddhist civil religion and monarchy resemble the pattern of the Britain and Western Europe of an earlier era. But if one follows Buddhism up into China and Japan, the scene changes. Here Buddhism shares cultural standing with other religious and nonreligious movements. Japan offers a particularly sobering example of a civil religion that attained dominance. The politically plotted state Shinto was devised out of traditional folk Shinto in the latter half of the nineteenth century and provided the cultural mobilization and legitimacy for Japanese industrialization and expansionism through World War II.

China poses a quite different challenge to civil religion, namely, the possibility of producing national cultural cohesion around a movement that may well be civil but is anything but religious. It is true that there are small communities of Buddhists and Christians—both official and unofficial—and that a sizable area of northwestern China is culturally Islamic. Moreover, virtually all Chinese respond at some level to the indigenous religions of Taoism and Confucianism, although the state derides the latter especially as politically incorrect in its social ethic. By now, it has become a cliché to treat communism as a secular religion in its own right. However, the functional and even organizational parallels are undeniable, and this includes its recent stage of so-called secularization.

Certainly China, the former USSR, and, to a lesser extent, Cuba and Turkey raise fundamental questions about just how important religion is to national cohesion. But then some also pose the issue for the United States. Insofar as the country continues to cohere, it may have more to do with the values and principles set forth in the Declaration of Independence and the Constitution than with the Bible. To put it another way, rather than regard traditional religion as the core of what is nationally civil, it may be increasingly appropriate to regard the politically civil as the core of what is tantamount to a national religion.

AMERICAN RELIGIOUS ORGANIZATIONS AND CONGREGATIONALISM

Few images of the stereotypical American community fail to include at least one corner church with steeple. Whether the white, frame icons of New England congregationalism, the neo-Gothic edifices of the Catholics and Episcopalians, the contemporary "ring-a-ding God-boxes" of the Lutherans and Jews, the storefront sites of urban neighborhoods in transition, or the new suburban campuses of conservative Protestant groups, these structures dot the American landscape in profusion. They also loom large in the country's institutional sector. Religious congregations provide critical support mechanisms for their members as communities within communities. They account for the lion's share of the nation's charitable giving and community service, and they represent a major source of political influence and mobilization.

All of this reflects a distinctively American confluence of Protestantism's founding theology and our localized and democratic community ethos. When Protestantism broke from Catholicism, it did what every successful movement must, namely, stress a problem to which it had the solution. In this case, the problem was the individual's suddenly unmediated relationship to God and all of the loneliness and anxiety that this entailed. The solution was nothing less than the congregation itself as a source of both fellowship and reassurance. Of course, the congregation was especially important in the rural areas and small towns of Europe and America, where it was often the only gathering point. The United States' particular emphasis on frontier self-reliance and local democracy gave congregational life a further thrust that was later carried back to the new frontiers of urbanization.

It was especially important that the most sophisticated versions of congregational life occurred among the liberal Protestant denominations, with all of their higher-status membership resources. In fact, the very existence of a self-proclaimed liberal church is one of the truly exceptional characteristics of American mainline religion. Liberals in most other faiths around the world quickly move outside of their faith structures and shift all the way to full-blown secularism. Here, however, this shift was slowed by such liberal American denominations as the Congregationalists, Episcopalians, Presbyterians, and Unitarians. Much of the secret lay in organizational complexes that combined liberalized religion with an array of compelling social and service activities. Early on, the resulting organizational stability gave important standing and influence to the liberalism that these churches embodied. More recently, this same organizational legacy has helped to brake their slippage.

The Protestant emphasis on congregational life has few equivalents in other world religions, though a number have recently begun to appropriate the model in various ways. Thus, much of the heralded "liberation theology" movement within Latin American Catholicism involves a move away from the patriarchal impersonality of large hierarchical parishes toward the more egalitarian intimacy of "base communities." The base communities have been among the most successful Catholic responses to Protestant Pentecostalism's own stress on tightly bonded (and highly feminized) congregations. In somewhat the same spirit, in Poland, the political cells of the Solidarity movement gave the Catholic church new contacts with the people during a decade of cooperation. Now that these contacts have largely disappeared, the church is suffering the consequences.

Neither the Islamic mosque nor the Hindu temple functions as congregations in the Protestant sense. Strictly speaking, the mosque is not one of the pillars of Islam, nor is it critical to the prayers that are essential but can be performed anywhere. With the family as the key Islamic institution, Muslim ritual life is not grounded in a wider network of social activity and support. The mosque is a special locus for prayer alone, and other activities within it are formally proscribed. In practice, it can take on educational functions and even serve as a mobilizing vehicle under the leadership of particular imams or mullahs. However, the gender segregation that is intrinsic to the mosque militates against a sense of full-blown congregational solidarity.

The Hindu temple is more a shrine to a particular god or goddess than a center of lay activity. In fact, Hindu rituals revolve more around the home in their concern for the purification of food and body. Rather than go to the priests, Hindus often have the priests come to them, and it is said that there is nothing two Hindus do together that one Hindu cannot do alone.

With this in mind, it is perhaps not surprising that both Islam and Hinduism have spawned a variety of extra-religious movements that provide more communality. Some are social, some are educational, and some are political. Indeed, precisely because these faiths lack a congregational base, they are vulnerable to movements that will perform some congregational functions. Virtually every Muslim nation has been fertile soil for so-called fundamentalist groups, though the term is misleading since even their religious programs can be more innovative than traditional, and for many participants religion provides a legitimate cover for a basic agenda that is more strictly secular. This is also suspected of many members and leaders of India's militant Hindu party, the BJP. Still there is no question that Hindutva extremism fills a void in the lives of even its most devout members.

Meanwhile, Buddhism has followed several slightly different paths, depending upon which Buddhism is in question. The Theravada Buddhism of Thailand and Southeast Asia is a purer, more elitist faith in which monastic monks hold the key to salvation and offer the laity opportunities to "make merit" by making donations of various sorts to the monks themselves. Temples are centers of religious observance but not lay organization. Although there is an elaborate national ecclesiastical structure called the *sangha* and some monks have considerable followings of their own, the laity is afforded little by way of a congregational life.

On the other hand, the Mahayana Buddhism to the northeast is more oriented to the laity. In China, Buddhist groups are often forced to take a sheltered congregational form as a protection against the Party and the state. In Japan, several lay Buddhist movements have adopted an explicitly congregational model. This certainly applies to the largest of them, the Soka Gakkai, whose membership is now estimated at anywhere from one-twentieth to one-tenth of all Japanese. The Soka Gakkai's intense recruitment has revolved around nested levels of lay organizations that once offered structured support and identity to rural working-class migrants to urban areas and now perform similar functions for an increasingly middle-class constituency.

This is yet another indication that other religions around the world are moving in the American direction in their organizational developments. In the meantime, however, America's own organizational forms of religion are undergoing change. In virtually every Christian faith, there is a widening gap between national denominations and local parishes. Many older liberal parishes have lost their younger generations and become increasingly geriatric in their membership and style. The new religious action occurs in new settings, whether the world of cults, of conservative evangelical churches, of massive congregations that offer more community and less religion per se, or of special and single-issue movements that bear little resemblance to the churches of yesterday as they struggle in more secular venues to realize their singular visions of tomorrow.

In sum, American religious organization continues to be distinctive in the world context, but it is not nearly as exceptional as it was even 25 years ago. Just as other religions have begun to take on related organizational characteristics, we are beginning to see changes in the very organizational patterns that once branded us unique.

DO PIOUS STATISTICS LIE?

It is not hard to find statistical evidence of the religious exceptionalism of individual Americans. Virtually any polling study of religious belief and behavior in various major countries will show the United States at or near the top in such matters as levels of church membership (close to 60 percent), weekly church attendance (better than 40 percent), belief in God (95 percent), and the experience of having encountered God (close to 75 percent) (cf. Ingelhart 1997).

Without actually pricking this balloon of national distinction, it is important to deflate it a bit. What is being compared in these studies is not just the religious penchants of differing individuals but the differing cultural expectations for religion and religiosity that apply from one society to the next. Thus it is paradoxical that participating in some form of American religion remains a generally compelling national norm even though we lack a formally established national religion to participate in. But disestablishment has put the onus on religious groups to develop at the grassroots level as expressions of community resolve molded to community needs. For many, church membership and church participation became an important part of community life itself. In addition, if there is no national establishment, there are surely local approximations, whether Catholic in the urban Northeast, Methodist in parts of the South, Baptist in much of the Southwest, and, of course, Mormon in Utah. Scholars disagree whether religious participation is highest in the context of a local religious monopoly or local religious competition (cf. Finke and Stark 1988; Blau, Redding, and Land 1997). However, there is little doubt that declaring oneself nonreligious is tantamount to an antisocial act in many circles.

Clearly, America's vaunted statistics of individual religiosity must be interpreted within this broader perspective. Without impugning the deep religious commitments of many American adherents, church membership does not necessarily entail regular church participation or personal religious commitment. Studies of belief in God are vulnerable to variations in the question and the context; in general, the levels of absolute belief decline when a respondent has more finely grained alternatives to choose from. One of the most significant, hence controversial, studies of individual religion in the last half-century involved a recent check to see whether people who claimed to have been in church on the previous Sunday could actually have showed up (Hadaway, Marler, and Chaves 1993). This study and subsequent refinements and replications show that actual levels of church attendance are less than half of those that are so widely cited. Are people lying? Perhaps a better way to put it is that many are telling the pollsters that they know what they ought to be doing and are anxious not to disappoint. Some respondents may also be wary of confessing nonbelief and nonparticipation to someone who may launch an evangelizing effort to enlist them to join the fold.

Just as context is important in America's putatively high levels of religious involvement, context is no less important in some of the low levels elsewhere. As we have already seen, the Judeo-Christian world is virtually unique in giving such emphasis to church or temple participation that it can become a central metric of religious behavior and devotion. To the extent that ritual and worship center on home and family in other faiths, they become more elusive. While one could always attempt to survey beliefs as opposed to behavior, this raises yet another source of troublesome variance. Christianity is very much a religion of the word; most other faiths are religions of the act where what one believes is far less important than what one does—not merely as a matter of ritual observance but also as part of one's overall ethical lifestyle.

Another problem in comparing levels of individual religiosity cross-nationally involves questions of religious identity. In many countries, religion has become more a matter of passive cultural heritage than active ongoing commitment. From Northern Ireland to Sweden and Poland

and on to Israel, I found many respondents uneasy when I asked about their personal religiosity. However, when I offered the category of cultural Protestant, Catholic, or Jew, they brightened and clutched the label eagerly. Although they regarded themselves as beyond the reach of conventional religious rounds, their religious legacies resonated in other important ways. Strict devotional criteria would exclude many Catholic Republicans of Northern Ireland as well as many radical but secular Zionists of Israel. Other criteria are more inclusive.

Similar cultural syndromes exist outside the Judeo-Christian orbit. High-status Muslims in Egypt, Turkey, Pakistan, India, and Indonesia all showed telltale traces. So did a number of Hindu intellectuals who were secular in most aspects of their lives but privately favored the ongoing effort to Hinduize India's secular government—again as a matter of broad culture rather than narrow religion. Perhaps less than 5 percent of Chinese are formally affiliated with either official or unofficial Buddhism, Islam, or Christianity. However, none of my Chinese respondents denied that virtually all Chinese carried strains of cultural Confucianism and Taoism, though most questioned whether either qualified as a religion.

The question of religious definition is especially apparent in understanding the Japanese case. Ask most Japanese whether they are religious, and the answer is no. But ask them if they participate in rituals at Shinto shrines, Buddhist temples, or their home, and the answer is gener-

ally a ready yes. After all, they will say, the latter only involve superstitions and invocations of good luck for students taking exams, family events, or the purchase of a new car or major appliance. On the other hand, being religious involves belonging to an actual religious group, and this is still rare despite the growth of such congregational movements as the Soka Gakkai.

However, there is another definitional difficulty in comparing Eastern religious experiences with our own. The Japanese are apt to engage in Shinto rituals concerning birth, Buddhist rituals involving death and ancestors, but Christian rituals for a wedding. The latter is less a matter of personal commitment and more a function of American television and the fact that Western white wedding dresses and ceremonial accoutrements are far less expensive than traditional Japanese kimonos and all that they entail.

This ritual syncretism through the life cycle suggests a major difference between two types of religious pluralism, one intergroup and the other intra-individual. When we speak of pluralism in the United States, we mean that the country is host to many different religious groups with distinct memberships. But when one observes pluralism in countries like Japan, China, and especially Indonesia, one finds individuals themselves hosting several different religions, which coexist internally. Thus it is true that Indonesia is the world's most populous Muslim nation. However, when asked their religion, many Indonesians will respond that they are not only Muslim but also part Buddhist, part Hindu, part Christian, and part indigenous animist. How does one even begin to tabulate neat statistics of religious affiliation and observance under these circumstances?

At the end of the day, cross-cultural comparisons of individual religious involvement yield less of a bottom line of clarity than a bottomless pit of ambiguity. They also offer a vast opportunity to indulge in interpretive license. In many countries, one could justify summary statistics of religious involvement that ranges from a low of 20 percent to a high of 90 percent. Sometimes I have been tempted to juggle the data to produce a constant universal fraction of people who are meaningfully involved in religion in any society—say, for example, 24.3 percent. But, of course, this would amount to more myth making instead of the myth breaking that is so important to the social science mission.

other nations, it is far preferable to probe how we are simply different. Moreover, while it is true that some of our differences have eroded due to changes here and abroad, it is also true that others remain. There is no question that our combined principles of civil religion and church-state separationism still confer a stamp of distinctiveness. Much the same is true of our emphasis on religious congregational life and our stress on church and temple participation as a basis of individual piety. Yet none of these is easily quantified in comparison with changing patterns in other nations around the world.

Perhaps the change most crucial to American religion, however, is its increasing realization that what is going on elsewhere is important. After all, the very phrase "American exceptionalism" suggests a self-congratulatory arrogance that has been this article's primary target.

CONCLUSION

Is America exceptional? Of course. At least in the sense that every society and culture is—in Emile Durkheim's classic phrase—sui generis. There is no question that the melding in the United States of national and religious heritages has produced a unique confection over the years. What is more questionable is whether this uniqueness is a matter of degree or kind.

The matter of American exceptionalism has tended to be miscast from the start. Instead of asserting that America and Americans are more or most religious when compared to

References

Bellah, Robert N. 1967. Civil Religion in America. *Daedalus* 96(Winter):1-21.

Blau, Judith R., Kent Redding, and Kenneth C. Land. 1997. Ethnocultural Cleavages and the Growth of Church Membership in the United States, 1860-1930. In *Sacred Companies: Organizational Aspects of Religion and Religious Aspects of Organizations*, ed. N. J. Demerath III, Peter D. Hall, Terry Schmitt, and Rhys H. Williams. New York: Oxford University Press.

Carter, Steven L. 1992. *Culture of Disbelief*. New York: Basic Books.

Demerath, N. J., III. 1991. Religious Capital and Capital Religions: Cross-Cultural and Non-Legal Factors in the

Separation of Church and State. *Daedalus* 120(Summer):21-40.

Demerath, N. J., III and Karen Straight. 1997. Lambs Among the Lions: America's Culture Wars in Cross-Cultural Perspective. In *Cultural Wars in American Politics*, ed. Rhys H. Williams. Chicago: Aldine de Gruyter.

Demerath, N. J., III and Rhys H. Williams. 1985. Civil Religion in an Uncivil Society. *The Annals* of the American Academy of Political and Social Science 480(July):154-66.

Demerath, N. J., III and Yonghe Yang. 1997. What American Culture War? A View from the Trenches as Opposed to the Command Posts and the Press Corps. In *Cultural Wars in American Politics*, ed. Rhys H. Williams. Chicago: Aldine de Gruyter.

Durkheim, Emile. 1912. *The Elementary Forms of the Religious Life*. New York: Free Press.

Finke, Roger and Rodney Stark. 1988. Religious Economies and Sacred Canopies. *American Sociological Review* 53(Feb.):41-49.

Hadaway, C. Kirk, Penny Long Marler, and Mark Chaves. 1993. What the Polls Don't Show: A Closer Look at U.S. Church Attendance. *American Sociological Review* 58(Dec.):741-52.

Hunter, James D. 1991. *Culture Wars: The Struggle to Define America*. New York: Basic Books.

Ingelhart, Ronald. 1997. *Modernization and Postmodernization: Cultural, Economic, and Political Change in 43 Societies*. Princeton, NJ: Princeton University Press.

Lipset, S. M. 1996. *American Exceptionalism: A Double-Edged Sword*. New York: W. W. Norton.

Neuhaus, Richard John. 1984. *The Naked Public Square: Religion and Democracy in America*. Grand Rapids, MI: Eerdmans.

Rousseau, Jean-Jacques. [1770] 1960. Of Civil Religion. In *Social Contract*, ed. Ernest Barker. New York: Oxford University Press.

Williams, Rhys H. and N. J. Demerath III. 1991. Religion and Political Process in an American City. *American Sociological Review* 56(Dec.):417-31.

Wuthnow, Robert. 1988. *The Restructuring of American Religion: Society and Faith Since World War II*. Princeton, NJ: Princeton University Press.

American Pilgrimage Landscapes

By JUAN EDUARDO CAMPO

ABSTRACT: In late-twentieth-century America, there is a surprisingly large and varied number of pilgrimage centers. This article organizes them into three groups (pilgrimages of organized religion, civil religion, and cultural religion) for comparative description. It includes descriptions of Catholic, Mormon, and Hindu pilgrimages, as well as the sites of Gettysburg, Mount Rushmore, and Graceland as pilgrimage centers. Modernity, rather than displacing pilgrimages, has actually been responsible for globalizing them, a process that involves their appropriation by expert systems, the fostering of diverse and sometimes contending interpretations of their significance, and the actual production of new pilgrimage landscapes. Drawing upon original fieldwork, published research, and resources on the World Wide Web, the author proposes that by placing pilgrimages in global perspective, we are better able to discern both the roles played by immigrant groups in the formation of American pilgrimage landscapes and the contours of American participation in pilgrimages abroad, such as the hajj to Mecca.

Juan Eduardo Campo is associate professor of history of religions, Islamic studies, and global and international studies at the University of California at Santa Barbara. He is currently writing a comparative study of pilgrimages in modernity based on research conducted in Egypt, Saudi Arabia, India, Malaysia, Mexico, and the United States.

PILGRIMAGE is a phenomenon that we might least expect to encounter in the United States. After all, how is it possible for a supposedly archaic, collective set of ritual practices connected with journeying to sacred places and monitored by religious experts to take root in a country conceived of as the future-oriented epicenter of the New World, where the individual reigns, secularism is the coin of the land, and organized rituals are eclipsed by a Protestant ethic? Indeed, pilgrimage appears to be at odds with our widely held belief in the progressive development of the West into a complex modern civilization based on science, technology, and reason, rather than on magic, religion, and irrationality.

Although these seem to be plausible expectations, they do not conform well with even a cursory examination of the evidence. Along with the story of human progress, the narrative of America's creation includes the story of Columbus, who, in seeking a new route to the Indies, attempted to reach Jerusalem itself, the goal of medieval Christian pilgrims and crusaders. Instead, he encountered in the New World what he thought was the edge of an earthly paradise—an idea that surfaces again and again in American perceptions of the wilderness. Our grade school textbooks recount the travails of the Plymouth Pilgrims, who, like Columbus, are remembered in our calendar of national holidays. Indeed, America served as a landscape for the reenactment of great biblical dramas: a promised land, a new Zion, a city on the hill. In an essay on the expansionist character of religion in the United States,

Sidney E. Mead (1963) described Americans as "a people in movement through space" who have so "celebrated the external and material side of their pilgrim's progress that they have tended to conceal even from themselves the inner, spiritual pilgrimage" (7-8). Not only are pilgrimage themes and metaphors thus inscribed in our national narratives, explicitly and implicitly, but our country's territory has come to incorporate a variety of actual pilgrimage centers and routes.

"Pilgrimage" is a word that is used with reference to many different kinds of journeys across geographic and textual space, entailing encounters with adversity and the unknown through which individuals undergo a process of self-discovery. These may truly be features of pilgrimage, but they do little to help delimit the scope of the subject. A more adequate concept of pilgrimage—one that facilitates the task of identifying American pilgrimages—has been reached by anthropologists and historians of religions, who view it as a set of ritual actions involving specific human communities, institutions, and organized travel to and from sacred places (for example, Turner 1973; Gold 1988; Eade and Sallnow 1991; Peters 1994; Dubisch 1995). American pilgrimages, like pilgrimages elsewhere, encompass various social groups and institutions and are directed toward an impressively diverse set of locations, at home and abroad: from the National Shrine of Our Lady of Sorrows in Belleville, Illinois; the Mormon Temple in Salt Lake City, Utah; and Mecca in Saudi Arabia, to centers of American civil religion such as the memorials dedicated to American veterans, Mount Rushmore, and the U.S. Holocaust Memorial Museum. Even travel to such secular but symbolically rich sites as Disneyland and Graceland deserves consideration in an account of American pilgrimages. It is with relation to such intersections of groups, institutions, travel routes, rituals, and holy places in changing pilgrimage landscapes that the inner experiences of individual pilgrims are best understood.

The variety of American pilgrimages, with their overlapping and contrasting meanings, provides strong support for the argument that no place (or journey) is intrinsically sacred (Smith 1982, 55). Most sacred sites in the United States, with the important exception of the Native American sites, have been fashioned during the twentieth century by communities and institutions in locales that are easily reached by paved highways, in full view of the media, visitors, and bureaucratic agencies. The word "landscapes" helps us think about the territories in which they are located because it captures the importance of humans in their creation, appropriation, organization, and representation—as when a culture defines a place by its architecture, or painters such as Thomas Moran determine the point of view and composition of presumably natural scenes in Yellowstone or on the Mountain of the Holy Cross that they depict on their canvases. Pilgrimages, like their landscapes, are made, not revealed. Once they are made, they can exercise a power over thought and action. It is through ritualization,

which differentiates them from other types of social action, and the working of the human imagination that they can acquire their timeless, mythic qualities and sacrality. Ritualization (or commemoration) and imagination enable pilgrimages to take place.

As human projects, pilgrimage landscapes undergo historical change, and never has the pace of this change been as breathtaking, nor its effects so profound, as during the modern era. Giddens described the intimate connection between modernity and the "disembedding" of traditional systems and local concepts of time and space, such that they become reorganized globally "across large time-space distances" (Giddens 1990, 17-29). Some pilgrimages might indeed be driven into extinction by modernity, but the institutions and landscapes of many traditional pilgrimages are being reshaped, and new ones are generated by global political and economic forces, industrialism, reliance upon expert systems of technology and transportation, and secular formations of knowledge. In other words, the modern nation-state, the world capitalist system, steel, plastic, the telephone, the locomotive, the automobile, the airplane, the television, and—yes—the computer are making it possible for greater numbers of people in more cultures to learn about, travel to, and see more sacred places faster than at any other time in human history. A significant result of this has been that the number and variety of sacred places have also increased dramatically.

There has been a tendency in the treatment of American religion to construe it as one grand national narrative, superseding and obscuring the plurality of distinct, alternative, and competing ones (Albanese 1992, xx-xxi). Likewise, interpretations of pilgrimage have overemphasized its unifying functions. Despite their attention to its multivocality and historical variety, the Turners stated that "pilgrimage is very much involved in [a] perennial, universal drama, cutting across cultures, societies, polities, language groups and ethnicities" (Turner and Turner 1978, 16). It is often viewed as a mechanism that integrates individual and local identities with superordinate national, even civilizational ones (Wolf 1958; Obeyesekere 1966, 23; Bhardwaj 1973). Recently, this consensus has been reassessed in light of a growing body of evidence that pilgrimage not only embodies competing social, cultural, and religious elements but that it can also engender or intensify the forces of conflict (Eade and Sallnow 1991; Campo 1991; van der Veer 1994).

In order to adequately grasp American pilgrimages, especially at the turn of the millennium, we need to consider them in a way that acknowledges both their variety and their relation to the forces of globalization. This means examining pilgrimages that occur in the United States and those that draw its citizens and residents to sacred sites in foreign lands. By doing this, we will discover not only how migrations of peoples from all over the world have contributed to the formation of many of America's pilgrimage landscapes but also how these peoples have engaged in travel "across large time-space distances" to sacred sites in Latin America, Europe, Africa, the Middle East, and Asia. The inward and outward flux of American pilgrimages represents in a significant way the paradoxes of modernity, an era when it seems, in the words of Marx, that "all that is solid melts into air."

DOMESTICATING PILGRIMAGE

At the conclusion of his memoir of an 18-month journey across the United States, William K. Zinsser observed, "America's iconic places remind us of our anchoring principles and our best ideals and intentions" (Zinsser 1992, 189). His quest for distinctively American places led him to 15 different locales, from Lexington and Concord in the Northeast to Montgomery, Alabama, in the South, from Hannibal, Missouri, in the Midwest to Disneyland and Pearl Harbor in the Pacific basin region.

Zinsser's account, though idiosyncratic, raises the important issue of how to identify and classify America's pilgrimage sites. Should this be done on the basis of historical development? In terms of the size or the popularity of the sites? Their locations? The religious or cultural groups with which they are affiliated? These are all avenues of inquiry that scholars of American religion and culture have only just begun to explore. They certainly call for more intense scrutiny than the practical limits of this study will allow. Let me then propose a working typology according to which American domestic pilgrimage can begin to be identified and compared.

The typology consists of the following divisions: (1) pilgrimages explicitly connected with organized religions in the United States; (2) pilgrimages connected with the values, symbols, and practices of American civil religion; and (3) pilgrimages connected with cultural religion (Albanese 1992, 463-99), or what others have called "implicit religion" (Reader and Walter 1993, 16-17). The second group, unlike the first and the third, is concerned primarily with the production of patriotic loyalty to the United States, and it benefits from sizable investments by governmental agencies. The third group comprises pilgrimages that in a significant way incorporate elements deriving from the sphere of cultural values and practices but that are distinct from those identified with organized religions and civil religion. They have been embraced neither by organized religions nor by the National Park Service. The majority of sites visited by Zinsser, such as Lexington, Concord, Montgomery, Yellowstone, and Pearl Harbor, involve American civil religion. The others, such as Rockefeller Center and Disneyland, are better understood as focal points on the landscape of America's cultural religion. Zinsser completely excludes pilgrimages connected with organized religions from his account, as have recent scholarly studies of American sacred places (Sears 1989; Chidester and Linenthal 1995). This, however, is where I will begin.

PILGRIMAGES OF AMERICA'S
ORGANIZED RELIGIONS

An idea of the variety of pilgrimage landscapes in this division of the typology can be gained by examining those of the Roman Catholics, the Mormons, and the Hindus. In all three communities, ritual activities are formalized and occur in or around shrines and temple complexes; authority is concentrated in a male priestly hierarchy; and the lay membership has had to accommodate to minority status within the wider American milieu. The sacred sites of all three do not attract only pilgrims from among their own members. Based on a limited number of sample surveys, they draw a mix of pilgrims, tourists, and visitors, including coreligionists and outsiders. This is not a distinctive feature of U.S. pilgrimages; from a global perspective, Christian shrines and many Indian pilgrimage sites are accessible to outsiders, as are Muslim mosques and shrines outside of Saudi Arabia. Up close, of course, each religion has its own distinctive pilgrimage characteristics, based not only on its own traditions and ritual codes but also on its encounters with other religions, institutions, value systems, and ideologies in America.

Catholics as a group claim the largest number of pilgrimages in this division, most established during the twentieth century. As many as 126 sites are involved, located mostly in the five regions of the country where there are large concentrations of Catholics: the Northeast, the Midwest, the Southwest, French Louisiana, and Florida. Half of these sites favor Marian devotions, and the greater share of these commemorate shrines dedicated to the Virgin in Europe, such as Lourdes (9 sites) and Fatima (4), and Mexico. Among the Mexican shrines, it is especially *La Morena*, the "dark" Virgin of Guadalupe (2), who is commemorated (Rinschede 1990, 96). The shrine of Our Lady of the Snows near St. Louis—a distinctive 200-acre complex of memorial gardens, walks, chapels, and other buildings that accommodates up to 1 million pilgrims and visitors—actually contains a two-thirds-scale model of the Lourdes Grotto (Giuriati, Myers, and Donach 1990, 158-59).

Although many other Catholic pilgrimage centers in the United States are dedicated to Jesus and saints not from America but from the early Christian era and medieval Europe, some are dedicated to a distinct group of American saints and martyrs. The National Shrine of the North American Martyrs in Auriesville, New York, for example, was initiated in 1885 to remember three seventeenth-century Jesuits who died while missionizing the Native American peoples in the area. In 100 years, it grew into a 600-acre complex comprising, in addition to the martyrs' chapel, several shrines to the Virgin (including Lourdes and Fatima replicas), a "torture platform crucifix," a museum, a coliseum for pilgrim gatherings, a path for the stations of the cross, a retreat house, a cafeteria, offices, and large parking lots. It is easily accessible via the New York State Thruway. Unlike Catholic pilgrimage sites based mainly on relics and saints transferred from Europe and the Middle East, this complex seeks to stake an unambiguous claim to a place in the American landscape. As the shrine's web page states,

Truly, here the blood of Martyrs was the seed of Christians in North America. . . . [It] bears witness to the Catholic dogma of the communion of saints. When the pilgrims make their way about the shrine grounds, they learn they are not alone. They are at one with the Christian saints who lived and suffered at Ossernenon [Auriesville] a third of a millennium ago. And they go away refreshed, renewed and hopeful. (Marzolf 1997)

The National Shrine of St. Jude in Chicago is a distinctively contemporary American pilgrimage center. Named after an obscure apostle, a cousin of Jesus, who was martyred in Persia, this shrine was founded in 1929 by the Claretian Fathers, a Spanish missionary organization, as part of a national campaign to raise funds for the building of Our Lady of Guadalupe Church, which served Mexican migrants drawn to Chicago by the steel industry (Orsi 1991). Promoted through the post office and the radio, this new devotion coincided with a rising tide of piety among Catholic immigrants from Europe who were beginning to move away from their old neighborhoods, seeking ways to blend their individual ethnic identities with the wider American society. St. Jude's shrine provided them with a way to participate in an ethnically inclusive pilgrimage and to do so by mail. The Claretians encouraged them to send their petitions and donations to the saint by post; they did not have to physically visit the shrine. It may well be the case that national space is what mattered at St. Jude's, not the local landscape (Orsi 1991, 219-20).

The Mormon church (the Church of Jesus Christ of Latter-day Saints

[LDS]) has interwoven its experiences in the American landscape with biblical themes. This means in particular that the migration of Joseph Smith and his followers from New York State to Missouri and Illinois in the 1830s and early 1840s, and of Brigham Young and his followers (including new converts from England) from Illinois to the Utah Territory in 1846-47 were interpreted in terms of the journeys of the Old Testament patriarchs and the Hebrew tribes. The Mormons speak of Young as a Joshua leading his people through the wilderness to a promised land and the construction of a new Zion. This narrative is rich in the themes of biblical pilgrimage: of tribulations, difficult journeys, and soteriological expectations (Davies 1990, 312-14; Albanese 1992, 225-27). Hence, it is not surprising to find that travel to temples and to the sites of key events in LDS history—such as Nauvoo, Illinois, the early Mormon settlement where Smith was buried—constitutes one of the foremost features of LDS religious practice, even though Mormons do not usually use the term "pilgrimage." Underscoring the importance of travel to sacred sites in this community is "temple work," rituals of baptizing the living for the dead and the "sealing" of the bonds between husband and wife and between parent and child to help their spirits, and those of deceased ancestors, attain full salvation in eternity (Davies 1990, 318-20; Albanese 1992, 229). Approximately 5 million Mormons go to temples—and especially to Temple Square, in Salt Lake City—to engage in these rites at least once annually (Jackson, Rinschede, and Knapp 1990, 42).

Pilgrimages, or *tirthayatras*, are among the most popular religious practices of India. They are a form of "sacred sightseeing" that involves the devotional worship of Hindu gods and goddesses at four types of sacred places: temples, river banks, mountains, and forests. S. M. Bhardwaj, who has studied Indian pilgrimages extensively, has posited, "The institution of pilgrimage in Hinduism is so deep rooted that it would be [a] surprise if it did not transfer to America" (Bhardwaj 1990, 96-97). He made this observation after visiting a number of the Hindu temples that had been constructed in various regions of the United States by Indians who arrived after the Immigration Act of 1965 went into effect. The successful transference of Roman Catholic pilgrimage traditions to America and their adaptation to the new land suggest that Bhardwaj's expectations were reasonable. In his study, he noted that several temples in or near urban areas were drawing donations and worshipers from beyond their immediate localities and that actual pilgrimage routes seemed to be developing in the late 1980s. For example, the Sri Venkateswara[1] temple in a suburb of Pittsburgh, inaugurated in 1976, drew 75 percent of its 1981-82 pilgrims from outside Pennsylvania, including some from Canada. It became a stop on routes connecting the Ganesha[2] temple in Flushing, New York, and Hindus in Canada with the new Vrindaban temple of the International Society for Krishna Consciousness[3] in rural Moundsville, West Virginia. The route also includes stops at other temples in the region, as well as Niagara Falls (Bhardwaj 1990, 85-87, 95).

It is too early to tell how deeply the roots of Hindu pilgrimages will grow into American soil during the next century. The early temples of the 1970s and 1980s were closely tied to temples, priests, and craftsmen in India, and the number of Hindus in the United States is small (less than 2 million). Pilgrimage sites will have to become less dependent on their connections to India in order to flourish here, a process that will be aided by the growth of the Indian immigrant community's size and wealth. Although there are no precise data, the number of visitors attending Hindu temples in the United States appears to be small compared to the numbers claimed by the larger American Catholic pilgrimage centers and the Mormons' Temple Square.

Islam is another major religion in which pilgrimage holds special significance. Indeed, pilgrimage to Mecca, known as the hajj, is a religious obligation for all Muslims to perform at least once in a lifetime if they are able to do so. It is striking, therefore, to note that, unlike Catholics, Mormons, and Hindus, Muslims have neither created new pilgrimage centers in the United States nor transferred pilgrimage traditions from their homelands. The lack of a Mecca in America for Muslims cannot be attributed to a lack of a sufficient population base. There are now between 4 and 6 million in the United States, and they may soon constitute the second-largest religious group here. The explanation lies elsewhere. First, it is easy to be exempted from the hajj requirement, allowing priority to be given to other forms of worship. Second, the detailed ritual code that governs it allows no room for transference to another location. Concomitantly, in this modern era of expert systems, Muslims who are inclined to undertake hajj can readily do so, thanks to the air travel industry and the establishment of Saudi consulates to handle visas in several locations in the United States (this convenience is largely due to each country's involvement with the oil industry). Prospective pilgrims can even download the hajj visa application from the World Wide Web. Third, Muslim worship here emphasizes congregational gatherings of fellow believers in mosques, and it shows no signs of establishing the devotional pilgrimages (*ziyarat*) to saints' shrines that are so ubiquitous in the Muslim cultures of Africa and Asia (Esposito 1995, s.v. "popular religion").

PILGRIMAGES OF AMERICAN CIVIL RELIGION

Meramec Caverns State Park, just west of St. Louis, consists of a complex of caves filled with unusual and colorful mineral formations. What is most remarkable is how such a natural site has become imbued with local and national significance. Guides inform visitors of its mythic past: its use as a Civil War ammunition storage area and hiding place by Quantrill's raiders, its connection with the life of Jesse James, and its use as a location for the filming of *The Adventures of Tom Sawyer* and *Lassie*. It was being readied as an atomic bomb shelter during the Cold War and has been used for Easter sunrise ceremonies. At the end of the tour, visitors are seated in a large cavern, facing the Stage Curtain, a spectacular wall of stalactites and stalagmites. Then, as an image of the American flag is projected onto this formation of colorful mineral deposits, they are regaled with a recording of Kate Smith singing "God Bless America," in memory of those who served in the armed forces during the Vietnam war.

Meramec contains all the elements that typify the pilgrimage sites of American civil religion: interconnection of God and country, commemoration of heroes (legendary and otherwise) and martyrs, and the attribution of patriotic significance to the natural landscape. Indeed, landscape itself is the prevailing feature of this division, more than for pilgrimages of organized religions in America. The ceremonial centers of American public life possess defined though often contested boundaries, are exempted from property taxes, and are supported by public funds (in addition to donations, admission fees, and income derived from business concessions). Indeed, a good way to begin to identify these sites is to peruse the listings of state and national parks and historical sites. The National Park Service currently lists nearly 400 sites, from Abraham Lincoln's birthplace to Zion National Park (National Park Service 1998). Here I will first discuss the Gettysburg National Military Park—identified in a late-nineteenth-century guidebook as "the most consecrated ground this world contains, except the path of the Savior of the world as he ascended the rugged heights of Calvary" (J. Howard Wert, quoted in

Linenthal 1991, 4)—and the Mount Rushmore National Memorial, America's so-called Shrine of Democracy. Then I will turn to consider sites connected with minority ethnic groups that have been incorporated into the country's civil sacred space.

The transformation of the Gettysburg Civil War battlefield in Pennsylvania farm country into a pilgrimage site occurred gradually between the actual event in early July 1863 and the centennial observances held in 1963. It was accomplished through acts of commemoration, monumentation, reunion, and reenactment (Linenthal 1991, chap. 3). These actions involved presidents, congressmen, governors, Civil War veterans, concerned citizens, the National Park Service, and, of course, ordinary visitors. Although a memorial association was founded just three months after the battle to commemorate the Union fighting men, it was Lincoln's address on 19 November 1863 that really initiated the process of sacralization.

The first monuments and statues at the site were restricted to the cemetery. This changed in the late 1870s, when monuments began to be erected on the field of battle, marking the heroic actions and deaths of officers and soldiers from both sides. The federal government took ownership of a part of the battlefield in 1895, and it was assigned to the National Park Service in 1933. Today, the site, which occupies six square miles of land, contains 1300 memorials, about 200 of which are Confederate ones (Linenthal 1991, 105, 123 n.48).

In the early days, many of the monuments were dedicated during reunions of the combatants on the anniversaries of the battle. These "elaborate rituals of reconciliation," as they are described by religious studies scholar Edward T. Linenthal, involved gatherings of up to 55,000 Civil War veterans who camped on the battlefield, related details of the action from memory, and reenacted key moments of the engagement. The last reunion occurred on the seventy-fifth anniversary, 1938, when about 2000 of the surviving veterans were joined by an estimated one-quarter million spectators. Franklin D. Roosevelt addressed this gathering and the nation in a broadcast that described Gettysburg as a shrine of American liberty (Linenthal 1991, 96-97). Even with the passing of the last veterans, the site continued to attract new generations of visitors, some of whom began to reenact the critical scenes of the conflict with enthusiasm and painstaking attention to detail. At the centennial anniversary, a crowd of about 40,000 watched as a group of 1000 men dressed as Union and Confederate soldiers staged the culminating engagement of the battle—a performance that ended with their joining together to sing the national anthem (Linenthal 1991, 99). Such reenactments continue to occur regularly to the present day.

Mount Rushmore stands apart from war memorials like Gettysburg, Lexington and Concord, the Alamo, the Little Big Horn, and Pearl Harbor as a pilgrimage center. As one religious studies scholar observed, this two-square-mile memorial site was not hallowed by the shedding of blood (Glass 1994, 266). Nor can it be lo-cated in a climactic moment in time, which limits opportunities for conducting distinctive commemorative observances at regular intervals, such as those that occur at battlefields. It is its own event: the sculpting of the colossal faces of "some sons of God"—Washington, Jefferson, Lincoln, and Theodore Roosevelt—into the solid granite of a mountain in the Black Hills of South Dakota. Originally intended to glorify America's western heroes, sculptor Gutzon Borglum created a monument that would arouse patriotic feelings "in every American." He also touted it as an income-producing tourist site. Borglum started work on the project in 1927; it was completed just months after his death in 1941. George Bush finally dedicated the site officially on Independence Day 1991. During the intervening years, commemorative observances often occurred in conjunction with the completion of some phase of the project itself (Glass 1995, 162-63). Administered by the National Park Service since 1933 and supported by a voluntary association, it now accommodates 2 million visitors each year.

This monument has been the focal point of conflicting interests and interpretations since its inception. While many people regarded Mount Rushmore as a national shrine, some local residents protested that it marred the natural beauty of the area. Corporations exploited its image in their advertisements. Early in the Cold War, Drew Pearson used it to rally Americans against what he saw as the rising tide of global communism, and, in 1987, activists from Greenpeace and Earth First! staged a protest there against industrial pollution.

Native Americans have been actively involved in contesting the significance of the site since the 1920s. Lakota medicine man Black Elk, who had a vision nearby, called upon the great spirits to protect Borglum and his workers. Others lamented that the project desecrated the beauty of the Black Hills, the Lakota homeland. In the 1970s, members of the American Indian Movement occupied the site several times, seeking to subvert its patriotic meaning by declaring that it stood for the crimes committed against Native Americans by "white America." Thus some called for transforming it into Mount Crazy Horse, in honor of the defender of the Black Hills and victor of the Little Big Horn. Concomitantly, the family of Borglum's assistant, Korczak Ziolkowski, was carving an even more colossal image of Crazy Horse on a nearby mountain that is now attracting visitors and the attention of the media (Glass 1995, 169-78).

The Martin Luther King, Jr., National Historical Site stands as an example of how black American protests against the injustices, violence, and racism of white America gave birth to a pilgrimage landscape that promotes the civil values of racial integration and nonviolence. Established by the National Park Service in 1980, the 23.2-acre complex occupies an urban neighborhood in Atlanta. Among its chief features are Martin Luther King's birthplace, the first black home to be included on the National Register; the Ebenezer Baptist Church, where he was co-pastor with his father; his tomb; and the Martin Luther King, Jr., Center for Nonviolent Social Change.

The Center for Nonviolent Social Change was founded by Coretta Scott King in the aftermath of King's assassination in 1968. It claims to receive 3.5 million visitors a year (Martin Luther King, Jr., Center 1997). This exceeds the numbers for many of the other sites on the roster of the National Park Service.

The recent appearance of new pilgrimage sites such as the King site and the United States Holocaust Memorial Museum (Linenthal 1995), near the National Mall, shows how the pain and suffering of distinct and influential ethnic groups in the United States can be changed into an affirmation of national values. We might expect to see the tribulations of other active ethnic groups in the United States achieve comparable recognition in the years to come. Public memorials for Native Americans, Japanese American internment camp victims, and Latino immigrants may well be established and develop into civil religion pilgrimage sites. Thus, rather than engendering division and conflict, as some assert, the forces of multiculturalism may actually contribute to the enrichment of public life in this country. The fact that this must come at the expense of inestimable human affliction, however, is a disturbing reminder that even the most democratic societies have a dark side.

PILGRIMAGES OF AMERICAN CULTURAL RELIGION

In this third division are pilgrimages that also involve ceremonial centers, ritualization, mythic figures, and journeys but which have not been absorbed by either an organized religion or the National Park Service. It includes theme parks such as Disneyland, celebrity haunts such as Graceland, and sporting events such as the Super Bowl and the Olympics. Many of these pilgrimages, though not necessarily all, entail both the commodification of culture and its invasive reproduction through the mass media. In their most excessive modality, they enrapture people with a seemingly endless parade of images and relics on television, in the cinema, and, most important, in shopping malls. For example, in 1996 alone, 28.8 million people visited either Disneyland or Walt Disney World (*Los Angeles Times* 22 Oct. 1997), making them the most frequently visited sites in the United States, if not the world. Why are we not surprised to discover billboards on the roads leading to Banaras, one of India's leading pilgrimage centers, inviting people to buy a Sony product and perhaps win a trip for two to Disney World and the 1996 Olympics in Atlanta? As a Japanese writer observed, Disneyland "has been transformed from simply being an amusement park and tourist spot, into a sacred space" (quoted in Reader and Walter 1993, 6).

When Elvis Presley died on 16 August 1977, his fans began to gather at Graceland, his family mansion in Memphis, Tennessee. This was the beginning of what has come to be known as Tribute Week or Elvis Week. The most popular event during this commemorative gathering is the Candlelight Vigil on the evening of 15 August each year, when up to 50,000

pilgrims pray and listen to Bible readings, sermons, and spirituals recorded by Elvis himself. This event was transmitted around the world by the electronic and print media in 1997, the twentieth anniversary of his death. It was capped by a sellout concert at Mid-South Coliseum starring Elvis himself, according to the Graceland web page, "singing lead vocal, via a large video screen suspended above the cast. . . . in person, in concert, now, today—after a twenty year absence" (Elvis Presley Enterprises 1997).

Though often the subject of American humor and tabloid journalism, postmortem Elvis is regarded as a saintly figure by many of his fans, and Graceland is his shrine. With the sanitizing of the messy details of his factual life, fans see parallels between the story of The King and that of Christ, and some have created portraits of him that are modeled after those of the white, Euro-American Jesus (Vikan 1994, 150; Rodman 1996, plates 28a-c, 120-121). In twenty years, Graceland itself has evolved into a 13.8-acre walled shrine complex consisting of an ornate melody gateway, a two-story Georgian Colonial-style mansion, administrative building, stables, swimming pool, and the Meditation Garden, with its Grecian columns, fountain, stained-glass windows, and angel statues (Davidson, Hecht, and Whitney 1990, 230-31; Marling 1996, 199-213). It is in the garden that Elvis was interred, together, in a sunburst pattern, with his mother, father, and paternal grandmother. There is also a memorial plaque for his twin brother, Jesse, who died at birth. An eternal flame burns at the head of his grave, and a statue of Jesus of the Sacred Heart overlooks it. Beside the grave many pilgrims leave their gifts: flowers, artificial roses, stuffed animals, flags, and homemade dioramas with scenes from Elvis's life. They are also encouraged to leave graffiti on the stone wall that fronts Elvis Presley Boulevard. Some are obscene; many, devotional in tone: "Elvis lives!" (over a radiant cross) and "I have seen Graceland. My life is complete. Miss you terribly" (Vikan 1994, 163, 166; Rodman 1996, 200-201, nn.33-34). At the souvenir stands nearby, tourists and pilgrims can also obtain maps showing the way to other Elvis sites, including his Tupelo birthplace, with its Elvis Presley Memorial Chapel. Although there is much here that is reminiscent of medieval saint veneration, as Gary Vikan argues, we cannot help but also take note of how much the commodification of the man's voice and image in the electronic media contributed to the development of this pilgrimage landscape.

PILGRIMS ABROAD

In order to fully appreciate the modern and global dimensions of American pilgrimages, it is fitting to conclude with some remarks concerning American pilgrimages to foreign lands. To do otherwise is to succumb to an exceptionalism that pervades too much of what has been written of American history, religion, and culture. I have already noted that numerous pilgrimage landscapes here have been created by immigrants from other regions of the world, that some are imbued with global significance, and that many attract foreign visitors. Toward what foreign meccas do Americans turn?

All three types of pilgrimage that I described previously have their global counterparts. Americans engage in visits to pilgrimage sites abroad connected with organized religions. Thus U.S. Catholics travel to Europe to visit the Vatican, Lourdes, Santiago de Compostela in Spain, or Medugorje in the former Yugoslavia. Mexicans and Chicanos not only venerate the image of the Virgin of Guadalupe in their homes and local churches here but also travel to her basilica on the outskirts of Mexico City. Jews, Protestants, Catholics, and Orthodox Christians visit holy sites in Jerusalem and elsewhere in Israel-Palestine. Hindu immigrants maintain close connections with pilgrimage centers in India. Several thousand American Muslims perform the hajj to Mecca each year or undertake a lesser pilgrimage before or after the hajj season. They are U.S. citizens and residents who are either converts or first- or second-generation immigrants from Muslim countries, and they even include U.S. armed forces personnel stationed in Saudi Arabia. Malcolm X's account of his experiences as a pilgrim in Mecca testifies to the involvement of African American pilgrims in the hajj, as well as to the profound effect it can have on their outlook (Malcolm X 1966, chaps. 17-18).

As we might expect, the number of sites abroad connected with American civil religion is very small. Perhaps the best known of these is the Normandy American Cemetery near

Omaha Beach, where President Clinton, World War II veterans, and foreign dignitaries gathered in June 1994 to commemorate soldiers who died fighting Nazi Germany. Fortunately, given the public's current reluctance to engage in long, bloody foreign conflicts, it is likely that we will see few if any additional sites of this sort in the near future.

Many Americans are attracted to sites abroad connected with cultural religion, however. In the global context, theme parks and celebrity sites are a minor aspect of this subgroup of pilgrimages. More important are visits to ancestral homelands in Africa, Europe, and Asia. For example, there are the journeys made by African Americans to Gorée Island, the former slave port off the coast of Senegal, to South Africa, and to Egypt. Babyboomer Americans motivated by a quest for individual spiritual experience and insight seek gurus at holy sites in India or gather at ancient monuments like Stonehenge and the Egyptian pyramids. Many of these locales provide American pilgrims access to what Indian writer Gita Mehta cynically called "the trance-inducing industry" (Mehta 1993, 139). The truly adventurous undertake pilgrimages that stress the journey itself rather than the destination, such as those who set out on solo voyages across the Pacific or scale the summits of the Himalayas and the Alps.

Is this not tourism, rather than pilgrimage? In the late twentieth century, the two are seldom easily distinguishable. Pilgrimage often invites tourism, while tourism entertains the possibility of pilgrimage experiences. Muslim travel agencies, for example offer a selection of hajj packages, including the "tourist hajj," with first-class transportation and accommodations. Likewise, other agencies tout Holy Land tours and excursions to the spiritual centers of India. A good sense of the fuzzy relationship between tourism and pilgrimage is conveyed in the following statement by the rector of the National Shrine of the Immaculate Conception in Washington, D.C.:

In nearly every part of the United States there is a place which has been designated as a national pilgrimage site.... *If you are planning a vacation*, include a visit to a shrine or place of pilgrimage on your itinerary as a way of enriching yours and your children's faith and appreciation for our Christian ancestry. *Not far from Disney World* in Orlando is the Mary, Queen of the Universe Shrine as well as shrines to Our Lady in Miami and St. Augustine. *A trip out west to California might include a tour* of the mission churches and shrines in San Diego, San Francisco, San Luis Rey and Ventura. (Emphasis added) (Bransfield 1996)

It is true that the experience of randomness and "no sense of place" is an aspect of modern life (Meyrowitz 1985). Yet the information I have assembled here demonstrates that modernity is also creating new senses of place in connection with the variety of American pilgrimage landscapes that have arisen or become disembedded and reembedded mainly during the last hundred years. The late-twentieth-century dominance of expert systems of political organization, transportation, and electronic communication (including the World Wide Web) has made it possible for the knowledge, imagery, and experience of these places to reach globally, in Giddens's words, "across large time-space distances." In the decades to come, they promise to have a significant effect upon the contours of American religious and social life, as well as upon peoples living in other regions of the world.

Notes

1. Venkateswara is worshiped as a form of the god Vishnu, protector of the universe, particularly at his south Indian temple in Tirupati.

2. Ganesha is the elephant-headed deity of the threshold, who removes obstacles and brings success. His New York temple is also known as the Vighaneswara temple.

3. Krishna is a form of the god Vishnu and embodies the qualities of divine love and playfulness. His Indian pilgrimage center is located in Vrindaban and the surrounding area of the Twelve Forests, south of New Delhi.

References

Albanese, Catherine L. 1992. *America: Religions and Religion*. 2d ed. Belmont, CA: Wadsworth.

Bhardwaj, Surinder Mohan. 1973. *Hindu Places of Pilgrimage in India: A Study in Cultural Geography*. Berkeley: University of California Press.

———. 1990. Hindu Pilgrimage in America. In *Social Anthropology of Pilgrimage*, ed. Makhan Jha. New Delhi: Inter-India.

Bransfield, Michael J. 1996. Pilgrims of God: A Church on the Move. Available on the World Wide Web from www. nationalshrine.com/NAT_SHRINE/pilgrims.htm.

Campo, Juan Eduardo. 1991. The Mecca Pilgrimage in the Formation of Islam in Modern Egypt. In *Sacred Places and Profane Spaces: Essays in the Geographics of Judaism, Christianity and Islam*, ed. Jamie Scott and Paul Simpson-Housely. New York: Greenwood.

Chidester, David and Edward T. Linenthal, eds. 1995. *American Sacred Space*. Bloomington: Indiana University Press.

Davidson, J. W., Alfred Hecht, and Herbert A. Whitney. 1990. The Pilgrimage to Graceland. In *Pilgrimage in the United States*, ed. Gisbert Rinschede and S. M. Bhardwaj. Geographia Religionum 5. Berlin: Dietrich Reimer Verlag.

Davies, D. J. 1990. Pilgrimage in Mormon Culture. In *Social Anthropology of Pilgrimage*, ed. Makhan Jha. New Delhi: Inter-India.

Dubisch, Jill. 1995. *In a Different Place: Pilgrimage, Gender, and Politics of a Greek Island Shrine*. Princeton, NJ: Princeton University Press.

Eade, John and Michael J. Sallnow, eds. 1991. *Contesting the Sacred: The Anthropology of Christian Pilgrimage*. London: Routledge.

Elvis Presley Enterprises, Inc. 1997. Elvis Week '97 Blows Minds and Breaks All Records! Available on the World Wide Web from www.elvispresley.com/newsp2.htm.

Esposito, John L., ed. 1995. *The Oxford Encyclopedia of the Modern Islamic World*. New York: Oxford University Press.

Giddens, Anthony. 1990. *The Consequences of Modernity*. Stanford, CA: Stanford University Press.

Giuriati, Paolo, Phyllis M. G. Myers, and Martin E. Donach. 1990. Pilgrims to "Our Lady of the Snows," Belleville, Illinois in the Marian Year: 1987-1988. In *Pilgrimage in the United States*, ed. Gisbert Rinschede and S. M. Bhardwaj. Geographia Religionum 5. Berlin: Dietrich Reimer Verlag.

Glass, Matthew. 1994. Producing Patriotic Inspiration at Mount Rushmore. *Journal of the American Academy of Religion* 62:265-83.

———. 1995. "Alexanders All": Symbols of Conquest and Resistance at Mount Rushmore. In *American Sacred Space*, ed. David Chidester and Edward T. Linenthal. Bloomington: Indiana University Press.

Gold, Ann Grodzins. 1988. *Fruitful Journeys: The Ways of Rajasthani Pilgrims*. Berkeley: University of California Press.

Jackson, Richard H., Gisbert Rinschede, and Jill Knapp. 1990. Pilgrimage in the Mormon Church. In *Pilgrimage in the United States*, ed. Gisbert Rinschede and S. M. Bhardwaj. Geographia Religionum 5. Berlin: Dietrich Reimer Verlag.

Linenthal, Edward Tabor. 1991. *Sacred Ground: Americans and Their Battlefields* Urbana: University of Illinois Press.

———. 1995. Locating Holocaust Memory: The United States Holocaust Memorial Museum. In *American Sacred Space*, ed. David Chidester and Edward T. Linenthal. Bloomington: Indiana University Press.

Malcolm X. 1966. *Autobiography of Malcolm X*. New York: Grove Press.

Marling, Karal Ann. 1996. *Graceland: Going Home with Elvis*. Cambridge, MA: Harvard University Press.

Martin Luther King, Jr., Center for Nonviolent Social Change. 1997. The King Center. Available on the World Wide Web from www.thekingcenter.com.

Marzolf, John G. 1997. Welcome to the National Shrine of the North American Martyrs. Available on the World Wide Web from www.klink.net/~jesuit/.

Mead, Sidney E. 1963. The American People: Their Space, Time, and Religion. In *The Lively Experiment: The Shaping of Christianity in America*. New York: Harper & Row.

Mehta, Gita. 1993. *Karma Cola*. New York: Penguin Books.

Meyrowitz, Joshua. 1985. *No Sense of Place: The Impact of Electronic Media on Social Behavior*. New York: Oxford University Press.

National Park Service. 1998. U.S. National Parks by Name. Available on the World Wide Web from www.nps.gov/parklists/byname.htm.

Obeyesekere, Gananath. 1966. The Buddhist Pantheon in Ceylon and Its Extensions. In *Anthropological Studies in Theravada Buddhism*, ed. Manning Nash. New Haven, CT: Yale University Press.

Orsi, Robert. 1991. The Center out There, in Here, and Everywhere Else: The Nature of Pilgrimage to the Shrine of Saint Jude, 1929-1965. *Journal of Social History* 25:213-32.

Peters, F. E. 1994. *The Hajj: The Muslim Pilgrimage to Mecca and the Holy Places*. Princeton, NJ: Princeton University Press.

Reader, Ian and Tony Walter, eds. 1993. *Pilgrimage in Popular Culture*. London: Macmillan.

Rinschede, Gisbert. 1990. Catholic Pilgrimage Places in the United States. In *Pilgrimage in the United States*, ed. Gisbert Rinschede and S. M. Bhardwaj. Geographia Religionum 5. Berlin: Dietrich Reimer Verlag.

Rodman, Gilbert B. 1996. *Elvis After Elvis: The Posthumous Career of a Living Legend*. London: Routledge.

Sears, John. 1989. *Sacred Places: American Tourist Attractions in the Nineteenth Century*. New York: Oxford University Press.

Smith, Jonathan Z. 1982. *Imagining Religion: From Babylon to Jonestown*. Chicago: University of Chicago Press.

Turner, Victor. 1973. The Center out There: Pilgrims' Goal. *History of Religions* 12:191-230.

Turner, Victor and Edith Turner. 1978. *Image and Pilgrimage in Christian Culture*. New York: Columbia University Press.

van der Veer, Peter. 1994. *Religious Nationalism: Hindus and Muslims in India*. Berkeley: University of California Press.

Vikan, Gary. 1994. Graceland as Locus Sanctus. In *Elvis + Marilyn: 2 × Immortal*, ed. Geri DePaoli. New York: Rizzoli.

Wolf, Eric. 1958. The Virgin of Guadalupe: A Mexican National Symbol. *Journal of American Folklore* 71:34-39.

Zinsser, William K. 1992. *American Places: A Writer's Pilgrimage to Fifteen of This Country's Most Visited and Cherished Sites*. New York: HarperCollins.

Mainline Protestantism 2000

By WILLIAM McKINNEY

ABSTRACT: For much of its history, mainline Protestantism has sought to mediate or bridge tensions present in the wider culture. In an increasingly polarized society, its churches struggle to find ways to provide moral leadership while holding themselves together. The postwar period has been difficult for mainline Protestantism's institutions. Membership declines and financial pressures continue. New communities of reference are replacing the denominational seminary as the primary locus of theological inquiry. Nonetheless, congregations are reemerging as centers of religious vitality, and there are signs of progress as mainline Protestantism adapts to a rapidly changing social context.

William McKinney is president and professor of American religion at Pacific School of Religion in Berkeley, California. His most recent book is The Responsibility People *(1994). He is an editor of* Studying Congregations *(forthcoming).*

WRITING of Cambridge, Massachusetts, some years ago, a *New Yorker* editor described the town as having a nineteenth-century sense of being right and open-minded at the same time. This is not a bad characterization of mainline Protestantism in the twentieth century.

"Mainline" is one of several labels (including "mainstream," "ecumenical," "public," "established," "old-line," and "liberal") used to refer to Protestant churches and sensibilities whose experience in America dates to the early years of European immigration. The term is theologically and sociologically imprecise but points to the fact that, in the U.S. setting today, even the term "Protestant" is problematic. Sociologically and theologically, the term "Protestant" has little meaning beyond suggesting what one is *not*: not Roman Catholic, not Jewish, not a religious "none." As Wade Clark Roof and I argued in *American Mainline Religion* (1987), there are at least three major Protestant subcommunities, each with distinctive histories and cultures. While one of these subcommunities, black Protestantism, is distinct in racial composition, the boundaries between mainline and evangelical Protestantism are a bit fuzzy, although few would argue that theologically and culturally the evangelical and mainline traditions have been on rather different trajectories since the late nineteenth century. Among the denominational groups usually seen as mainline are the churches of the early British immigrants (Congregationalists, Presbyterians, and Episcopalians), the Reformed and Lutheran churches of the major waves of European immigration in the eighteenth and nineteenth centuries, and the more homegrown American Protestant churches of the frontier expansion (Methodists and Disciples of Christ). American Baptists and a number of smaller religious bodies, most identified with the National Council of the Churches of Christ in the U.S.A., round out the mainline family.

This family of churches and sensibilities is distinguished as much by an ethos and series of interrelationships as by doctrine, demographics, or organizational structure. Most of the nation's leading educational institutions and thousands of national and local cultural and social service institutions were founded by mainline Protestant churches and laity. William Hutchison (1989) points out that, even into the twentieth century, the social networks of Protestant clergy and leaders of business, culture, and government remained strong. While most of the official ties between institutions like Ivy League and liberal arts colleges, art museums, and benevolence agencies and their founding churches are gone, they nonetheless have origins and values in common.

Part of the genius but also a source of the contemporary struggle of mainline Protestantism is its determination to bridge or mediate seemingly conflicting ideas and relationships. Its instincts lead it to seek common ground between what seem to be irreconcilable concepts or ideas. Early on, these tensions were between European church roots and the needs and possibilities of the new land. Could, for example, churches founded to serve specific ethnic populations reach out to persons of varied national backgrounds? Later, tensions were evident between faithfulness to Christian orthodoxy and accommodation to the new insights and possibilities of philosophy and science. One can see the split between evangelical and mainline Protestantism as a division over the degree to which churches ought to accommodate to cultural changes. Throughout this century, mainline Protestantism has sought to affirm loyalty to nation while pressing for a new sense of global interdependence. Today its churches struggle to affirm traditions they helped to shape while taking responsibility for the sins of its earlier position of privilege.

This impulse toward finding common ground amid conflict is partly due to the composition of the churches themselves. With their membership often crossing national, class, regional, and ideological lines, these churches embraced the challenge of leaving room for dissent. Like American political parties, they have balanced the need for independent identity with the need for inclusiveness. As is true of the political parties, these churches struggle to find a common voice on public issues that will avoid dividing their own constituents.

As American political culture has become more contentious, polarized as some suggest into warring camps of progressivist versus orthodox worldviews, mainline Protestantism's attempt to remain a "big tent" has been challenged (see, for example, Wuthnow 1988; Hunter 1989; and, for another perspective, Sine

1995). On issues ranging from Christian doctrine to economics to sexuality, its members reflect the diversity of the wider society. In contrast with the seemingly more theologically and ideologically united religious Right, mainline Protestantism struggles to find ways to provide moral leadership while holding itself together.

MAINLINE PROTESTANTISM'S INSTITUTIONS

The decades since the 1960s have been difficult for the institutions of mainline Protestantism, including denominational structures. Its churches have lost members nearly every year since 1965. These declines have reduced the membership of some denominations by a third or more. David A. Roozen and Kirk Hadaway (1993) report that, in 1990, eight leading mainline Protestant churches included 22.6 million members, down 6.4 million from 1965. Over four decades, these churches' share of the U.S. religious market fell from 15.9 to 9.1 percent.

In addition, membership declines, combined with inflation and the desire on the part of local churches and members to have more choice in allocating mission support dollars, have increased the financial pressure on national and regional church bodies.[1] As denominations have faced financial difficulties, they have reduced contributions to regional, national, and worldwide ecumenical agencies.

One response to financial difficulties has been to attempt to reduce the psychological distance between national church settings and local churches. By the 1980s, a long-term trend toward locating denominational offices in New York City, close to the offices of the National Council of the Churches of Christ in the U.S.A. at 475 Riverside Drive, had been reversed. Presbyterians relocated to Louisville, the new Evangelical Lutheran Church in America to Chicago, and the United Church of Christ to Cleveland (McKinney 1991). The size of the National Council's program and staff was reduced radically as this national symbol of mainline Protestant cooperation struggled to find a new direction.

While organized ecumenism has experienced great stress in recent decades, interchurch cooperation has continued to flourish. In 1983 the Presbyterian Church (U.S.A.) brought together the northern and southern branches of Presbyterianism, which had been divided since Civil War times. The new Evangelical Lutheran Church in America, founded in 1987, united three major Lutheran streams. The United Church of Christ and the Christian Church (Disciples of Christ) have covenanted to share several ministries, including their overseas mission work. Further, these churches have reached important ecumenical agreements leading to mutual recognition of members and ministries.

MAINLINE PROTESTANTISM AND THEOLOGY

During World War II and in the years that followed, Protestant theology experienced an upswing. While never quite becoming household names, Paul Tillich, Dietrich Bonhoeffer, Karl Barth, Reinhold Niebuhr, H. Richard Niebuhr, and others were major intellectual figures with a sizable public following. Theology and ethics were taken seriously. As these major figures passed from the scene, there has been a sense that their successors are somehow not of the same stature.

Questions of quality and public recognition aside, there have been significant changes on the mainline Protestant theological scene. The denominational seminary has receded further as the principal source of theological scholarship. Increasingly, the university-related divinity school and the university departments of religious studies have become centers of scholarly activity. Mainline Protestantism is represented in these settings (some would say overrepresented), but the community of reference has changed, with far greater attention to the context out of which theology arises. New communities of reference have been spawned, and race, ethnicity, gender, and sexual orientation increasingly take the place of the denomination as context and conversation partner in constructive theology. Thus, black theology rises out of the context of the African American struggle for equal rights and justice, Latin American liberation theology has its roots in the experience of colonialism, and feminist theology begins with women's experience of patriarchy and cultural marginality.

Among theologians who influence mainline Protestantism today, Harvey Cox remains an important bellwether figure. Robert McAfee Brown, Martin Marty, Walter Brueggemann, John Cobb, William Willimon, and Stanley Hauerwas have sizable followings. Letty Russell and Elizabeth Schussler Fiorenza are important feminist theologians, joined by Rebecca Chopp, Katie Geneva Cannon, Susan Brooks Thistlethwaite, and Rita Nakashima Brock from a younger generation of feminist scholars. Cornel West, James Cone, C. Eric Lincoln, and Vincent Harding are important interpreters of the African American religious experience.

It is difficult to measure the impact of popular religious writers on the mainline Protestant laity. The larger denominations maintain active publishing programs, but this community has not produced authors who are explicitly recognized as spokespersons or representative of the movement itself. It lacks a Charles Colson or a James Dobson, who function as popular interpreters of evangelical Protestantism. Writers like Robert Fulgham and Forrester Church (both Unitarian Universalists) and Madeleine L'Engle (an Episcopalian) have sizable followings, as does M. Scott Peck. Perhaps mainline Protestantism's relative inattention to broadcast and electronic media has left it without the distribution systems through which its theological and intellectual leaders can reach larger audiences.

CONGREGATIONS

As is true of other religious traditions, most mainline Protestants express their faith commitments through participation in congregations.

While evangelical Protestantism has developed an elaborate infrastructure of para-church organizations (missionary movements, publishing houses, schools, even record companies and radio and television networks), the mainline churches have relied on more traditional forms of organization. These structures are increasingly centralized bureaucratic organizations accountable to formal, usually representative bodies of laity and clergy at the regional and national levels (Dykstra and Hudnut-Beumler 1992).

It is easy to overstate the contrast between evangelical Protestantism's growing institutional infrastructure with what seems to be a lack of social and cultural capital on the part of mainline Protestantism. As a dominant religious force through much of the nation's development, the Protestant churches felt free to release control of the institutions they had spawned, assuming that these colleges, hospitals, social service agencies, and advocacy movements would continue to reflect their interests and values. For better or worse, mainline Protestants felt confident that their interests and values would remain well represented in an increasingly pluralistic America.[2]

The mainline Protestant churches have retained an elaborate series of ecclesiastical and mission institutions. These structures vary across denominational lines, and their shape and purposes have changed over time. However, it is through thousands of congregations across the country that most adherents experience their faith tradition most directly. Most of these congregations are small and average fewer than 100 participants in weekend worship services. Even in churches with a connectional polity (for example, the Episcopal, United Methodist, and Presbyterian churches), congregations have considerable autonomy. Most are free to call their own clergy leadership and to shape their own budgets and programs.

As national church organizations have struggled for support in recent years, increasing attention has been given to the relatively small number of large local churches in strategic locations. For example, a network of Episcopal cathedrals has organized to convene electronically connected gatherings in cities across the country. Individual congregations with significant endowed resources have become centers of philanthropic activity, and the churches have come to look to individual congregations for leadership on public issues. This has long been true of churches like Riverside Chapel and the Cathedral of Saint John the Divine in New York City, Fourth Presbyterian Church in Chicago, and First Methodist Church, Dallas. Increasingly, scholars and religious journalists are recognizing that the future of American church life is being shaped from the ground up.

In a study centering on three growing conservative, congregationally based Christian religious movements, Donald Miller (1997, 183-87) has suggested the rise of a new paradigm. "New paradigm churches," he summarizes, have

eliminated many of the inefficiencies of bureaucratized religion by an appeal to the first-century model of Christianity; this "purged" form of religion corresponded to the countercultural world view of baby boomers, who rejected institutionalized religion; with their bureaucratically lean, lay-oriented organizational structure, new paradigm churches developed programs sensitive to the needs of their constituency; new paradigm churches offered a style of worship that was attractive to people who were alienated from establishment religion because it was in their own idiom; this worship and the corresponding message provided direct access to an experience of the sacred, which had the potential of transforming people's lives by addressing their deepest personal needs.

Miller, who is an Episcopalian, suggests that mainline Protestantism needs to take the new paradigm seriously. To remain competitive in the new religious marketplace, he argues, established churches must "radically reinvent themselves" by returning the ministry to the people, creating a much flatter organizational structure, and becoming "vehicles for people to access the sacred in profound and life-changing ways."

DIAGNOSING THE MAINLINE

As public recognition of the changing shape of mainline Protestantism has grown, scholars, foundations, and consultants have given a good deal of attention to its current situation and future prospects. This attention has run the gamut from the analytical[3] (changing birthrates, shifting denominational priorities, and so on) to the angry (who failed to lead the churches and why) (see Oden 1995; Wilke 1986; Willimon and Wilson 1987) to the prescriptive (what to do next) (see Coalter, Mulder, and Weeks 1996; Hadaway and Roozen 1993; Mead 1991).

From the early 1970s (with the publication of Dean M. Kelley's *Why Conservative Churches Are Growing* [1997]) through the 1980s, this attention tended to be sociological in character. By the 1990s, mainline Protestantism was receiving greater attention from historians and theologians. Multidisciplinary studies, including a seven-volume study of the Presbyterian Church (U.S.A.) (Coalter, Mulder, and Weeks 1990-92), an extended volume on the Christian Church (Disciples of Christ) (Williams 1991), and multi-authored volumes on United Methodism (Lawrence, Campbell, and Richey, forthcoming; Richey, Campbell, and Lawrence 1997), represent an important resource for understanding this movement.

What is the future of mainline Protestantism in North America? Several things seem clear. Low internal birthrates, the slow growth of its traditional constituencies, and the relatively low priority given to evangelism and membership growth make dramatic changes in its long-term pattern of declining market share unlikely. Recent growth among racial, ethnic, and immigrant populations should help stem declines.

Often overlooked in discussions of the plight of mainstream Protestantism are important positive changes that have taken place in the past two decades in the internal life of these historical churches. One such change is a rediscovery of the churches' social ministry. Prompted in part by decreasing public support for social programs in the Reagan-Bush era, many congregations found themselves able to make a concrete difference in the lives of their communities and neighborhoods. Recently, sociologist Nancy Ammerman (1997) has documented encouraging signs of congregations' capacity for adaptation in the midst of rapid social change.

Second, these churches have opened opportunities in ministry for women and in senior leadership roles for women and members of racial or ethnic minorities to a degree some thought unimaginable as recently as two decades ago. In doing so, often in contrast with other professions, the churches themselves have shown a capacity for change and not just assimilation. There are signs that the historical suppression of the ministerial gifts of gay men and lesbians are beginning to give way as well. No one would argue that the churches have achieved recognition of the full equality of women, members of racial and ethnic minorities, and gays and lesbians, and issues of patriarchy, racism, and homophobia are alive across the religious spectrum, but there is clear movement toward greater acceptance and affirmation.

Third, the mainline churches are giving considerable attention to the ministry of the laity. This has led to a reshaping of lay and clerical roles as clergy take more responsibility for helping empower men and women for their ministries in the family, the workplace, and public life. This shift has been accompanied by a further shift from judgment to education and dialogue on public policy issues.

Fourth, the churches have given considerable attention to issues of globalization, placing greater emphasis on global interdependence and partnerships with overseas churches. Increasingly, mission is conceived as involving both the sending and receiving of missionary personnel. Greater attention is given to interfaith dialogue.

Fifth, there has been a rediscovery of hymnody and worship. Virtually every denomination has published new books of worship and new hymnals. How a church worships—what and how churches sing and pray together—has become a new and sometimes conflictual locus of theological discussion in which all members are theologians.

Finally, mainline Protestantism has given birth to some new institutions. These range from abuse counseling and shelters for battered women, to alternative forms of theological education, to large social service institutions such as Habitat for Humanity and World Vision, to nonprofit organizations such as the Alban Institute and Leadership Network.

Even more interesting than the future of its institutions is the question of the future of mainline Protestantism's ethos and value system. In a more pluralistic, competitive, and adversarial public square, this community's historical impulse to bridge conflicting ideas and movements becomes a greater challenge than was

true when these churches enjoyed a privileged position in the society. The idea that these churches have a special responsibility for promoting ways in which diverse groups can coexist in relation to one another is questioned from within and without. It has been an important component of the history and current identity of mainline Protestantism, and the need for bridging and mediating institutions continues. No question is more important to these churches as some of them enter their fourth century on America's shores.

Notes

1. Several recent publications document the churches' financial struggles. See, for example, Hoge et al. 1996; Ronsvalle and Ronsvalle 1996. Robert Wuthnow 1997 traces the churches' fiscal crisis to a spiritual malaise growing from mainline churches' inability to come to grips with its middle-class origins and base.

2. Higher education provides a fascinating case study of mainline churches and the institutions they have created. See Bass 1989 and Marsden 1994 for two different perspectives on these relationships.

3. Representative are Roof and McKinney 1987; Wuthnow 1988, 1989; Roof and Michaelsen 1986; Finke and Stark 1992; Roozen and Hadaway 1993.

References

Ammerman, Nancy T. 1997. *Congregations and Community*. New Brunswick, NJ: Rutgers University Press.

Bass, Dorothy C. 1989. Ministry on the Margin: Protestants and Education. In *Between the Times: The Travail of the Protestant Establishment in America*, ed. William R. Hutchison. New York: Cambridge University Press.

Coalter, Milton J., John M. Mulder, and Louis Weeks. 1990-92. *The Presbyterian Presence*. Louisville, KY: Westminster, John Knox.

——. 1996. *Vital Signs: The Promise of Mainline Protestantism*. Grand Rapids, MI: Eerdmans.

Dykstra, Craig and James Hudnut-Beumler. 1992. The National Organizational Structures of Protestant Denominations. In *The Organizational Revolution: Presbyterians and American Denominationalism*, ed. Milton J. Coalter, John M. Mulder, and Louis Weeks. Louisville, NY: Westminster, John Knox.

Finke, Roger and Rodney Stark. 1992. *The Churching of America, 1776-1990: Winners and Losers in Our Religious Economy*. New Brunswick, NJ: Rutgers University Press.

Hadaway, Kirk and David A. Roozen. 1993. *Rerouting the Protestant Mainstream*. Nashville, TN: Abingdon.

Hoge, Dean R. et al. 1996. *Money Matters: Personal Giving in America's Churches*. Louisville, KY: Westminster, John Knox.

Hunter, James Davison. 1989. *Culture Wars: The Struggle to Define America*. New York: Basic Books.

Hutchison, William R. 1989. Protestantism as Establishment. In *Between the Times: The Travail of the Protestant Establishment in America, 1900-1960*, ed. William R. Hutchison. New York: Cambridge University Press.

Kelley, Dean M. 1997. *Why Conservative Churches Are Growing*. 2d ed. New York: Harper & Row.

Lawrence, William B., Dennis M. Campbell, and Russell E. Richey, eds. Forthcoming. *The People(s) Called Methodist: Forms and Reforms of Their Life*. Nashville, TN: Abingdon.

Marsden, George. 1994. *The Soul of the American University: From Protestant Establishment to Established Unbelief*. New York: Oxford University Press.

McKinney, William. 1991. The NCC in a New Time: Finding a Place in the Culture. In *Ethics in the Present Tense: Readings from Christianity and Crisis, 1966-1991*, ed. Leon Howell and Vivian Lindermayer. New York: Friendship Press.

Mead, Loren B. 1991. *The Once and Future Church*. Bethesda, MD: Alban Institute.

Miller, Donald E. 1997. *Reinventing American Protestantism: Christianity in the New Millennium*. Berkeley: University of California Press.

Oden, Thomas C. 1995. *Requiem: A Lament in Three Movements*. Nashville, TN: Abingdon.

Richey, Russell E., Dennis M. Campbell, and William B. Lawrence, eds. 1997. *Connectionalism, Mission and Identity*. Nashville, TN: Abingdon.

Ronsvalle, John and Sylvia Ronsvalle. 1996. *Behind the Stained Glass Window: Money Dynamics in the Church*. Grand Rapids, MI: Baker Book House.

Roof, Wade Clark and William McKinney. 1987. *American Mainline Religion: Its Changing Shape and Future*. New Brunswick, NJ: Rutgers University Press.

Roof, Wade Clark and Robert Michaelsen, eds. 1986. *Liberal Protestantism*. New York: Pilgrim.

Roozen, David A. and Kirk Hadaway. 1993. *Church and Denominational Growth*. Nashville, TN: Abingdon.

Sine, Tom. 1995. *Cease Fire: Searching for Sanity in America's Culture Wars*. Grand Rapids, MI: Eerdmans.

Wilke, Richard B. 1986. *Are We Yet Alive?* Nashville, TN: Abingdon.

Williams, D. Newell, ed. 1991. *A Case Study of Mainstream Protestantism: The Disciples' Relation to American Culture, 1880-1989*. Grand Rapids, MI: Eerdmans.

Willimon, William H. and Robert L. Wilson. 1987. *Rekindling the Flame: Strategies for a Vital United Methodism.* Nashville, TN: Abingdon.

Wuthnow, Robert. 1988. *The Restructuring of American Religion.* Princeton, NJ: Princeton University Press.

———. 1989. *The Struggle for America's Soul.* Grand Rapids, MI: Eerdmans.

———. 1997. *The Crisis in the Churches.* New York: Oxford University Press.

ANNALS, *AAPSS*, **558**, July 1998

Contemporary Evangelicals: Born-Again and World Affirming

By MARK A. SHIBLEY

ABSTRACT: Because conservative Protestant activism in the 1970s and 1980s was motivated by moral concerns—a reaction to the further disestablishment of so-called traditional Christian values in American society—and because explanations of church growth have also centered on values and boundary maintenance—the strict-churches-grow thesis—resurgent evangelicalism has come to be understood as a reactionary social movement, that is, as though most evangelicals are fundamentalists. Serious students of religion know this is not the case, but it is easy to confound explanations of the popularity of born-again Christianity and the cultural politics of the new Christian Right. In this article, three features of contemporary American evangelicalism are examined that suggest born-again Christians are becoming more like their fellow Americans in their comfort with popular culture, which is to say they are less culturally conservative. Whether contemporary evangelicalism is understood to be sectarian or world affirming is consequential for explaining the prosperity of born-again Christianity and for discerning its future role in public life.

Mark A. Shibley is assistant professor of sociology at Southern Oregon University. He is author of Resurgent Evangelicalism in the United States: Mapping Cultural Change Since 1970 *(1996) and several articles and book chapters on contemporary evangelicalism. Currently, he is researching the role of religious organizations in the environmental movement.*

EVANGELICALISM is flourishing in the United States as the twentieth century draws to a close. What accounts for this prosperity? The literature says that evangelical churches attract and retain members more effectively than do liberal Protestant churches, which are in decline, because they demand complete loyalty, unwavering belief, and rigid adherence to a distinct lifestyle (see, for example, Kelley 1972; Iannaccone 1994). This thesis—that strict churches grow—more or less accurately describes aggregate church membership trends during the middle decades of this century: Southern Baptists did outgrow Congregationalists, Presbyterians, and Episcopalians, and the former are theologically and culturally more sectarian. Nonetheless, the recent emergence of new evangelical associations like Vineyard Christian Fellowship, Willow Creek Community Church, and the Metropolitan Community Church, together with new evidence that oldline evangelicals like Southern Baptists are no longer driving the growth of born-again Christianity (Shibley 1996), invites a reassessment of evangelical vitality. There are two specific reasons for this reassessment.

First, because the church membership data on which most growth studies are based are supplied to researchers by denominational offices, the data exclude information on new and independent religious organizations (see, for example, Bradley et al. 1992). We know nondenominational churches are the fastest-growing segment of American religion (Thumma 1996), and yet groups like Vineyard, Willow Creek, and the Metropolitan Community Church are excluded from these growth studies. Moreover, while these vibrant churches are evangelical, they are not sectarian. This is the second problem with conventional explanations of church growth and decline. Not all evangelical churches are alike in their efforts to keep tradition and differentiate themselves from the wider culture.

However, maintaining moral boundaries is precisely what animates the most vocal and visible segment of evangelical Protestantism, the new Christian Right. Phillip E. Hammond's 1985 article for *The Annals* argued convincingly that conservative Protestants reemerged in public life in the late 1970s to defend core values that they felt were being undermined by the social revolutions of the previous decade, particularly regarding greater individual freedom with respect to gender roles and sexuality. There is no doubt about the efficacy of Hammond's historical thesis as a cultural explanation for Christian Right activism, but because the most compelling explanations for Christian Right activism and evangelical growth have centered on resistance to moral relativism in the surrounding culture, there is a tendency to confound these two different phenomena. Focusing on reactionary Christian politics while seeking to understand evangelicalism's current prosperity obscures the degree to which born-again Christians have grown comfortable with the wider culture.

Drawing on my own fieldwork in a wide range of evangelical churches (from traditional to contemporary) and a review of recent social scientific literature on born-again Christianity, the present article argues that contemporary evangelicalism is a world-affirming faith, that its ability to adapt to the surrounding culture has been essential to its recent growth, and that therefore the assumption that its popularity signals a revitalization of traditional Christian values in American life is inaccurate. My claims depend on a somewhat nuanced understanding of the varieties of American evangelicalism, to which I now turn.

DEFINING CONTEMPORARY EVANGELICALISM

Generally, the term "evangelical" refers to a broad group of believers who (1) have had a born-again (conversion) experience resulting in a personal relationship with Jesus Christ; (2) accept the full authority of the Bible in matters of faith and the conduct of everyday life; and (3) are committed to spreading the gospel by bearing public witness to their faith. While all born-again Christians share these theological markers to some degree, American evangelicalism is historically, ethnically, and geographically diverse (see, for example, Balmer 1989; Dayton and Johnston 1991; Shibley 1996). Not all evangelicals are fundamentalists; they are increasingly not of Anglo-Saxon or European descent; and born-again Christians in California's beach communities bear little resemblance to their evangelical kin in the rural South. Recognizing this diversity is essential for explaining resurgent evangelicalism, understanding its effect on the wider culture, and

assessing its prospects in the next century.

Within American evangelicalism there are at least four distinct subcultures—fundamentalists, Pentecostals, charismatics, and neo-evangelicals. Fundamentalists constitute the doctrinally and culturally strict subculture within evangelicalism that began in the early twentieth century as an opposition movement against the gradual acceptance of biblical criticism, evolutionary theory, and the social gospel in Protestant seminaries and among denominational leaders. The movement was a reaction to the demise of theological orthodoxy. Fundamentalists, therefore, have always insisted on biblical inerrancy and the literal interpretation of Scripture. Unable to win the theological battle with modernism, fundamentalists turned inward, isolating themselves ideologically from the influence of the wider culture. In so doing, the fundamentalist movement became a repository for nineteenth-century Protestant morality as well as theology. Thus fundamentalists are socially conservative.

Pentecostals are theologically and culturally akin to fundamentalists, but their identity centers on religious experience and testimony rather than a defense of doctrine. Pentecostalism also arose at the turn of the century and was inspired by scriptural accounts of the Day of Pentecost, when the Holy Spirit became manifest among believers. Following conversion, Pentecostals experience a "baptism in the Holy Spirit," signaled by spiritual gifts: the ability to speak in tongues, prophecy, and divine healing. This emphasis on continuing revelation put the movement theologically at odds with fundamentalism, and Pentecostals, too, formed their own exclusive organizations.

In H. Richard Niebuhr's social class analysis of denominationalism in the United States ([1929] 1965), fundamentalists and Pentecostals were the "churches of the disinherited." They were working class, were less educated than other Protestants, lived in rural areas, and were generally suspicious of secular trends in American society. Together these two sectarian subcultures were the primary source of the reactionary politics of the new Christian Right as it emerged in the 1970s. Economically and politically disenfranchised and increasingly offended by the so-called new morality (that is, by the further disestablishment of Protestant values in American society) (see Hammond 1992), these conservative Protestants were ripe for political mobilization. The Reverend Jerry Falwell, cofounder of the Moral Majority, is a fundamentalist, as are many but by no means all of his fellow Baptists. Television evangelists Jim Bakker and Jimmy Swaggert came out of the Pentecostal tradition and were affiliated with the Assemblies of God, its flagship denomination. Their high visibility in public life in the early 1980s, prior to the scandalous collapse of their ministries, resulted from their success in rallying troops of already committed conservative Protestants rather than spreading the Gospel among nonbelievers (Hadden 1982).

While these two conservative Protestant subcultures were clearly the social source of new Christian Right activism in the late 1970s and early 1980s, there is simply no evidence that the current growth of born-again Christianity emanates from them. On the contrary, a transformed, culturally contemporary style of evangelicalism accounts for born-again Christianity's vitality in recent decades. It is driven by charismatic Christians and the descendants of the neo-evangelical movement.

Charismatics, a third subculture, constitute a nondenominational movement within mainline Protestant churches and Catholic parishes to reinvigorate congregational life through the practice of their spiritual gifts. In this respect, they are more ecumenical than either fundamentalists or Pentecostals. Charismatics (sometimes called neo-Pentecostals) are the spiritual heirs to Pentecostalism but are more middle class and theologically less dogmatic. Like Pentecostals, religious experience and revelation are at the core of their evangelical identity; thus worship is often an emotional event. Vineyard Christian Fellowship, one of the newest and fastest-growing evangelical associations, is a charismatic movement, as are many so-called megachurches.

A fourth subculture within American evangelicalism started as a countermovement that broke with fundamentalism in the 1940s. Calling themselves neo-evangelicals, they affirmed the basic tenets of conservative Protestant belief but rejected the extreme anti-intellectual and sectarian tendencies of fundamentalism. Whereas their conservative Protestant forebears rejected the values of the wider society, the new evangelicals sought to reengage the outside world. They did so by creating a sub-culture separate from fundamental-ism and closer to the world. Wheaton College, Fuller Seminary, the Na-tional Association of Evangelicals, Intervarsity Christian Fellowship, and World Vision International were part of a new organizational infra-structure for the neo-evangelical movement, and Billy Graham was the movement's most prominent leader. Like the charismatic renewal, the neo-evangelical movement cut across denominational boundaries, and by the 1970s, neo-evangelical in-stitutions had redefined the cultural center of American evangelicalism, moving it away from fundamentalism.

When George Gallup, Jr., dubbed 1976 "The Year of the Evangelical," he was marking the popularity of born-again Christianity in the United States and thereby acknowledging the success of the neo-evangelical and charismatic movements. Re-markably, these contemporary evan-gelicals, as I will henceforth refer to the new generation of born-again Christians, are comfortable in the world. They take for granted many of the cultural norms of middle-class life as it is being redefined by the baby-boom generation (Roof 1993).

In *The Worldly Evangelicals* (1978), Richard Quebedeaux ad-vanced the thesis that evangelical Protestantism's engagement with the world (charismatic renewal and the neo-evangelical movement) was "liberalizing" the tradition, cultur-ally and theologically. He observed that evangelicals were becoming more middle class, more educated, more ecumenical, more interested in

historical biblical scholarship, more feminist, less tolerant of racism, less tolerant of social injustice abroad, and less homophobic. But very soon after the publication of *The Worldly Evangelicals*, the Moral Majority was launched and Ronald Reagan was elected president with notable sup-port from conservative white evan-gelicals in the South. Since the new Christian Right was tapping a cul-tural reservoir of conservative Prot-estantism (namely, fundamentalists and Pentecostals), it was easy in the political climate of the 1980s to lose track of worldly evangelicalism. Moreover, journalists in the 1980s largely focused on the sensational features of American evangelicalism: raucous anti-abortion protests, du-plicitous television evangelists, fun-damentalist gay-bashing, school board debates over teaching evolution ver-sus creationism, and the stealth po-litical tactics used by the new Chris-tian Right. Taken together, these selective images misrepresent the re-lationship that most contemporary evangelicals have with the wider cul-ture and are therefore no basis for assessing what we can expect from evangelicals in the future.

My own work on evangelical Prot-estantism, which began in the early 1980s as an assessment of the role of white born-again Christians in presi-dential elections, eventually led to the conclusion that the most impor-tant feature of contemporary Ameri-can evangelicalism is its transforma-tion into a world-affirming faith. This basic process was briefly eclipsed by the regressive cultural politics of the Christian Right, but even that move-ment radically changed in 20 years.

Three facets of contemporary evangelicalism show just how at-home in the broader world evangelicals have become: (1) it fits comfortably with many aspects of popular culture; (2) its entrepreneurial leadership and innovative organizational forms self-consciously emulate new marketing and corporate management strategies; and (3) as the new Christian Right has grown in political sophistication, its reactionary agenda has moderated.

AT EASE IN THE WORLD

The world-affirming character of contemporary evangelicalism is most clearly illustrated in the cultural realm where evangelical convictions and habits of action increasingly resemble those of other Americans. It has been observed that

religious relevance is a function of achieving in each new historical epoch a compromise between the radical teachings of primitive religion and the culture in which the religion is now being practiced. Religious institutions that do not change inevitably decline; churches that survive and grow will adapt to their culture. (Miller 1992, 3)

Whether intended or unintended, contemporary evangelicalism is blending with elements of popular culture in surprising ways, driven by the need to be relevant for a new generation. John Wimber (1990), the charismatic leader of the Vineyard Christian Fellowship, put it this way:

The prewar generation is beginning to pass from the evangelical church scene without replacing itself. Few churches are effectively reaching the young—those who do not feel comfortable with the life-

style, music or jargon of establishment Christianity. We are reaching them. As a young church, we experience all of the opportunities and problems which accompany youth. Our young 18 to 25 year old attenders are providing the spiritual dynamic which enables us to reach out to a young culture and relate the Gospel to them. Because we are young, we are current. We speak the language of these people. Our sermons and songs are familiar and acceptable. We find ourselves communicating eternal truths in a contemporary style. (19)

A contemporary evangelical church, then, is nondenominational and embraces youth-oriented popular culture. Congregants' dress and demeanor are decidedly casual. Contemporary Christian music can even make Sunday morning worship feel a bit like a rock concert. But how fundamental are these changes? Is evangelical adaptation to contemporary culture merely cosmetic, or does it reflect a change in core values? The answer is both. Contemporary evangelicals are Bible believers, but a short anecdote will illustrate the degree to which new evangelical churches accommodate to lifestyle choices that would be unthinkable in more traditional Christian contexts.

The setting was a Halloween costume party in October 1992 in an upper-middle-class, southern California neighborhood. The guests were mostly professionals in their thirties and forties. They were college educated; some had children; most were part of two-income families; few were California natives. The hosts, recent migrants from New England, had no church affiliation. If anything, they were antagonistic toward organized religion. Midway through the evening, two women and two men congregated for conversation on a backyard patio. These guests knew each other, though they had come to the party separately. Three of the four were smoking cigarettes, and all were drinking alcohol, either beer or a heavily spiked Halloween punch. One of the men steered the conversation in a bawdy direction, and for perhaps thirty minutes they laughed and exchanged dirty jokes. There is nothing unusual about smoking, drinking, and telling colorful stories at a party, but it turns out, all four people in the conversation were born-again Christians—adult converts—and they all attended Calvary Chapel. These Calvary members were indulging in behavior that would be condemned as sinful in more traditional evangelical settings. Indeed, [an Assemblies of God congregation in the neighborhood], fearing the evil connotations even of a Halloween celebration, hosted an alternative Christian party in their church basement on Halloween night. . . .

When asked what was appealing about [Calvary Chapel], one of the women replied simply and without hesitation, "They preach the truth." The truth of salvation through Jesus Christ, she meant, as revealed in the Bible. Theologically, she sounded like a fundamentalist, but she is a worldly woman—a well-paid professional, twice married, articulate, supremely self-confident, and perfectly comfortable in the secular world of a yuppie Halloween party. (Shibley 1996, 85-86)

Evangelicals are embracing, or at least tolerating, many of the worldly mores their conservative Protestant forebears strenuously resisted. Even feminism has penetrated the evangelical world.

Prominent evangelical theologians have absorbed and since the 1970s taught feminist ideas (Bendroth 1993), but the influence of feminism goes well beyond the self-conscious engagement of some evangelical leaders. Recent surveys reveal an emerging ethic of gender equality among contemporary evangelicals, particularly young people, and, even more remarkably, ethnographies of evangelical life are revealing patterns of gender equality in practice.

Ten years ago, James Davison Hunter's study (1987) of the coming generation of evangelicals found a surprising mix of conservative and feminist attitudes toward gender and family relationships. While a majority claimed that the husband should have the final say in a family's decision making, most also found images of assertive, self-reliant women and sensitive, gentle men as appealing as stereotypical images of women and men. Most of Hunter's respondents thought a women should put her husband and children ahead of her career, but most also disagreed with the statement that "a married woman should not work if she has a husband capable of supporting her." Hunter also found a dramatic cohort difference; younger evangelicals are far less satisfied with traditional gender roles in family life (94-100).

The point is not that evangelicals are now feminists; some are, but most are not. Rather, I am suggesting that contemporary evangelicals are increasingly like other modern Americans for whom an ethic of gender equality is a taken-for-granted feature of ordinary life. Judith Stacey calls this a "postfeminist" ideology. In *Brave New Families* (1990), Stacey found that domestic upheaval in postindustrial America is producing new forms of family life, including a reformulation of gender roles, and, to her surprise, she found born-again Christianity at the center of these changes. For some women, evangelicalism was a flexible ideological resource for reconstituting gender and kinship relationships. Stacey called this postmodern mingling of conservative Protestant theology and distinctly modern family arrangements "new wave evangelicalism." More recently, Donald E. Miller (1997) found a similar pattern in his study of contemporary evangelicalism. While there were no women clergy in any of the congregations he studied, postfeminism so thoroughly pervaded evangelical youth culture that wifely submission—the scriptural basis for traditional gender roles among fundamentalists—was effectively stripped of hierarchical and authoritarian meaning (114-16).

In short, the changing economic conditions of family life in contemporary America (the necessity of dual-income families and the reality of single-parent families), feminist politics (a modern social movement), and the intellectual resources of modernism (historical and critical study of biblical texts) have collided in contemporary American society, and, as a result, evangelicals are reinventing Protestant theology and morality. Most born-again Christians are still pro-family, but the meaning of that symbolic badge is gradually changing as ordinary evangelicals reconstruct patterns of belief and practice in their own gendered relationships.

To summarize, evangelicals are in the world and, strategically or unwittingly, have absorbed many of the core values of contemporary American culture. This portrait of changing gender roles and family structure is no anomaly. The same pattern of cultural adaptation has occurred in many other aspects of evangelical life. For example, secular rock and roll (once the devil's domain) has become Christian rock music; psychology and the therapeutic culture have become Christian self-help books and twelve-step programs; the scientific method is utilized in historical biblical scholarship and creation science (as in the archeological search for Noah's ark); materialism and consumer culture become name-it-and-claim-it theology (one can have worldly success if one prays hard enough). In this way, evangelicalism has fused with American popular culture, thus making the tradition accessible to non-Christians in new ways. Paradoxically, it is also now possible to be a born-again Christian without being very different from other Americans.

NEW ORGANIZATIONAL FORMS

It is now clear that contemporary evangelicalism's vitality is located in congregations that operate outside old denominational structures. In *Reinventing American Protestantism* (1997), Donald E. Miller calls these organizations "new paradigm churches." "Like upstart religious groups of the past," he observes,

they have discarded many of the attributes of establishment religion. Appropriating contemporary cultural forms, these churches are creating a new genre of worship music; they are restructuring the organizational character of institutional religion; and they are democratizing access to the sacred by radicalizing the Protestant principle of the priesthood of all believers. (1)

Arguing that the cultural and organizational changes he observed transcend categories like evangelical, fundamentalist, charismatic, and Pentecostal, Miller sees another Protestant reformation on the horizon. Perhaps so. At the very least, these rapidly growing born-again Christian movements—like Vineyard and Willow Creek—are transforming American evangelicalism.

Seeking to serve a post--World War II generation, these churches are shaped by the antiestablishment and therapeutic values that baby boomers and post-boomers take for granted. The prototypical new evangelical congregation is not denominationally affiliated, is organized around a charismatic leader, and has a relatively decentralized authority structure. Clergy, who may not have seminary training themselves, recruit and mentor lay leadership rather than hire professional staff. As the church grows, lay people have a great deal of autonomy in developing and leading ministries they feel called to, from Bible study and prayer groups to soup kitchens, computer clubs, and aerobics classes. Contemporary evangelical churches are structured around these small groups, which are designed to address individuals' felt needs (physical, social, and psychological as well as spiritual) and embed members in Christian community.

Typically, these congregations meet for Sunday worship in a rented movie theater, school auditorium, or converted warehouse, wherever they can find a large, affordable space. When a congregation is established enough to buy or build its own facility, it is likely to resemble in architectural style the corporate parks and shopping malls that characterize the suburban landscapes in which these churches flourish. While their meeting places generally lack overt Christian symbols (even a cross) and dress is casual, making Sunday morning an informal affair, the leadership will often use sophisticated audio, visual, and computer technology to create an engaging multimedia worship experience. These gatherings are much more celebratory than solemn. Unencumbered by liturgical traditions that come with denominational affiliations, clergy have enormous freedom to structure worship in ways that appeal to a generation of young people turned off by establishment religion.

One of the key organizational innovations in contemporary evangelicalism has been the use of market surveys, pioneered by a young evangelical pastor named Bill Hybels. Like any thoughtful entrepreneur, Hybels surveyed potential consumers in his suburban market to ascertain what type of religion they would buy and what it would take to sell it to them. In less than two decades, his congregation—Willow Creek Community Church, in Barrington, Illinois—has become one of the country's largest churches (15,000 members) and is a model for church growth being emulated by countless other evangelical pastors.

Hybels found that his market base was largely unchurched and uninterested in traditional forms of Christian worship but that there was some interest in cultivating a spiritual life. So he created a "seeker service" that would be comfortable for middle-class, suburban baby boomers. He drew in the unchurched by simplifying the message ("Christianity 101"), putting it in contemporary, often psychological terms, delivering it in an entertaining format (humor, beautiful music, and dramatic theater), and requiring nothing from visitors in return. They were instructed to sit back, enjoy the service, and ignore the offering plate when it came around. When visitors attend regularly and begin to feel at home, they are invited to join.

By catering to the cultural preferences of baby boomers, new-paradigm churches have had tremendous success in attracting newcomers. However, Gregory Pritchard's ethnography of Willow Creek's seeker service (1994) shows that a contemporary faith shaped by a market analysis of consumer preferences cuts two ways. Evangelical Protestantism is being revitalized by these culturally innovative organizations, but it is also changed in the process. Pritchard concludes his study with a series of paradoxical observations that make his point, and mine, succinctly:

— as Willow Creek markets Christianity, Willow Creek's Christianity is shaped by this marketing strategy;
— as Willow Creek Christianity becomes relevant, it is in danger of becoming irrelevant;
— as Willow Creek Christianity becomes more psychological, it also becomes less Christian; and
— most poignantly, as Willow Creek seeks to evangelize those in the world to Christianity, it also evangelizes Willow Creek Christians to the world (806-11).

The market survey is one of the tools by which evangelical Protestantism has reformulated itself to fit contemporary culture, with intended and unintended consequences. Evangelicalism is more world affirming because, in order to grow, church leaders gave people what they wanted—a contemporary faith.

Scott L. Thumma (1996) estimates that there are roughly 400 megachurches in the United States (that is, churches with at least 2000 members), most of them having emerged in the last two decades. In other words, there are hundreds of churches like Willow Creek, and many more that want to be like Willow Creek. For years now, Willow Creek and other successful megachurches (such as Saddleback Valley Community Church, in Orange County, California) have sponsored church growth seminars and leadership conferences, disseminating their successful growth model. Completely new associational structures have emerged linking these contemporary evangelical churches.

Some new evangelical associations, like Vineyard Christian Fellowship and Calvary Chapel, are more like social movement organizations than denominations. They are nonhierarchical and have a mission-oriented evangelical vision that goes beyond growing a large church like Willow Creek, even though the large congregations that anchor these movements fit the megachurch profile described previously. A key feature of these movements is that they continually seek opportunities to plant new churches by spinning off gifted lay leaders who feel called to church development ministries.

It is tempting to capture this franchising activity with the "McDonaldization" metaphor (Ritzer 1996), but Miller cautions that such a characterization can misrepresent the motivations of many contemporary evangelicals. Not all "new paradigm groups think of religion as a business in which they are selling a product," Miller says.

Quite the contrary. They believe they are responding to the "calling" of the Holy Spirit, and their efforts at starting new churches are part of the "Great Commission" to share the message of salvation. . . . Furthermore, the most successful efforts at evangelism, such as those by Calvary Chapel, are self-consciously hostile to church growth techniques, demographic studies, and various "how to" manuals. They see their growth as the work of the Holy Spirit. (1997, 160)

Some contemporary evangelical churches do self-consciously think of themselves as businesses, while others, including the new-paradigm movements Miller studied, do not. Churches like Willow Creek model themselves after modern corporations and employ market surveys; Vineyard and Calvary Chapel model their organizations after the first-century Christian church. There are important differences between Vineyard Christian Fellowship and megachurches like Willow Creek Community Church (for example, worship in Vineyard churches is experiential while worship at Willow Creek is more entertainment), but,

most important, neither is sectarian. These are the new institutional forms of world-affirming evangelicalism; they are culturally contemporary.

One final organizational component of contemporary evangelicalism bears mention. While revivals are not an innovation, new-paradigm churches sponsor and/or participate in Christian revivals that fill stadiums across the land. Most participants are already saved but come to celebrate their faith, listen to inspirational speakers, and rededicate themselves to Christ. These events also produce a steady flow of converts. New-paradigm churches feed on the energy generated in festive, large-scale gatherings, and Sunday worship in a megachurch is an only slightly smaller scale version of these stadium events.

Some of these events are Christian music festivals. For twenty years, Jesus Northwest, which takes place at the Clark County fairgrounds in Washington State, has drawn tens of thousands of young people from up and down the West Coast to a summer weekend of Christian rock bands and inspirational speakers. Some of these events are public crusades. In the early 1990s, evangelist Greg Laurie, with Calvary Chapel's support, organized the Harvest Crusades in the manner of Billy Graham but designed specifically to appeal to young people. These crusades attracted hundreds of thousands of people in their teens, twenties, and thirties. Some of these events are part of the Promise Keepers, a new Christian men's movement focused primarily on strengthening families by encouraging men to be more responsible husbands and fathers. Its founder, Bill McCartney, is a participant in Boulder, Colorado's Vineyard Fellowship.

While distinctly evangelical and with participants who are, as a group, mostly white, all these gatherings downplay denominational and racial differences, thus making them more ecumenical and ethnically diverse than most religious gatherings in America. Embracing diversity in this way distinguishes contemporary evangelicals from old-line conservative Protestants who resist pluralism as a matter of principle. Among contemporary evangelicals, racial diversity is not just tolerated; it has become a core value, one of the guiding principles of the Promise Keepers (Abraham 1997). Even the Christian Right is speaking of "racial reconciliation," and it is their transformation that provides the most striking evidence of cultural adaptation on the part of evangelicals.

THE TRANSFORMATION OF THE CHRISTIAN RIGHT

A central point in this article is that, as evangelicals engage the world, they are becoming more like the world. This change, visible in the new cultural and organizational forms of contemporary evangelicalism, is also apparent in the gradual transformation of the new Christian Right from a largely sectarian social movement to a nonsectarian political organization. The leaders, the issues, and the tactics have changed significantly in twenty years, and the changes amount to a kinder, gentler Christian Right.[1]

The movement to become political at all was a revolutionary step into the temporal world. Many evangelical Protestants had to overcome a pietism and an other-worldly theology that militated against activity in the public sphere; good Christians worried about getting right with God, not changing the world. Billy Graham, the country's most prominent evangelical, played a public role as counselor to presidents during the 1960s and 1970s that favored the cause of social conservatives, but he tried assiduously to remain nonpartisan and keep spiritual goals in the forefront of his ministry. Since Goldwater's defeat in 1964, however, the new Right had courted conservative Christians in support of Republican candidates. When conservative Protestants in the South became disillusioned with President Jimmy Carter, a self-professed born-again Christian, new-Right operatives finally succeeded in persuading prominent evangelicals like Jerry Falwell to help mobilize conservative Christians for political purpose.

In the 1960s, Falwell had openly criticized religious leaders for their involvement in the civil rights movement. Yet, extraordinary times called for extraordinary measures. With support from the new Right and the cooperation of other conservative Protestant leaders, Jerry Falwell launched the Moral Majority, a religious political lobby. The marginality of evangelicals in Washington, exemplified by, among other things, the Internal Revenue Service's challenge to the tax-exempt status of Christian schools in the mid-1970s, and their growing sense of moral outrage at the erosion of "traditional family values" in American society turned Christian leaders like Falwell toward politics and made it easy by the late 1970s to persuade rank-and-file fundamentalists that resisting Godless liberalism in the public square was their Christian duty.

The Moral Majority and related groups accomplished two things in the early 1980s that helped revolutionize evangelicals' understanding of their potential role in civil society. First, it helped convince them that they ought to participate as Christians in the public life of the nation. It took inspirational leaders and some ideological work to change the apolitical tune of Protestant fundamentalism. The Moral Majority effectively used direct-mail campaigns to warn conservative Christians that "our Grand Old Flag is going down the drain," that "we are losing the war against homosexuals," and the like (Martin 1997, 205). The second thing that the Moral Majority accomplished was to convince conservative Christians that they were not marginal, that conservative politicians like Ronald Reagan were listening to Christian leaders, and that they could shape the country through political action.

The Moral Majority did not produce notable electoral victories in its seven-year life span, but it did teach conservative Protestants to think of themselves as political actors, and it shaped the social agenda of the Republican Party and the nation during the 1980s.

Three things ultimately limited the Moral Majority's effectiveness. Most prominently, it failed to develop effective grassroots political organizations, which are essential to sustained success in the electoral process. Second, closely aligned with television evangelists like Jim Bakker, the Moral Majority suffered a credibility problem when several television ministries were rocked by scandal in the mid-1980s. Third, despite the new Right's strategy to unite religious conservatives from different traditions, the Moral Majority was essentially sectarian in that its leaders primarily were drawn from the fundamentalist wing of Protestantism. In founding the Moral Majority, Falwell made an effort to overcome separatist impulses by announcing that it was a political, not a religious, organization and that it welcomed Jews, Catholics, Protestants, Mormons, and even nonreligious people who shared their views on family values (Martin 1997, 204). In practice, however, it was dominated by southern white fundamentalists who were not accustomed to participating in ecumenical or interfaith organizations.

To save his own diminishing credibility, in 1986 Falwell disassembled the Moral Majority, which had become ineffective. Soon thereafter, Pat Robertson, proprietor of the Christian Broadcasting Network and host of *700 Club*, a still-thriving television ministry, became the focal point of Christian Right activism. His role was pivotal in moving the Christian Right a step further in a nonsectarian direction. Robertson had not been included in Moral Majority activities, but as a prominent, socially conservative evangelical, he was present on the fringes of Christian Right organizing during those early years.

In 1981, Robertson established an organization called the Freedom Council. Its purpose was, he said, "to fight for the rights of believers and to teach evangelical Christians, primarily, but also Orthodox Jews and Roman Catholics, how they could be effective in the political process" (Martin 1997, 259). His goal was to train activists in every precinct around the country and thus build an organization that would be effective for the long haul, locally and nationally, but, unlike Falwell and the Moral Majority, he did not seek media attention. While Robertson, like other evangelical leaders, was initially reluctant to lead his charismatic flock into politics, he turned out to be politically more savvy than many of his fundamentalist allies on the Christian Right. He was a Yale Law School graduate, and his father had been a U.S. congressman. The Freedom Council, with its emphasis on grassroots organizing, was the basis for Robertson's presidential bid in 1988 and the precursor to the Christian Coalition, now the most politically sophisticated religious lobby in the country.

Theological differences between Robertson and Falwell are significant in that Robertson's background and worldview made the ecumenical work of political coalition building easier. He graduated from college Phi Beta Kappa and has a degree from New York Theological Seminary. By comparison, Falwell's education at Baptist Bible College in Springfield, Missouri, was far more sectarian. Because Robertson's charismatic faith emphasizes experience and ongoing

revelation more than defense of doctrine, as in Falwell's fundamentalism, creating a coalition of social conservatives from different religious traditions could be justified by the authority of revelation, bypassing church doctrine altogether. A Freedom Council organizer in Michigan, Marlene Elwell, illustrated the importance of the differences between Robertson's and Falwell's organizations. Elwell, a Roman Catholic, reported:

In the Jerry Falwell days, I looked into Moral Majority. I attended a couple of their meetings. I was pursued by some of their leadership, but that was not a movement I could embrace, because there was no openness to someone of my faith. It was very narrow in its thinking. There was a lot of anger, a lot of judgment. Frankly, I found it very scary. . . . That was just the opposite of what I experienced with Pat Robertson. (Quoted in Martin 1997, 336)

Thus, despite his failed presidential bid, Robertson successfully mobilized religious conservatives at the grass roots, something that the Moral Majority failed to accomplish. In 1989, Robertson relinquished the reigns of his nascent movement by founding the Christian Coalition and anointing Ralph Reed executive director. Reed's work with the Christian Coalition between 1989 and 1997 in effect transformed the Christian Right into a modern political organization, both tactically and ideologically.

Reed was a campus activist before becoming a born-again Christian in 1983. He served a stint as the national director of the College Republicans and worked in the mid-1980s to enlist Christian students on college campuses in the conservative cause. He subsequently earned a Ph.D. in American history from Emory University. Thus he has keen political instincts and a clear sense of the secular mechanics of American politics. Born in 1961, he is also part of the new generation of born-again Christians who were not reared in a fundamentalist subculture. Reed is a contemporary evangelical with an essentially political vocation.

The Christian Coalition initially built on Robertson's grassroots organizing success in two ways. It sponsored leadership training workshops that equipped grassroots activists to run Christian candidates for local office, and it used direct mail (a Moral Majority practice) to outrage its constituency with sensational accounts of offenses against religion and morality committed by homosexuals, liberals, or the government. It organized around the same family-values agenda that animated Moral Majority constituents a decade earlier, and it had some success winning in local elections by distributing voter guides that caricatured the "liberal incumbents" and by running phone banks to get out the vote in key precincts.

In two well-known cases in the early 1990s where the Christian Right helped elect a majority to local school boards—in San Diego County, California, and Lake County, Florida—candidates campaigned on conservative but relatively mainstream educational platforms. When, however, the newly elected Christian majorities began censoring library books that they found offensive and began moving to introduce creationism into the curriculum, they sparked an immediate backlash that, in both cases, led to their own demise in the next election (Martin 1997, 318-19, 335-37).

Notwithstanding the new influence of conservative Christians in local politics, often facilitated by the Christian Coalition, Reed's most important contribution to the broader movement to politicize conservative Christians has been his willingness to compromise on controversial issues and to broaden the issue base.

Following the Republican Party's impressive congressional gains in 1994, Reed endorsed the Contract with America and unveiled, six months later, the Contract with the American Family. The latter was distinctly conservative and "pro-family" (for example, it called for reductions in the tax burden on families; increased controls on pornography; school vouchers; a religious equality amendment that would relax Supreme Court restrictions on public prayer and other religious expressions; and the like), but it was not belligerent (Christian Coalition 1995). It did not call for a human life amendment outlawing abortion and made no mention of gays and lesbians at all. Reed described the document as a political agenda of limited scope, not a Christian agenda or theological statement (Martin 1997, 364). The Christian Coalition, under Reed's leadership, was no longer behaving as a reactionary movement. It was proactive and reasonable.

Convinced that the religious Right must give ground or risk irrelevance, Reed's book *Active Faith* (1996a) cautioned religious conservatives to "resist the temptation to replace the social engineering of the left with the social engineering of the right by forcing compliance with the moral principles that motivate us so deeply." Religious conservatives, he said, "must shun harsh language on critical issues—chiefly abortion, Clinton-bashing, and homosexuality—and learn to speak of our opponents with charity" (Reed 1996b, 28).

Reed angered anti-abortion advocates in 1996—notably, Randall Terry of the anti-abortion group Operation Rescue—by endorsing presidential candidate Bob Dole when he appeared likely to select a pro-choice running mate. Reed's decision was perfectly consistent with his ultimate goal to build a political organization that would be a player in mainstream politics in the long run. His book, in fact, tried to persuade religious conservatives that it was not politically expedient to be intransigent on abortion. As one fellow evangelical leader observed:

Ralph Reed realizes both the importance of pragmatism and the need for principle and, [in light of] the excesses of the last fifteen years, he is trying to lead [evangelicals] in a wiser direction. But of course, he's riding a populist tiger, and he has people above who are insisting on certain things, such as the name "Christian Coalition," which I believe he strongly disagrees with, but cannot change. So he is a much more thoughtful leader than those who went before. (Martin 1997, 365)

Reed clearly has a vision of the role of religious conservatives in politics that is broader than the sectarian movement he inherited.

Nowhere is this clearer than in the Christian Coalition's recent efforts to court minorities and broaden its issue base. In January 1997, Reed unveiled the coalition's Samaritan Project. The coalition's most ambitious program to date, the Samaritan Project is both a legislative agenda—it promotes bills offering scholarships, tax credits, urban empowerment zones, and other measures designed to improve poor black and Latino communities—and a concerted effort to broaden its support (Fulwood 1997). The coalition pledged to raise $10 million over three years to support outreach ministries in black and Latino churches. Reed justified the program in this way:

For too long, our movement has been primarily—and frankly almost exclusively—a white, evangelical, Republican movement, whose center of gravity focused on the safety of the suburbs. The Samaritan Project is a bold plan to break that color line and bridge the gap that separates white evangelicals and Roman Catholics from their Latino and African American brothers and sisters. (Fulwood 1997)

Cynical observers and critics of the Christian Right have dismissed the program as disingenuous, yet it is quite consistent with the new ethic of racial healing and diversity now found in many contemporary evangelical organizations.

The Christian Coalition is trying to secure a prominent place in the public square by softening its position on controversial issues and expanding its constituency. Most evangelicals are still conservative on moral issues, but changes on the Christian Right suggest they are learning to behave strategically and with civility in political arenas. Looking back over the last quarter-century, this amounts to a sea change in Christian Right politics. The new generation of politically active evangelicals are people of faith who, like their liberal Protestant counterparts, seem increasingly willing to concede the secular authority of the state to adjudicate the affairs of a culturally pluralistic society (Casanova 1994).

In summary, this article advances a simple but important thesis: namely, not all born-again Christians are culturally conservative; in fact, contemporary evangelicals are remarkably liberal in their openness to the world. This is visible in evangelical popular culture, in the new organizational forms of contemporary evangelicalism, and in the transformation of the Christian Right. I am not arguing that most evangelicals are contemporary, only that the most vibrant and fastest-growing segment of evangelical Protestantism is culturally hip. But so what? As I said in my introduction, this observation—that contemporary evangelicalism is not hostile toward the surrounding culture— has important implications for explaining the popularity of born-again Christianity and for discerning its future role in public life. Let me now specify these implications, first by suggesting why I think evangelicalism is growing and then by looking to the future.

WHY EVANGELICAL PROSPERITY?

It seems to me that there are four essential reasons for evangelical prosperity. First, being born-again can be profoundly life transforming. People for whom the faith is a choice

rather than an inheritance—that is, converts—are often discontent with their pre-conversion lives. Time and again, ethnographies of born-again Christians recount stories of lives in crisis, healed by the grace of God. I found in my research that adult conversions tend to occur at times of personal crisis when people are unhappy and struggling to make sense of their lives without a supporting and affirming community (1996, 72-76). Evangelicals minister effectively to broken individuals, and their contemporary churches design elaborate programs to meet people's social, psychological, spiritual, and even physical needs.

Second, contemporary evangelical churches are essentially religious organizations. Thus these churches facilitate self-transcendence—the experience of the sacred. Religious experience is central to worship in new-paradigm churches, and Miller argues that it accounts for their vitality: "The real staying power of new paradigm churches is that they are mediating deeply felt religious experiences, and doing this much more effectively than many mainline churches" (1997, 16). Indeed, most contemporary evangelicalism is infused with religious energy. The vibrant new organizations previously described often have a charismatic flavor. This religious dimension is typically not appreciated by social scientists but is obvious to any good ethnographer and clearly relevant for explaining the popularity of contemporary evangelicals.

A third source of evangelical strength is that these congregations provide a distinct identity and relatively clear guidelines for organizing a new life, which is particularly appealing for people unhappy with their old life. Born-again Christians literally change themselves; they develop a new understanding of who they are and where they fit in the world, made viable in a self-reinforcing community of believers. Relatively clear rules for Christian living, and some effort to hold adherents accountable to those standards, make contemporary evangelical churches strong congregations. Christian Smith develops this subcultural identity theme in his book *American Evangelicalism: Embattled and Thriving* (1998).

The strictness thesis, which has dominated church growth research, offers a variation on this third theme in that it highlights tension with the surrounding culture. The logic is as follows: In contrast to liberal Protestantism, evangelicals are doubt-free and morally strict congregations. They know who they are and how they are different from non-Christians. A clear identity and unambiguous conduct codes strengthen the community, which in turn leads to prosperity. Yet, as my work shows, not all evangelical churches are alike in their efforts to keep tradition and differentiate themselves from the wider culture. Contemporary evangelicals are remarkably comfortable with the diversity of contemporary American life.

This article is an effort to counterbalance the impression, derived from the strictness thesis and the social conservatism of the Christian Right, that evangelical vitality is a function of cultural rigidity, that born-again Christians are essentially moral traditionalists. My point is that there is enormous fluidity in the moral (and even theological, though I did not make that argument here) character of evangelicalism because, like all religion, it must continually adapt to the host culture, which varies considerably across time and place. Core values, along with dress code and organizational form, are reinvented in each generation; Scripture is reinterpreted. Churches that succeed in the long run grow in step with the surrounding culture. This cultural currency is the fourth source of evangelical vitality today. Given this, what can we expect from born-again Christians in the near future?

BORN-AGAIN CHRISTIANS IN THE NEXT CENTURY

First, evangelicalism will continue to flourish in culturally current forms. Evangelical churches that provide engaging worship experiences and supportive community in terms that resonate with young people—boomers and post-boomers—will continue to prosper. Evangelical churches that fail in this regard will join many liberal Protestant congregations in their drift toward irrelevance for the next generation, regardless of the clarity of their religious vision or how resolute their conduct codes. This is already happening to many old-line evangelical congregations.

Second, evangelical morality, which varies greatly from one subculture to another, will continue to change as born-again Christians adapt to a changing world. Drinking, dancing, and divorce provoked a moral crusade by fundamentalists a generation ago, but such behavior is commonplace in American culture today, even among born-again Christians. If the righteous fervor regarding those issues dissipated over time, why should we not expect a similar loss of energy on the issues that animated the Christian Right in the 1980s (for example, pornography, homosexuality, and abortion)? Are the moral precepts concerning these issues nonnegotiable? I think not, particularly for a faith tradition based on experience, ongoing revelation, and the priesthood of all believers. Organizers of the openly gay and distinctly evangelical Metropolitan Community Church (with 20,000 members nationwide), for example, managed the ideological work of fitting evangelical theology with their sexuality and life experience (Warner 1995).

Most contemporary evangelicals are still rather conservative with regard to sexuality and gender roles, and their congregations are family oriented, but "family values" as a political issue simply are not featured in congregational life, as they came to be in many fundamentalist churches in the 1980s (Shibley 1996, 103). The provocative strategies used by the new Christian Right to tap the cultural anxieties of an older generation of conservative Protestants will therefore not work on contemporary evangelicals. New-paradigm churches are not about cultural warfare; they are about religious experience, personal transformation, and community. These concerns do not directly translate into a political agenda, but their influence on the wider culture may be felt in other ways, such as the realm of race relations.

Contemporary evangelicals are more racially diverse than most congregations in the United States,[2] and they are committed to a vision of multiracial harmony, starting in their own congregations (Shibley 1996, 101-3). This is reason enough not to dismiss overtures of racial reconciliation by the Christian Coalition and the Promise Keepers as mere political posturing. The long history of racial segregation in this country is reflected in religious institutions. Yet it is also true that blacks, whites, Hispanics, and Asian Americans increasingly share a religious language. Along with a new evangelical majority among white Protestants, church-going African Americans are overwhelmingly evangelical, Pentecostalism is the fastest-growing religion among Hispanics, and second-generation Asian immigrants are finding new-paradigm churches more attractive than their parents' ethnic congregations. Born-again Christianity is an increasingly multiracial phenomenon, and this bears watching. Perhaps the new generation of evangelicals will provide moral if not political leadership on race issues.

In conclusion, this article is not a secularization thesis. There is a sense in which contemporary evangelicals are more modern and more liberal than other conservative Protestants if by "modern" and "liberal" we mean simply that they have a higher level of comfort with cultural pluralism and a willingness to concede the authority of a secular state. There is, however, no meaningful sense in which evangelical adaptation to contemporary culture is eroding religious authenticity; contemporary evangelicals are not somehow less born-again. Nevertheless, I am suggesting that the midcentury effort of neo-evangelicals to reengage the world and the efforts of new-paradigm churches to be culturally current has both intended and unintended consequences. Being contemporary facilitates growth and leads to change. Sociologically speaking, it is impossible to be in the world and not of the world.

Notes

1. Many of the historical details in my account of the transformation of the Christian Right are drawn from William Martin's excellent social history of the religious Right in America, *With God on Our Side* (1997). The interpretation of historical events offered in this article—that changes in the movement amount to Christian Right moderation—is my own, however.

2. Miller found the following racial mix in new-paradigm churches: 75 percent white, 2 percent black, 13 percent Hispanic, 7 percent Asian, and 3 percent other (1997, 195).

References

Abraham, Ken. 1997. *Who Are the Promise Keepers? Understanding the Christian Men's Movement.* New York: Doubleday.

Balmer, Randall Herbert. 1989. *Mine Eyes Have Seen the Glory: A Journey into Evangelical Subculture in America.* New York: Oxford University Press.

Bendroth, Margaret Lamberts. 1993. *Fundamentalism and Gender, 1875 to the Present.* New Haven, CT: Yale University Press.

Bradley, Martin B., Norman M. Green, Jr., Dale E. Jones, Mac Lynn, and Lou McNeil. 1992. *Churches and Church Membership in the United States, 1990.* Atlanta, GA: Glenmary Research Center.

Casanova, Jose. 1994. *Public Religions in the Modern World.* Chicago: University of Chicago Press.

Christian Coalition. 1995. Contact with the American Family. *Christian Century,* 24-31 May, 560.

Dayton, Donald W. and Robert K. Johnston. 1991. *The Variety of American Evangelicalism.* Knoxville: University of Tennessee Press.

Fulwood, Sam. 1997. Christian Coalition Courts Minorities. *New York Times,* 31 Jan.

Hadden, Jeffrey. 1982. *Prime Time Preachers: The Rising Power of Televangelism.* Reading, MA: Addison-Wesley.

Hammond, Phillip E. 1985. The Curious Path of Conservative Protestantism. *The Annals* of the American Academy of Political and Social Science 480(July):53-62.

———. 1992. *Religion and Personal Autonomy: The Third Disestablishment in America.* Columbia: University of South Carolina Press.

Hunter, James Davison. 1987. *Evangelicalism: The Coming Generation.* Chicago: University of Chicago Press.

Iannaccone, Laurence R. 1994. Why Strict Churches Are Strong. *American Journal of Sociology* 99:1180-1211.

Kelley, Dean M. 1972. *Why Conservative Churches Are Growing.* New York: Harper & Row.

Martin, William. 1997. *With God on Our Side: The Rise of the Religious Right in America.* New York: Broadway Books.

Miller, Donald E. 1992. Hope Chapel: Revisioning the Foursquare Gospel. Paper presented at the annual meeting of the Society for the Scientific Study of Religion, Washington, DC.

———. 1997. *Reinventing American Protestantism: Christianity in the New Millennium*. Berkeley: University of California Press.

Niebuhr, H. Richard. [1929] 1965. *The Social Sources of Denominationalism*. New York: Meridian.

Pritchard, Gregory A. 1994. The Strategy of Willow Creek Community Church: A Study in the Sociology of Religion. Ph.D. diss., Northwestern University.

Quebedeaux, Richard. 1978. *The Worldly Evangelicals*. San Francisco: Harper & Row.

Reed, Ralph. 1996a. *Active Faith: How Christians Are Changing the Soul of American Politics*. New York: Free Press.

———. 1996b. We Stand at a Crossroads. *Newsweek*, 13 May, 28-29.

Ritzer, George. 1996. *The McDonaldization of Society: An Investigation into the Changing Character of Contemporary Social Life*. Thousand Oaks, CA: Pine Forge Press.

Roof, Wade Clark. 1993. *A Generation of Seekers: The Spiritual Journeys of the Baby Boom Generation*. San Francisco: HarperCollins.

Shibley, Mark A. 1996. *Resurgent Evangelicalism in the US: Mapping Cultural Change Since 1970*. Columbia: University of South Carolina Press.

Smith, Christian. 1998. *American Evangelicalism: Embattled and Thriving*. Chicago: University of Chicago Press.

Stacey, Judith. 1990. *Brave New Families: Stories of Domestic Upheaval in the Late Twentieth Century America*. New York: Basic Books.

Thumma, Scott L. 1996. The Kingdom, the Power, and the Glory: The Megachurch in Modern American Society. Ph.D. diss., Emory University.

Warner, R. Stephen. 1995. The Metropolitan Community Churches and the Gay Agenda: The Power of Pentecostalism and Essentialism. In *Sex, Lies, and Sanctity: Religion and Deviance in Contemporary North America*, ed. Mary Jo Neitz and Marion S. Goldman. Greenwich, CT: JAI Press.

Wimber, John. 1990. Zip to 3000 in 5 Years. *Signs & Wonders Today* 13-20.

ANNALS, *AAPSS*, **558**, July 1998

Christian Violence in America

By MARK JUERGENSMEYER

ABSTRACT: As the millennium approaches, the wave of antimodernism that has brought violent movements of religious nationalism in its wake around the world has arrived at America's shores. In the United States, attacks on abortion clinics, the killing of abortion clinic staff, and the destructive acts of members of Christian militia movements are chilling examples of assaults on the legitimacy of modern social and political institutions, based on the theological frameworks of reconstruction theology and Christian Identity thinking. These examples of Christian militancy present a religious perception of warfare and struggle in what is perhaps the most modern of twentieth-century societies. The secular political order of America is imagined to be trapped in vast satanic conspiracies involving spiritual and personal control. This perception provides Christian activists with both the justification and the obligation to use violent means to fulfill their understanding of the country's Christian mission—and at the same time offers a formidable critique of Enlightenment society and a reassertion of the primacy of religion in public life.

Mark Juergensmeyer is professor of sociology and director of global and international studies at the University of California, Santa Barbara. He has been a fellow of the Harry Frank Guggenheim Foundation, the U.S. Institute of Peace, and the American Council of Learned Societies. He is author or editor of ten books, including Violence and the Sacred in the Modern World *and* The New Cold War? *named by the* New York Times *as one of the most notable books of 1993. He is currently writing a book on religious terrorism.*

THE Islamic Revolution in Iran in 1978 heralded a new kind of religiously motivated political violence and protest, a wave of disaffection from modern forms of secular political authority throughout the world that ultimately reached American shores. Writing in 1993, I could characterize this as largely a Third World, postcolonial phenomenon (Juergensmeyer 1993, 19-20). As the millennium approaches, however, this wave of antimodernism has increasingly come to such industrialized and thoroughly modern countries as Japan, which suffered a nerve gas attack in Tokyo subways by the Aum Shinrikyo religious movement; France, where militant supporters of the Islamic Party in Algeria have placed bombs in Parisian subways; and, perhaps most surprising, the United States, where the bombing of the World Trade Center, attacks on abortion clinics and the killing of abortion clinic staff, and the destruction of the Oklahoma City federal building are chilling examples of assaults on the legitimacy of modern social and political institutions.

The examples of Christian militancy in America are especially noteworthy, for they present a religious perception of warfare and struggle in what is perhaps the most modern of twentieth-century societies. It is not totally uncharacteristic of Christianity to have a violent side, of course: the bloody history of the faith—the Crusades, the Inquisition, and the holy wars—has provided images as disturbing as those provided by Islam, Hinduism, or Sikhism. What is significant about the recent forms of Christian violence is not so much the violence as the ideology that lies behind it: the perception that the secular social and political order of America is caught up in satanic conspiracies of spiritual and personal control. These perceived plots provide Christian activists with reasons for using violent means.

The social history of Christianity—and theological positions based ultimately on the Bible—provide legitimacy for the worldviews of a variety of contemporary Christian subcultures. Some of them emerged from mainstream denominations; others are fiercely independent from traditional forms of organized Christianity. In the case of recent attacks on abortion clinics, the theological justification and the social vision associated with it are firmly rooted in Protestant reformation theology. Such is the position of the Reverend Michael Bray, for instance. He is a Lutheran pastor who has been convicted of a series of abortion clinic attacks and defends the use of lethal weapons against abortion clinic staff.

ABORTION CLINIC BOMBINGS

The Reverend Bray recalled that it was "a cold February night" in 1984 when he and a friend drove a yellow Honda from his home in Bowie to nearby Dover, Delaware. The trunk of the car held a cargo of ominous supplies: a cinder block to break a window, cans of gasoline to pour in and around a building, and rags and matches to ignite the flames. The road to Delaware was foggy that night, and the bridge across the Chesapeake Bay was icy. The car skidded and a minor accident occurred, but the pair was determined to forge ahead. "Before daybreak," Bray recalled, "the only abortion chamber in Dover was gutted by fire and put out of the business of butchering babies" (Bray 1994, 9). The following year, Bray and two other defendants stood trial for destroying seven abortion facilities in Delaware, Maryland, Virginia, and the District of Columbia, totaling over $1 million in damages. He was convicted of these charges and served time in prison until 15 May 1989.

When I talked with the Reverend Bray in his suburban home in Bowie in April 1996, there was nothing sinister or intensely fanatical about him. He was a cheerful, charming, handsome man in his early forties who liked to be called Mike. Hardly the image of an ignorant, narrow-minded fundamentalist, Mike Bray enjoyed a glass of wine before dinner and talked knowledgeably about theology and political ideas (Bray 1996).

It was a demeanor quite different from his public posture. As a leader in the Defensive Action movement, he advocated the use of violence in anti-abortion activities, and his attacks on abortion clinics were considered extreme even by members of the pro-life movement. The same has been said of his writings. Bray publishes one of the country's most militant Christian newsletters, *Capitol Area Christian News*, which focuses on abortion, homosexuality, and what Bray regards as the Clinton administration's pathological abuse of government power.

Bray was the spokesman for two activists who were convicted of murderous assaults on abortion clinic staffs. On 29 July 1994, Bray's friend, the Reverend Paul Hill, killed Dr. John Britton and his volunteer escort, James Barrett, as they drove up to the Ladies Center, an abortion clinic in Pensacola, Florida. Several years earlier, another member of Bray's network of associates, Rachelle ("Shelly") Shannon, a housewife from rural Oregon, confessed to a string of abortion clinic bombings as well as being convicted of attempted murder for shooting and wounding Dr. George Tiller as he drove away from his clinic in Wichita, Kansas. Bray wrote the definitive book on the ethical justification for anti-abortion violence, *A Time to Kill*, which defended his own acts of terrorism, the murders committed by Hill, and the attempted murders committed by Shannon (Bray 1994). Yet, in person, the Reverend Michael Bray was in many ways an attractive and interesting man.

Mike Bray had always been active, he told me, having been raised in a family focused on sports, church activities, and military life. His father was a naval officer who served at nearby Annapolis, and Mike grew up expecting to follow in his father's military footsteps. An athletic hero in high school, he took the most popular girl in class to the senior prom. Her name was Kathy Lee, and later she became an actress and a nationally televised talk show host, receiving top billing on her own daytime show with Regis Philbin. Mike's own career was marked by less obvious attributes of success. He attended Annapolis for a year and then dropped out, living what he described as a "prodigal" life. He searched for religion as a solution to his malaise and was for a time tempted by the Mormons, but then the mother of his old girlfriend, Kathy Lee, steered him toward Billy Graham and the born-again experience of evangelical Christianity. Mike was converted and went to Colorado to study in a Baptist Bible college and seminary.

Yet Bray never quite rejected the Lutheranism of his upbringing. So when he returned to Bowie, he rejoined his childhood church and became the assistant pastor. When the national Lutheran churches merged, Bray led a faction of the local church that objected to what it regarded as the national church's abandonment of the principle of scriptural literalism. Seeing himself as a crusader, Mike and his group of 10 families split off and formed their own Reformed Lutheran church in 1984, an independent group affiliated with the national Association of Free Lutheran Congregations. Over 10 years later, Bray's church remained a circle of about fifty people without its own church building. The church operated out of Bray's suburban home: Bray remodeled the garage into a classroom for a Christian elementary school, where he and his wife taught a small group of students.

Increasingly, Mike Bray's real occupation became social activism. Supported by his wife, members of the church, and his volunteer associate pastor, Michael Colvin—who held a Ph.D. in classics from Indiana University and worked in the federal health care administration—Mike and his followers launched several anti-abortion crusades and tapped into a growing national network of like-minded Christian activists. They became consumed by the idea that the federal government—particularly the attorney general, whom Mike called "Janet Waco Reno"—was involved in a massive plot to undermine individual freedom and moral values. He saw American society as being in a state of utter depravity, over which its elected officials presided with an almost satanic disregard for truth and human life. He viewed President Clinton and other politicians as latter-day Hitlers, and the Nazi image pervaded Bray's understanding of how ethically minded people should respond to such a threat. Regarding the activities that led to his prison conviction, Bray had "no regrets." "Whatever I did," he said, "it was worth it."

According to Bray, we live in a situation "comparable to Nazi Germany," a state of hidden warfare. The comforts of modern society have lulled the populace into a lack of awareness of the situation, and Bray was convinced that if there were some dramatic event, such as economic collapse or social chaos, the demonic role of the government would be revealed, and people would have "the strength and the zeal to take up arms" in a revolutionary struggle. What he envisioned as the outcome of that struggle was the establishment of a new moral order in America, one based on biblical law and a spiritual, rather than a secular, social compact.

Until this new moral order was established, Bray and others like him who were aware of what was going on and had the moral courage to resist it were compelled to take action. According to Bray, he had the right to defend innocent "unborn children," even by use of force, whether it involved "destroying the facilities that they are regularly killed in, or taking the life of one who is murdering them." By the latter, Bray meant killing doctors and other clinical staff involved in performing abortions.

When I suggested that such violent actions were tantamount to acting as both judge and executioner, Bray demurred. Although he did not deny that a religious authority had the right to pronounce judgment over those who broke the moral law, he explained that his actions in attacking abortion clinics and the actions of his friend, the Reverend Paul Hill, in killing abortion doctors were essentially defensive rather than punitive acts. According to Bray, "There is a difference between taking a retired abortionist and executing him, and killing a practicing abortionist who is regularly killing babies." The first act is, in Bray's view, retributive; the other, defensive. According to Bray, the attacks that he and Hill committed were not so much aimed at punishing the clinics and the abortionists for their actions as at preventing them from "killing babies," as Bray put it.

APPROPRIATING BONHOEFFER
AND NIEBUHR

Bray found support for his position in actions undertaken during the Nazi regime in Europe. His theological hero in this regard was the German theologian and Lutheran pastor Dietrich Bonhoeffer. Bonhoeffer abruptly terminated his privileged research position at Union Theological Seminary in New York City in order to return to Germany and clandestinely join a plot to assassinate Hitler. The plot was uncovered before it could be carried out, and Bonhoeffer, the brilliant young ethical theorist, was hanged by the Nazis shortly before the end of the war. His image of martyrdom and his theological writings have lived on, however, and Bonhoeffer is often cited by moral theorists as an example of how Christians can undertake violent actions for a just cause and how occasionally Christians are compelled to break laws for a higher purpose.

These are positions also held by one of Bonhoeffer's colleagues at Union Theological Seminary, Reinhold Niebuhr, whom Bray similarly admired. Often touted as one of the greatest Protestant theologians of the twentieth century, Niebuhr wrestled with one of Christianity's oldest ethical problems: when is it permissible to use force—even violence—in behalf of a righteous cause? Niebuhr began his career as a pacifist, but in time grudgingly began to accept the position that a Christian, acting for the sake of justice, could be violent (Niebuhr 1932, 1942).

Niebuhr showed the relevance of just war theory to contemporary social struggles in the twentieth century by relating this classic idea— a notion first stated by Cicero and later developed by Ambrose and Augustine—to what he regarded as the Christian requirement to fulfill social justice. Viewing the world through the lens of "realism," Niebuhr was impressed that moral suasion was not sufficient to combat injustices, especially when they are buttressed by corporate and state power. For this reason, he explained in a seminal essay, "Why the Christian Church Is Not Pacifist" (1940), it was at times necessary to abandon nonviolence in favor of a more forceful solution. Building his case on Augustine's understanding of original sin, Niebuhr argued that righteous force was sometimes necessary to extirpate injustice and subdue evil within a sinful world, and that small strategic acts of violence were occasionally necessary to deter large acts of violence and injustice. If violence is to be used in such situations, Niebuhr explained, it must be used sparingly and as swiftly and as skillfully "as a surgeon's knife" (1932, 134).

Bray borrowed this theological logic for justifying violence from Niebuhr and Bonhoeffer, but where Bray radically differed from these thinkers was in his interpretation of the contemporary political situation that made the application of the logic credible. In a conceptual sleight of hand that Bonhoeffer would have regarded as inconceivable, Bray compared America's democratic state with Nazism. In a manner that would have sent Niebuhr reeling, Bray insisted that only a biblically based religious politics, rather than a secular one, was capable of dispensing social justice. Both of these positions would be rejected not only by these but also by most other theologians within the mainstream of Protestant thought. Bonhoeffer and Niebuhr, like most modern theologians, accepted the principle of the separation of church and state. They felt the separation was necessary for the integrity of both institutions. Niebuhr was especially wary of what he called "moralism," the intrusion of religious or other ideological values into the political calculations of statecraft.

RECONSTRUCTION THEOLOGY

To support his ideas about religious politics, therefore, Bray had to look beyond mainstream Protestant thought. He found intellectual company in a group of recent writers associated with dominion theology, the theological position that Christianity must reassert the dominion of God over all things, including secular politics and society. This point of view—well articulated by such right-wing Protestant spokespersons as the Reverend Jerry Falwell and Pat Robertson—has led to a burst of social and political activism on the Christian Right in the 1980s and 1990s.

The Christian anti-abortion movement is permeated with dominion theology ideas. Randall Terry, the founder of the militant anti-abortion organization Operation Rescue, writes for the dominion magazine *Crosswinds* and has signed its Manifesto for the Christian Church, which asserts that America should "function as a Christian nation." The manifesto opposes such "social moral evils" of secular society as

abortion on demand, fornication, homosexuality, sexual entertainment, state usurpation of parental rights and God-given liberties, statist-collectivist theft from citizens through devaluation of their money and redistribution of their wealth, and evolutionism taught as a monopoly viewpoint in the public schools. (Berlet 1996, 8)

At the extreme right-wing of dominion theology is a relatively obscure theological movement that Mike Bray has found particularly appealing: a movement known as reconstructionist theology, whose exponents long to create a Christian theocratic state. Leaders of this movement trace their ideas to Cornelius Van Til, a twentieth-century Presbyterian professor of theology at Princeton Seminary who took seriously the sixteenth-century ideas of the Reformation theologian John Calvin regarding the necessity for presupposing the authority of God in all worldly matters. Followers of Van Til, including his former students, the Reverend Greg Bahnsen and Rousas John Rushdoony, and Rushdoony's son-in-law, Gary North, have adopted this presuppositionalism as a doctrine, with all its implications about the role of religion in political life.

Reconstructionist writers have regarded the history of Protestant politics since the early years of the Reformation as having taken a bad turn, and they were especially unhappy with the Enlightenment formulation of church-state separation. They felt that it was necessary to "reconstruct" Christian society by turning to the Bible as the basis for a nation's law and social order. To propagate their views, the reconstructionists established an Institute for Christian Economics in Tyler, Texas, and published a steady stream of literature on the theological justification for interjecting Christian ideas into economic, legal, and political life (for example, Rushdoony 1973).

According to the most prolific reconstructionist writer, Gary North, it was "the moral obligation of Christians to recapture every institution for Jesus Christ" (North 1984, 267). This was especially so in the United States, where secular law as construed by the Supreme Court and defended by liberal politicians has taken what Rushdoony and others regard as a decidedly un-Christian direction, particularly in matters regarding abortion and homosexuality. What the reconstructionists ultimately wanted, however, was much more than the rejection of secularism. Like other dominion theologians, they utilized the biblical concept of dominion, reasoning further that Christians, as the new chosen people of God, were destined to dominate the world.

The reconstructionists have a postmillennial view of history. That is, they believe that Christ will return to earth only after the thousand years of religious rule that characterizes the Christian idea of the millennium, and therefore Christians have an obligation to provide the political and social conditions that would make Christ's return possible. Premillennialists, on the other hand, hold the view that the thousand years of Christendom can come only after Christ returns, an event that will occur in a cataclysmic moment of world history, and therefore they tend to be much less active politically. Postmillennial followers of reconstructionist theology such as Mike Bray, dominion theologians such as Pat

Robertson, and many of the leaders of the politically active Christian Coalition believe that a Christian kingdom can be established on earth before Christ's return, and they take seriously the idea of Christian society and the eruption of religious politics that would make biblical code the law of the land.

In our conversation, Bray insisted that the idea of a society based on Christian morality was not a new one, and he emphasized the "re" in "reconstruction." Although Bray rejected the idea of a pope, he appreciated much of the Roman Catholic church's social teachings and greatly admired the tradition of canon law. Only recently in history, he observed, had the political order not been based on religious concepts. For that reason, Bray labeled himself an "antidisestablishmentarian." He was deeply serious about his commitment to bring such religious politics into power. He imagined that it was possible, under the right conditions, for a Christian revolution to sweep across the country, bringing in its wake constitutional changes that would allow for biblical law to be the basis of social legislation. Failing that, Bray envisaged a new federalism in America that would allow individual states to experiment with religious politics on their own. When I asked Bray which state might be ready for such an experiment, he hesitated and then offered the names of Louisiana and Mississippi, or, he added, "maybe one of the Dakotas."

CHRISTIAN IDENTITY

A somewhat different set of theological justifications lay in the background of another anti-abortion activist, Eric Robert Rudolph. Rudolph was the subject of a well-publicized manhunt by the Federal Bureau of Investigation early in 1998 for his alleged role in bombing abortion clinics in Birmingham, Alabama, and Atlanta, Georgia; blasting a gay bar in Atlanta; and exploding a bomb at the 1996 Atlanta Olympics. He subscribed to the theology of Christian Identity. The thinking of Christian Identity has been part of the background of such movements as the Posse Comitatus, the Order, the Aryan Nation, the supporters of Randy Weaver at Ruby Ridge, Herbert Armstrong's Worldwide Church of God, and the Freeman Compound. It also has been popular in many militia movements throughout the United States.

Christian Identity ideas were most likely a part of the thinking of Timothy McVeigh, the convicted bomber of the Oklahoma City federal building. McVeigh was exposed to Identity thinking through the Michigan militia with which he was once associated and which had a strong Christian Identity flavoring, and through his visits to the Christian Identity encampment, Elohim City, on the Oklahoma-Arkansas border. He also imbibed Christian Identity ideas through the book *The Turner Diaries* (Macdonald 1978), which he treated virtually as a bible and which was strongly influenced by Christian Identity ideas.

McVeigh had distributed *The Turner Diaries* at rallies and had contacted the author shortly before the Oklahoma City blast. A copy of the book was found in his car when it was intercepted leaving Oklahoma City within an hour of the attack. The anti-Semitic novel, which was written by William Pierce under the pseudonym Andrew Macdonald, tells the story of the encroachment of government control in America and the resistance by a guerrilla band known as the Order, which attacked government buildings using a modus operandi almost exactly the same as the one McVeigh used in destroying the Oklahoma City federal building. Pierce, who received a Ph.D. from the University of Colorado and for a time taught physics at Oregon State University, once served as a writer for the American Nazi Party and in 1984 proclaimed himself the founder of a new religious group, the Cosmotheist Community (Solnin 1995, 8). Although Pierce denied affiliation with the Christian Identity movement, he knew the literature well, and his own teachings were virtually synonymous with those associated with the movement.

Pierce, like many members of the Christian Identity militia groups, distrusted ordinary Christian churches for their liberalism and lack of courage. He claimed that in the future described in his novel, the "Jewish takeover" of the Christian church would be "virtually complete" (Macdonald 1978, 64). The members of the fictional Order in his novel were characterized as being intensely religious, having undergone an initiation similar to that of joining a monastic order. The narrator in the novel tells of being required to take an oath, "a mighty Oath, a moving Oath that shook me to my bones and raised the hair on the back of my neck" (Macdonald 1978, 73). With this oath the members of the Order were spiritually armed to be "bearers of the Faith" in a godless world (Macdonald 1978, 74). According to Pierce, such missionary efforts were necessary because of the mind-set of secularism that had been imposed on American society as a result of an elaborate conspiracy orchestrated by Jews and liberals who were hell-bent on depriving Christian society of its spiritual moorings. In formulating his own version of this view, McVeigh had read Pierce and *The Turner Diaries*; Pierce, in turn, had read thinkers associated with Christian Identity.

Although the writers associated with the Christian Identity movement distrusted most modern churches, they railed against the separation of church and state—or, rather, religion and state—and longed for a new society governed by religious law. They were strongly anti-Semitic, held an apocalyptic view of history, and possessed an even more conspiratorial view of government than the reconstructionists. Christian Identity originated in the movement of British Israelism in the nineteenth century. According to John Wilson, whose central work, *Lectures on Our Israelitish Origin*, brought the message to a large British and Irish middle-class audience, Jesus had been an Aryan, not a Semite; the migrating Israelite tribes from the northern kingdom of Israel were in fact blue-eyed Aryans themselves who somehow ended up in the British Isles; and the "Lost Sheep of the House of Israel" were none other than present-day Englishmen (Barkun 1994, 7). Adherents of this theory hold that those people who claim to be Jews are imposters—according to one variation of the theory, they are aliens from outer space—who pretend to be Jews in order to assert their superiority in a scheme to control the world. Their plot is allegedly supported by the secret Protestant order of Freemasons.

British Israelism came to the United States in the twentieth century through the teachings of the evangelist Gerald L. K. Smith and the writings of William Cameron, who was the publicist for the famous automobile magnate, Henry Ford (Zeskind 1986, 12). Ford himself supported many of Cameron's views and published a book of anti-Semitic essays written by Cameron but attributed to Ford, *The International Jew: The World's Foremost Problem*. Central to Cameron's thought were the necessity of the Anglo-Saxon race in the United States to retain its purity and political dominance, and the need to establish a biblical basis for governance. These ideas were developed into the Christian Identity movement in America by Bertram Comparet, a deputy district attorney in San Diego, and Wesley Swift, a Ku Klux Klan member who founded the Church of Jesus Christ—Christian in 1946. This church was the basis for the Christian Defense League, organized by Bill Gale at his ranch in Mariposa, California, in the 1960s, a movement that spawned both the Posse Comitatus and the Aryan Nation (Zeskind 1986, 14).

In the 1980s and 1990s, the largest concentration of Christian Identity groups has been in Idaho—centered on the Aryan Nation's compound near Hayden Lake—and in the southern Midwest near the Oklahoma-Arkansas-Missouri borders. In that location, a Christian Identity group called the Covenant, the Sword, and the Arm of the Lord established a 224-acre community and a paramilitary school which it named the Endtime Overcomer Survival Training School (Zeskind 1986, 45). Nearby, Christian Identity minister Steven Millar and former Nazi Party member Glenn Miller established Elohim City, whose members stockpiled weapons and prepared themselves for "a Branch Davidian–type raid" by the U.S. government's Bureau of Alcohol, Tobacco and Firearms (Baumgarten 1995, 17). It was this Christian Identity encampment that Timothy McVeigh visited shortly before the Oklahoma City federal building blast.

The American incarnation of the Christian Identity movement contained many of its British counterpart's paranoid views, updated to suit the social anxieties of many contemporary Americans. For instance, in the American version, the United Nations and the Democratic Party were alleged to be accomplices in a Jewish-Freemason conspiracy to control the world and deprive individuals of their freedom. According to a 1982 Identity pamphlet, Jews were described as "parasites and vultures," who controlled the world through international banking (Mohr 1982). The establishment of the International Monetary Fund, the introduction of magnetized credit cards, and the establishment of paper money not backed by gold or silver were the final steps in "Satan's Plan" (Aho 1990,

91). Gun control was also an important issue to Christian Identity supporters, since they believed that Jewish, U.N., and liberal conspirators intended to remove the last possibilities of rebellion against their centralized power by depriving individuals of the weapons they might use to defend themselves or free their countrymen from a tyrannical state. The views of Timothy McVeigh, although less obviously Christian and anti-Semitic than most Christian Identity teachings, otherwise fit precisely the paradigm of Christian Identity thought.

THE HIDDEN WAR

The world as envisioned by both reconstructionist theology and Christian Identity was a world at war. Identity preachers cited the biblical accounts of Michael the Archangel's destruction of the offspring of evil to point to a hidden, albeit "cosmic war" between the forces of darkness and the forces of light (Aho 1990, 85). "There is murder going on," Mike Bray explained, "which we have to stop." In the Christian Identity view of the world, the struggle was a secret war between colossal evil forces allied with U.N., U.S., and other government powers, on the one hand, and a small band of the enlightened few who recognized these invisible enemies for what they were—in their view, satanic powers—and were sufficiently courageous to battle against them. Although Bray rejected much of Christian Identity's conspiratorial view of the world and specifically decried its anti-Semitism, he did appreciate its commitment to struggle

against secular forms of evil and its insistence on the need for a Christian social order. Both Christian Identity and reconstructionist thought yearned for a version of American politics rooted in Christian values and biblical law.

As Mike Bray explained, the destruction of abortion clinics was not the result of a personal vendetta against agencies with which he and others have had moral differences, but the consequences of a grand religious vision. His actions were part of a great crusade conducted by a Christian subculture in America that has seen itself at war with the larger society and, to some extent, victimized by it. Armed with the theological explanations of reconstruction and Christian Identity, this subculture has seen itself justified in its violent responses to what it perceives as a violent repression waged by secular (and, in some versions of this perception, Jewish) agents of a satanic force. Mike Bray and his network of associates around the country saw themselves engaged in violence not for its own sake but as a response to the institutional violence of what they regarded as a repressive secular state. When he poured gasoline on rags and ignited fires to demolish abortion clinics, therefore, Mike Bray was firing the opening salvos in what he envisaged to be a great defensive Christian struggle against the secular state, a contest between the forces of spiritual truth and secular darkness, in which the moral character of America as a righteous nation hung in the balance.

In this regard, the Reverend Bray joined a legion of religious activists from Algeria to Idaho who have come to hate secular governments with an almost transcendent passion, and dream of revolutionary changes that will establish a godly social order in the rubble of what the citizens of most secular societies regard as modern, egalitarian democracies. Their enemies seem to most of us to be benign and banal: modern secular leaders and such symbols of prosperity and authority as international airlines and the World Trade Center. The logic of their ideological religious view is, although difficult to comprehend, profound, for it contains a fundamental critique of the world's post-Enlightenment secular culture and politics.

After years of waiting in history's wings, religion has renewed its claim to be an ideology of public order in a dramatic fashion: violently. In the United States, as in other parts of the world, religion's renewed political presence is accompanied by violence in part because of the nature of religion and its claims of power over life and death. In part, the violence is due to the nature of secular politics, which bases its own legitimacy on the currency of weapons and can be challenged successfully only on a level of force. In part, it is due to the nature of violence itself. Violence is a destructive display of power, and in a time when competing groups are attempting to assert their strength, the power of violence becomes a valuable political commodity. At the very least, the proponents of a religious ideology of social control such as those American activists associated with the ideas of reconstruction theology and Christian Identity have to remind the populace of the godly power that makes their ideologies potent. At their destructive worst, they create incidents of violence on God's behalf.

References

Aho, James. 1990. *The Politics of Righteousness: Idaho Christian Patriotism.* Seattle: University of Washington Press.

Barkun, Michael. 1994. *Religion and the Racist Right: The Origins of the Christian Identity Movement.* Chapel Hill: University of North Carolina Press.

Baumgarten, Gerald. 1995. *Paranoia as Patriotism: Far-Right Influences on the Militia Movement.* New York: Anti-Defamation League.

Berlet, Chip. 1996. *John Salvi, Abortion Clinic Violence, and Catholic Right Conspiracism.* Somerville, MA: Political Research Associates.

Bray, Michael. 1994. *A Time to Kill: A Study Concerning the Use of Force and Abortion.* Portland, OR: Advocates for Life.

———. 1996. Interview by author. Bowie, MD, 25 Apr. 1996.

Juergensmeyer, Mark. 1993. *The New Cold War? Religious Nationalism Confronts the Secular State.* Berkeley: University of California Press.

Macdonald, Andrew [William Pierce]. 1978. *The Turner Diaries.* Arlington, VA: Alliance National Vanguard Books.

Mohr, Gordon "Jack." 1982. *Know Your Enemies.* N.p.

Niebuhr, Reinhold. 1932. *Moral Man and Immoral Society.* New York: Scribner's.

———. 1940. *Why the Christian Church Is Not Pacifist.* London: Student Christian Movement Press.

———. 1942. *The Nature and Destiny of Man.* New York: Scribner's.

North, Gary. 1984. *Backward, Christian Soldiers? An Action Manual for Chris-*

tian Reconstruction. Tyler, TX: Institute for Christian Economics.

Rushdoony, Rousas John. 1973. *Institutes of Biblical Law*. Nutley, NJ: Craig Press.

Solnin, Amy C. 1995. *William L. Pierce: Novelist of Hate*. New York: Anti-Defamation League.

Zeskind, Leonard. 1986. *The "Christian Identity" Movement: Analyzing Its Theological Rationalization for Racist and Anti-Semitic Violence*. New York: National Council of Churches of Christ in the U.S.A., Division of Church and Society.

Plenty Good Room: Adaptation in a Changing Black Church

By CHERYL TOWNSEND GILKES

ABSTRACT: The contemporary black church is a product of the social movements of the 1960s. Alongside the rapid growth of mega-churches, there are several important features shaping the church of the twenty-first century: (1) a transformation of consciousness that combines black consciousness with Christian ethics; (2) a rapid expansion of the black middle class and the geographic and social relocation of the new middle class; (3) the professionalization of a highly literate laity in terms of the quality of services it demands and the professionalized voluntarism it offers; and (4) changing gender relations evidenced by a continued dependence on women's work and growing numbers of women in ministry, along with a focus on the social problems of black males, especially among the urban poor. The tradition of adaptation to change remains strong as these new features are utilized to combine the work of traditional religion with efforts to pursue social justice and economic equity.

Cheryl Townsend Gilkes is a MacArthur Associate Professor of African American Studies and Sociology and director of the African American Studies Program at Colby College. She is also an associate minister at the Union Baptist Church in Cambridge, Massachusetts. Her articles on sociology of religion, African American women, W.E.B. Du Bois, and African American religious traditions have appeared in several journals and anthologies.

NOTE: Earlier versions of this article were presented to the Howard University School of Divinity, Harvard University's Center for Literary and Cultural Studies, and the Eastern Sociological Society.

There's plenty good room
Way in the Kingdom. . . .
Choose your seat and sit down!
—Traditional Negro spiritual[1]

Two-thirds of the way through the twentieth century, the activisms of the 1960s changed the entire society and its diverse spectrum of religious experiences. Some thought these changes significant enough to be called a revolution (Killian 1975). The black community, in many ways, most directly experienced many of the problems—for instance, Jim Crow, poverty, institutional racism, and conscription for the war in Vietnam—that gave rise to the movements of the 1960s. While civil rights and black power activism in the black community provided models for other groups as they addressed their particular hurts and needs (McAdam 1984; Glazer 1973; Deloria 1970), these revolutions and movements of the 1960s sparked controversies and conversations within the religious communities of black America and encouraged the growth of a new black consciousness (Lincoln and Mamiya 1990, 164-95). As a result, the denominations and congregations controlled by black people in the United States underwent profound changes; the Negro church ceased to be and the black church was born (Lincoln 1974).

Influenced by Malcolm X, leaders of the Student Nonviolent Coordinating Committee started a black power movement that sought to increase the economic position, political power, and cultural self-awareness of black Americans (King 1987; Carmichael and Hamilton 1967). That movement mobilized, reorganized, and inspired black people to transform old organizations and create new ones within the communities they sought to control. In the context of continued subordination, powerlessness, and aggressive state repression, black churches and mosques maintained their historical role as the public sphere (Higginbotham 1993), while the convocations of the black church addressed this new emphasis on power and self-definition and coped with social change.

The most visible recent change in American religion was the emergence of the megachurch (Thumma 1996, 429-526). Although African Americans compose only 12 percent of the U.S. population, they constitute 25 percent of its megachurch congregations. These congregations are bursting with crowds of black baby boomers, or so-called buppies, who have "come home" to church (Lawrence 1996; Roof 1993). The fascination on the part of the press with these very prominent churches often has obscured the older traditions on which they are built and the deeper networks in which they are embedded—traditions and networks that have historically nurtured and challenged American religious culture. Although megachurches are harbingers of more profound changes affecting all black churches in the United States, their newness is more apparent than real. The emergence of a wide variety of new churches and the dramatic transformation of a significant number of old ones at a time when the black community itself is experiencing a major socioeconomic restructuring invites questions about the current state of African American religion. This article seeks to identify significant features shaping the contemporary black church (Lincoln and Mamiya 1990) or "the church of what's happening now"[2] (Gilkes 1995, 180-86).

The civil rights and black power movements changed black communities, and the subsequent rise in black consciousness shook black churches to their very foundations. These changes in consciousness occurred when the consequences of the civil rights movement fostered the economic and occupational mobility of a significant segment of the black population (Wilson 1978). At the same time that this indigenous black middle class grew, changes in the immigration laws opened the doors to an African and Caribbean immigration that changed black neighborhoods, churches, and cultural expression, reinforcing the Afrocentric emphases of many congregations. The mobility—both socioeconomic and geographic—of younger black people meant that, as had happened during earlier migrations, significant numbers of black Americans switched congregations, carrying diverse denominational and local traditions into the more Anglo-conformist, mainstream congregations and thus reorganizing and sometimes reinventing African American tradition. Their increased education contributed to the professionalization of the laity. The larger numbers of church members with graduate and professional degrees offered and demanded new levels of teaching and service, contributing to a proliferation of innovative and diverse ministries and sending their pastors into doctoral and other graduate programs in response to these new demands.[3] As has been the case historically, gender relations were profoundly implicated in all of these changes. Controversies and conflicts surrounding the black family, intimate relations, and sex roles engendered both an assertive emergence of the black church's historical womanist infrastructure and rhetorical and organizational attention to the problems of black males.

Overall, this black church "of what's happening now" is an absorbent and adaptive institution that both fosters social change, pursuing the "dual agenda" of social justice and economic equity (Hamilton and Hamilton 1997), and mediates and interprets the impact of structural transformations on diverse, dynamic, and disadvantaged black communities. As Roof (1993) and others have pointed out, major social changes since World War II have reshaped and restructured American religion overall. However, the demographic trends pointing to a shrinking white American mainline have not applied to black churches. These churches held their memberships during and after the crises of the 1960s (Glenn 1977), but those segments of the black church often dismissed as "sects and cults" and portrayed as deviant (Washington 1973)—preferably referred to as the "Sanctified Church"[4] by black Christians—actually grew in size and in prestige, sharing equally in the status and culture of the black church's denominational mainstream (Lincoln and Mamiya 1990). After sketching the impact of the 1960s on the black church, this article points to these changing trends—heightened cultural and sociopolitical consciousness, rapid mobility, revitalization, professionalization, and gender relations—as aspects of church organization and ethos that both reflect and nurture, through a dynamic and adaptive interaction, the growth and revitalization of congregational life and community presence.

BEYOND THE BLACK MEGACHURCH

There has always been an edifice complex in the study of black churches in the United States. First it was storefront churches; now it is megachurches. The emergence of megachurches in black communities builds upon an older but unrecognized feature of black church history. At key points in the history of black Americans, the large congregations of the black church have been the primary gathering place from which black Americans asserted their humanity and adapted to changing conditions in a racist society.

Social scientists and journalists tend to define a megachurch as a congregation of more than 3000 members (Thumma 1996; Harris 1997; Banks 1997; Caldwell 1997). However, the black church has a tradition of large churches that precedes the Civil War. Albert Raboteau (1978, 196) points out, "Town churches . . . drew slaves from both town and country, swelling in size to hundreds and in a few instances, thousands of members." One could perhaps persuasively argue that First African of Richmond, Virginia, with its membership of 3260 in 1860 would certainly qualify as a megachurch. Clarence Taylor, in his model study *The Black Churches of Brooklyn* (1994), identifies a fair number of congregations whose memberships exceeded 3000 in the first half of the twentieth century. Before 1940, northern migration brought the memberships of Holy Trinity, Bethany, Concord, and Mount Lebanon Baptist churches to memberships of 3100, 3600, 8600, and over 4000, respectively (86, 144). When the late Adam Clayton Powell, Jr., assumed the pastorate of New York City's Abyssinia Baptist Church in 1937, "the church had ten thousand members and was one of the largest Baptist congregations in America" (Haygood 1998, 26).

Contemporary black megachurches have usually grown quite rapidly, attracting quite a bit of attention and, occasionally, hostility in their communities. Although they are manifestly middle-class, their worship style reflects the older tradition of the Sanctified Church and other shouting churches. Their music is the best gospel music, and the preaching there is some of the best biblically based preaching to be heard. Furthermore, most black megachurches offer a high degree of affirmation of a black identity in a hostile white society. The church reminds its members "who they are and whose they are," as a counterforce to oppressive social, economic, and cultural circumstances that may make them want to forget.

These megachurches are the most visible evidence of a revitalization and reorganization of black church life that has been taking place since the late 1960s. There are many other black churches that have experienced explosive growth in both inner-city and suburban locations without becoming megachurches. Their rapid rates of growth point to other, more complex features shaping trends in black churches. These other features—such as congregational culture, volunteer and professional roles, class structure, and theological and cultural values—may point to a larger set of concerns throughout the black community and provide a better portrait of religion in the entire African American experience since "the revolution" has come.

CIVIL RIGHTS, EMPOWERMENT, AND BLACK CONSCIOUSNESS

"When the revolution came,"[5] according to the poet Carolyn Rodgers (1976), a new generation of African Americans questioned the political relevance of black Christian organizations, beliefs, and practices, especially the love ethic of the civil rights movement, challenging the hegemony of the black church in African American life and culture. The Black Muslims (the Nation of Islam), "the largest indigenous population of Americans who have become Muslims," nurtured this challenge (Lincoln and Mamiya 1990, 388-89; Lincoln 1973). Members of the Nation of Islam often engaged in a practice called "fishing," where they stood outside of black Christian congregations as the Sunday service ended, haranguing church members about the contradictions of Christianity in white America. Spike Lee's film *Mal-colm X* depicted Malcolm X as offering one such typical challenge:

You think you are Christians, and yet you see your so-called white Christian brother hanging black Christians on trees. . . . That white man . . . has done every evil act against you. He has everything while he is living and tells you to be a good slave and when you die you will have more than he has in Beulah's land. We so-called Negroes are in pitiful shape. . . . Come out of the sky. Build heaven on earth. Islam is the black man's true religion. (Lee with Wiley, 1992, 246)

The Black Muslims directly addressed the discontents of the ghetto and dissented from the ethical emphases of Martin Luther King, Jr., and the Southern Christian Leadership Conference.

The civil rights movement changed America, achieving what Lewis Killian (1975) called an "impossible revolution" by overthrowing a body of law in a nation supposedly under the rule of law. The civil rights revolution was the most significant mobilization of the black church (Morris 1984); it brought the ethics, traditions, and practices of the black church into the foreground, placing a harsh spotlight on the segregated Sundays of American Christians. Violent reaction to a decidedly Christian civil rights movement was usually expressed in church burnings and bombings, and the dissenters pointed to such violence as more reason to criticize and belittle the love ethic of black Christianity. The Black Muslims' criticisms were carried forward by Malcolm X, the Student Nonviolent Coordinating Committee, and others in what came to be called the black power movement.[6] They articulated the problems of institutional racism, internal colonialism, and economic justice as the central issues to be addressed by black power. They also countered the cultural humiliation and assaults on self-esteem embedded in America's history of racism with calls for black pride.

Black churches responded with organized challenges to white churches through the National Committee of Black Churchmen and demands for reparations as they promoted a black theological revolution within (Wilmore and Cone 1980). The transformation was so profound that C. Eric Lincoln (1974) described the moment as a change from Frazier's "Negro Church" ([1963] 1974) to "the Black Church." He wrote:

The "Negro Church" that Frazier wrote about no longer exists. It died an agonized death in the harsh turmoil that tried the faith so rigorously in the decade of the "Savage Sixties," for there it had to confront under the most trying circumstances the possibility that "Negro" and "Christian" were irreconcilable categories. The call to full manhood, to *personhood*, and the call to Christian responsibility left no room for the implications of being a "Negro" in contemporary America. . . . The Negro Church accepted death in order to be reborn. Out of the ashes of its funeral pyre there sprang the bold, strident, self-conscious phoenix that is the contemporary Black Church.[7] (105-6)

The successes of the civil rights movement highlighted deeper social problems and revealed a legacy of economic inequality, political exclusion, and cultural humiliation. Voter registration and political organization revealed the connections between political powerlessness, eco-

nomic disadvantage, miseducation, and the larger structured outcomes that came to be called institutional racism (Carmichael and Hamilton 1967; Knowles and Prewitt 1969; King 1987; Wilhelm 1971; Wilson 1973; Malcolm X and Haley 1964). The new militant black power rhetoric also masculinized the language of black liberation at precisely the same moment that white women began to challenge sexism in America and the U.S. government published a report on black families that vilified black women, interpreting their labor history as a force emasculating black men (Cade 1970; Gilkes 1987, 1990).

New and expanded opportunities changed the class configurations and collective consciousness of congregations and other organizations as professionalized activists and activist professionals joined the leadership class formerly monopolized by pastors and their allies. "When the revolution came," brothers and sisters in black churches were forced to reposition themselves in a space that was itself shifting. While black churches, in contrast to white churches, did not lose their memberships, the generation we now call baby boomers experimented with a wide variety of organizations and spiritual perspectives before returning "home" (Lawrence 1996; Trescott 1997).

MOBILITY, MIGRATION,
AND THE CRISIS OF
CONNECTEDNESS

Shortly after World War I, a Baptist deacon in Little Rock, Arkansas, had admonished his daughter as she prepared to migrate north with her husband, a Pullman car porter, "Don't ever forget your church and the NAACP [National Association for the Advancement of Colored People]." As I recorded her life history, I was surprised at how similar was my own father's admonition during the 1960s as I prepared to leave home for college: "I don't care what you decide to believe, remember you can't get anything done in the community without the church." The perception of the church as a source of connection and activist efficacy had not changed across those two generations as the 87-year-old community and church mother and the 27-year-old sociology graduate student faced each other across a cassette tape recorder.

Migration, mobilization, and movement are themes and events that define and describe the black experience and that cluster around the points in black history where class composition and black occupational attainment changed substantially. According to Bart Landry (1987, 19-20), 90 percent of the black population remained in agricultural and service work until World War I. Two world wars and restrictive immigration made black northern migration and entry into the industrial sector possible. The actual "emergence of a new black middle class" was prompted by "two simultaneous and powerful forces within American society: prosperity and the civil rights movement" (70). In the 1960s, this middle class doubled to 28.6 percent of the black population and then grew during the 1970s and early 1980s to 37.4 percent (194, 218). These changing class configurations changed black churches. Greater educational opportunities and career choices fos-

tered a great deal of geographic mobility. This new prosperity also prompted suburbanization, and, as large black middle-class populations moved to the suburbs, usually black suburbs, some churches followed.

The old and new black middle classes met in the churches. Some of the most vibrant black megachurches had former identities as "silkstocking" congregations of the "old" black elite or black bourgeoisie (Frazier 1957) and were transformed by massive infusions of these economically mobile younger people. They were historic congregations and small, having fewer than 100 members. They were part of either predominantly white denominations or established black denominations when a new pastor, who represented the civil rights and black power generation's consciousness, was either called or assigned. While methods of recruitment and revitalization varied, these pastors drew members of the new black middle class who were college students, former members of the Nation of Islam, newly affluent middle-income families, self-critical members of the black bourgeoisie, and migrant and immigrant black professionals seeking a new church home. In some cases, these congregations were spaces where the new and old middle classes and elites had the opportunity to integrate and socialize with each other. In one southern congregation, whose leadership was historically tied to a black-owned insurance company, the church's revitalization and transformation was so sudden and abrupt that working-class members of other churches would come to visit just to see for themselves that the members were really shouting and saying "Amen" and that a more vibrant worship style was actually taking place. The church had outgrown its building and moved to a larger, more suburban setting. At the end of a particularly exciting church service at the new site, a church leader, a member of the old elite, said to me, with tears of joy streaming down his face, "This used to be the First Church of the Frigidaire!"

Some churches in deteriorating inner-city locations made a conscious effort to reach out to newer networks in the neighborhood as the older church population became commuters from suburban locations. Such centrally located churches also attracted black professional members from the suburbs whose only experience of a black majority was in their Sunday morning service. For black professionals who worked in overwhelmingly white settings, the cultural comfort of these black churches provided therapeutic relief from the micropolitics of being black in a white and unpredictably hostile world; this was especially true for women (Gilkes 1980; Wiggins 1997).

African Americans have traditionally felt deep anxiety over social class divisions, and such anxiety is evident in the popular culture. The negative interpersonal consequences of social mobility where children return from college ashamed of their parents' speech patterns and country ways and where middle-class congregations attempt to suppress the ecstatic expression of their members are sung about in gospel music and preached about from pulpits. E. Franklin Frazier's critique of the old black middle class, *The Black Bourgeoisie* (1957),

was so well popularized among African Americans that a pejorative term, "bourgie," emerged and became a hit record by rhythm and blues singer Gladys Knight.

A culturally relevant religious explanation of one's good fortune in the face of so many who had been left behind became necessary. The nature of black social mobility is so precarious ("one paycheck away from poverty") that prosperity is both a blessing and a problem in theodicy. Some of the newer churches or newly expanded congregations became places where an explicit doctrine of prosperity was preached. For African Americans, such a doctrine was a departure from more traditional liberationist and perseverance themes. Such preaching facilitated psychological relocation and integration in the world of affluence.

Mobility in the black community, in terms of both geographic and social relocation, has always produced a crisis in connectedness. For members of Frazier's "black bourgeoisie," staying connected to the African American mainstream sometimes meant membership in two churches, what black people jokingly called a church of "the masses" and a church of "the classes." The rhetoric of civil rights and black power fostered a moral position of solidarity across social class. Affluent black Americans felt more direct social pressures than their white counterparts to maintain a bond with their "brothers and sisters" who did not have their talents, skills, education, or simply good luck. Because of the recency of middle-class expansion, the vast majority of members in the black middle class have siblings and other kin who are not only not middle class but who also embody the problems of disadvantage, disorganization, and deprivation. The crises of these poor relations may punctuate and disrupt the lives of the affluent, whose response may be shaped by a deep sense of obligation to unusually strong kinship bonds (Hill 1997).

Since before the end of slavery, black communities have enforced the expectation that the educated should lead by teaching and sharing skills. Churches became the settings where connections across class boundaries were fostered. In the revived and expanded churches, this may be done through a wide variety of social programs or ministries. In some cases, black churches have developed private schools. After-school and career-day programs for young people provide mentors who serve as models for occupational attainment and success. Overall, the church became the site for personal, social, and cultural integration and reintegration as class configurations changed.

REORGANIZATION
AND REINVENTION
OF TRADITION

The growth and mobility of the black middle class in the context of a post-civil-rights- and post-black-power-era church sparked a rediscovery of black tradition. One heard a renewed and transformed gospel music shaped by musicians trained in both the folk traditions of the Sanctified Church and the classical music theory of the conservatories.[8] The black power movement's insistence on black pride prompted many African Americans to cease feeling ashamed of their old-time religious ways. The

cultural renewal that came with celebrations of Black History Month and the emphases on black theology in the academy also encouraged a reinvention of the black church as a social and cultural center. Such cultural renewal prompted Trinity United Church of Christ in Chicago to declare that its members were "unashamedly Black" as well as "unapologetically Christian." Murals and stained-glass windows with black and brown faces appeared in place of or alongside more traditional images of a white Jesus.

The reorganization and reinvention of tradition were manifested in the revitalization and revival of churches often labeled "seditty,"[9] "bourgie," or "dead." In their study of over 2000 churches, Lincoln and Mamiya (1990, 385-88) noted the rise of what they called "neo-pentecostalism" in black churches. Styles of worship that had come to be associated with the Holiness and Pentecostal denominations and congregations "over in the Sanctified Church" could be seen and heard in the traditionally middle-class churches of the 1970s and 1980s. Although Lincoln and Mamiya focused on the rise of this phenomenon in the African Methodist Episcopal (AME) Church, it was something that occurred in churches of various denominations and sizes that experienced growth and revitalization as their middle-class memberships grew. Congregations in historically black denominations changed, and black congregations in historically white denominations became more "black," defining their blackness in terms of their commitment to the traditional ecstatic style that emphasized what Du Bois ([1924] 1975, 320-40) called "the religion of the Spirit."

College men and women who grew up in the Sanctified Church attended black and white colleges all over the United States. Like most college students, the break from home sometimes meant a break from the home church. The revived and renewed black churches often provided a special call to come home, albeit to a new place, and also provided a space to be black without white hostility and pejorative assumptions. Bishop John Bryant of the AME Church, identified by Lincoln and Mamiya (1990, 385-86) as an exemplar for this neo-Pentecostal movement, recruited undergraduate, graduate, and professional school students to one of his early pastorates, a pastorate that became a magnet for a nationally connected corps of new clergy. In addition to AME students, his efforts attracted Pentecostal, Holiness, Baptist, and other students who brought with them a love of ecstatic worship and a wide variety of talents, including musical ones. These new members reclaimed traditions familiar to those raised in "shouting churches" and essentially revived a dead church. Members of the local community jokingly referred to the church as "AMEP" or "African Methodist Episcopal Pentecostal." Sometimes the term "Bapticostal" was also used.

Another source of transformation and revitalization of mainline black churches came from seminarians crossing denominational lines in order to complete internships in approved church settings. Since many black male seminarians arrived at seminary fully ordained, they were not bound to their denominational body in order to fulfill the internship requirements for graduation. Black female students seeking ordination were able to seek out less sexist and more welcoming settings in which to explore their vocations and become ordained. Students from the Sanctified churches often found that there were no approved settings in their own traditions but their preaching skills and other talents opened doors for them in the approved mainline Baptist, Methodist, and African Methodist traditions. These seminarians articulated an ecstatic tradition that older members longed for, securing opportunities for pastoring early in their careers. The permeability of black denominational boundaries that facilitated the adjustment to urbanization and migration for earlier generations served the same purposes for "the golden cohort" as they moved into new church settings with their upwardly mobile age peers— as both ministers and congregants. Combined with an emphasis on the Spirit, these relocations led to denunciations of denominationalism, reflecting a resolution to what Lincoln and Mamiya have called "the challenge of black ecumenism" (1990, 391).

PROFESSIONALIZATION OF THE LAITY

There is a saying in the black church that "your gifts will make room for you." A larger educated and talented black middle class meant a larger pool of talent available to serve their churches. The quality of services available and this educated laity's demands for professionalized, high-quality service, especially from their clergy, increased dramatically. These demands coincided with the challenge of black power advocates to assume "community control" and to build "black institutions." The poet Carolyn Rodgers describes this process better than any sociologist when she writes the following:

and when the revolution came
the militants said
. . . .
. . . we got to
build black institutions where our children
call each other sister and brother
and can grow beautiful, black and strong
    and grow in black grace. . . . (1976, 66)

Well-educated black professionals, whose sensibilities and spirituality had been shaped by the zeitgeist of black power, returned to church either with the realization that the church embodied the ideals they had valorized through their political activities or with the determination to make the church fulfill its potential in the black community and the world. Rodgers described these consequences in her poetry:

. . . the militants looked around
after a while and said hey, look at all
these fine buildings we got scattered
    throughout
the black communities some of em built wid
    schools and nurseries
who do they belong to?

and the church folks said, yeah.
we been waiting fo you militants
to realize that the church is an eternal rock
now why don't you militants jest come on in
we been waiting for you
we can show you how to build
    anything that needs building
and while we're on our knees, at that. (1976,
    66-67)

The dramatic increase in black participation in higher education that followed the civil rights movement provided a more highly credentialed clergy. Historically, a significant portion of African American clergy pursued their religious vocations as adults engaged in other occupations, often, as jokes and folklore implied, while plowing, planting, or picking in the hot sun. Now African American women and men were answering their calls to Christian ministry while "trespassing" in the corporations and institutions of hostile white privilege where the taint of affirmative action dismissed and trivialized their considerable educational and professional achievements (Parker 1997).

Revival and renewal within these churches challenged members to use their gifts and talents in the service of the church. Those gifts and talents came with a larger number of graduate and professional degrees. Church nurses' units no longer consisted of only nurses' aides and licensed practical nurses but also registered nurses with college degrees. Their tradiional roles as attendants to worshippers overcome by the Spirit continued, but they added blood pressure screenings, health fairs, and health education to their repertoire. Doctors and lawyers offered their services as mentors to young people. Accountants and other business professionals assumed roles on trustee boards and as church treasurers. Young professionals with children willingly taught Sunday school, and large churches staffed their independent schools from their congregations. Church social service and counseling centers also found highly talented and credentialed professionals among their members.

Pastorates in Protestant churches had always represented what sociologists call a "two-person career" (Papanek 1973). They comprised pastors and their wives. Pastors' wives were often missionaries, music directors, stewardesses, deaconesses, and other highly visible church workers who functioned as leaders of the female infrastructure that was the proverbial backbone of the church. They taught the Sunday school and represented their churches at the conferences and convocations that constituted the black church regionally and nationally. Usually the pastors' wives also had professional employment outside the church as nurses, teachers, or social workers. More recently, those second persons in the clergy career had graduate degrees and professional careers in law, medicine, and business; they were a resource for the church and a model for the members. An increasing number of these women discovered their own vocations for Christian ministry, carving out new careers as their husbands' co-pastors or in settings independent of their husbands.

The black church had always been characterized by its traditions of biblical literacy. Even during slavery and immediately afterward, those few who could read made it their business to teach others and to read the Bible for themselves and their communities (Cornelius 1991; Litwack 1979). The rise of the Sanctified Church beginning at the end of Reconstruction in the South was accompanied by elaborate biblically based defenses of

that church's ecstatic worship, "in the Spirit," which included shouting and the holy dance (Gilkes 1984; Mason 1969, 36-37). These same shouting saints pushed their children and grandchildren to secure as much education as circumstances would allow. The countercultural dimensions of black religion and the effectiveness of preaching depended heavily on an understanding and knowledge of the Bible that was widely and deeply shared. In the aftermath of the civil rights movement, black church members were as well educated as the majority of their clergy or sometimes better educated. The emphasis on Bible study and on teaching in the context of preaching was not simply an expression of Bible-believing fundamentalism (Ammerman 1987, 87); rather, this emphasis represented an extension of a highly elaborated biblically based worldview (Gilkes 1989, 1994). The "churches of what's happening now," the churches with reorganized and revived traditions and a newly expanded professionalized laity, emerged as congregations with an explicitly stated thirst for sophisticated biblical knowledge.

MILITANT MANHOOD AND WOMANIST INFRASTRUCTURE IN CONFLICT

One of the most poignant and lasting images of the civil rights movement is a long line of garbage workers in Memphis, Tennessee, wearing signs saying, "I AM A MAN." Between 1965 and 1968, black power advocates transformed the language of America, nearly erasing the term "Negro" and replacing it with the term "black." The problem of the Negro became the problem of "the Black Man" and the rhetoric of black revolution was heavily masculinized. The Nation of Islam had long claimed the term "black," accepting the label "Black Muslims" and declaring Islam to be the "religion of the Black Man" (Lincoln 1973). Indeed, the organization of African American religion became so gendered that Lincoln and Mamiya (1990, 391) point to "the phenomenon of more black males preferring Islam while more black females adhere to traditional black Christianity" as a serious challenge facing the black church. The challenge of Islam, with its male-centered analysis of the black condition, entered the mainstream of black struggle at precisely the same moment that U.S. government reports and social policy targeted the black family and the too-prominent role of educated black women in their families and society (Gilkes 1990).

Ironically, the proportion of black men entering the ministry dropped even as black church memberships stayed stable and began to grow (Glenn 1977). As Lincoln and Mamiya (1990, 401) point out, "there has been an increased interest in the ministry among black women, and the decade of the 1980s has shown the largest and most dramatic increases in black women seminarians in major divinity schools." Although, Lincoln and Mamiya continue, "black women are stepping forward to offer their participation in the leadership of the most historic and most independent institution in the black community" (401), they do so, in the words of AME pastor Vashti Murphy McKenzie (1996), "not without a struggle."

Women historically have been the most important agents of organizational integrity in the black churches and communities (Du Bois [1924] 1975; Gilkes 1993). Their role as educators shaped the leadership of women's departments and auxiliaries throughout the diverse denominations (Higginbotham 1993; Barnett 1978; Hall 1997). Church women took early responsibility for leadership, first during slavery as preaching women and through a specialized "women's network" (Andrews 1986; Collier-Thomas 1997; White 1985) and later in the local and national communities through an elaborate network of clubs, national organizations, community education, and sophisticated political lobbying (Giddings 1984; Dodson and Gilkes 1986). Secular and sacred organizations have been served by and have depended upon an extensive "womanist" infrastructure that remained "committed to survival and wholeness of entire people, male and female" (Walker 1983, xi). Much of the leadership of these church women took place in settings outside the church precisely because they were blocked from the pulpits within the church. Rather than defecting from their churches, women stayed and built additional organizations that accommodated their gifts for leadership.

The masculinization of the civil rights and black power struggle came precisely at the wrong moment in African American history. Targeted by both social science and popular culture as deviant and emasculating, black women were challenged to justify their femininity (Cade 1970) at the same time that they were making the greatest gains ever in education (Landry 1987, 207-9) and a large feminist movement helped to increase the occupational and professional attainment of all women. College-educated black women, unusually suited to take advantage of these new opportunities, began closing the income gaps between themselves and white women and accounted for the economic gains experienced by working-class and middle-class black families.

Emile Durkheim (1995, 167) once observed that "all the men . . ., on the one hand, and, on the other, all the women form what amounts to two distinct and even antagonistic societies." In spite of their competition, "these two sexual corporations" saw themselves as mystically joined together through a common totem. Durkheim's observation almost defines gender relations in the black church. Historical ritual rivalries through Men's and Women's Days, with women usually eclipsing men in their ability to raise funds, are merely hints of deeper antagonisms, what sociologist Orlando Patterson (1995) calls African Americans' "gendered burden of history" (93).

The revitalized churches of late-twentieth-century black America contain large groups of exceptionally well-educated women at the same time that the concern for the crisis surrounding black men has gripped all of black consciousness. Many black megachurches have large staffs that include women. One newsmagazine story featured the picture of the ministerial staff of an 18,000-member church, where the pastor's wife served as co-pastor and nearly half of the staff was female (Harris 1997). Although most black megachurches have a men's ministry or fellowship, where wives serve as co-pastors, there are vibrant women's ministries whose annual conferences and convocations attract a national network of women leaders and participants (Flake 1995). Probably the most masculinist of the black megachurches, St. Paul Community Baptist Church in Brooklyn, pastored by the Reverend Dr. Johnny Ray Youngblood, has a ministry to men, the Eldad and Medad ministry, that speaks explicitly to the reclamation and healing of black men. This church also employs a minister to women as part of its professional staff.

Black women take seriously their own issues and problems, and they also pay special attention to the problems of black males in their conferences, national organizations, writings, and everyday lives (Golden 1995; Vanzant 1996). Ironically, the concern that black women evince for the emergencies facing black men—criminalization, joblessness, poverty, hyperghettoization, and social isolation (Wilson 1987)—is not reciprocated by a similar concern for black women by the male leadership of black churches. The perception that black women have survived and succeeded obscures the realities of poverty, welfare, social isolation, joblessness, and single parenting that create unparalleled stress in black women's lives (Flake 1995; Browne 1997). The irony is that while some social scientists may argue that the better mental health of black women indicates that black men "are not only far behind their white male counterparts, but also significantly worse off than African American women" (Patterson 1995, 61), women's better mental health and educational achievement may indeed be a product of their overwhelming commitment to their churches. For black women, the black church not only continues to function as a therapeutic community (Gilkes 1980), but it also reinforces women's sense of importance by thriving because of women's gifts and support in ways that are observable to the entire community in spite of the institutional sexism.

CONCLUSION: MIGHTY CAUSES ARE STILL CALLING

African American Christianity, in spite of, and perhaps because of, dissenting and competing perspectives, remains a vital cultural force in the United States (Du Bois [1924] 1975; Hatch 1989; Holloway 1990; Wills 1997); its style and leadership have profound impacts on American religion and the larger society. As America turns to the twenty-first century, the black church is advancing through its third century. The new types of twenty-first-century churches and their practices are embedded in a historical self-consciousness that encourages the elaboration and revitalization of African American folk traditions. The highly visible and vibrant black megachurches have their antecedents in the institutional churches that responded to "the great migration," but they incorporate and exploit the growth of education, skills, and middle-class mobility at a larger scale that is new and unprecedented. Because churches are the sites for the working and reworking of tradition, they provide a unique opportunity for understanding human agency in the context of changing social forces and structures. The success of the civil rights movement, the new movements and consciousness it produced, the newly expanded middle class, and the changed institutional arrangements serve to make the black church a more complicated and conflicted context for human agency and creative spirituality.

These changes and their incorporation point to the continuing importance of the black church as a dynamic and adaptive site for the production of culture and social changes. Praying at Atlanta University between 1909 and 1910, W.E.B. Du Bois (1980) declared, "Mighty causes are calling us—the freeing of women, the training of children, the putting down of hate, murder, and poverty—all these and more" (21). Du Bois's prayer articulated the tasks facing the black church at the beginning of the twentieth century. The "mighty causes" that call us now are remarkably similar; they remain the "dual agenda" of economic equity and social justice (Hamilton and Hamilton 1997). Addressing these social needs must be done at the same time that the black church does the taken-for-granted work of religion: producing and defending the sacred over against the profane, creating and maintaining appropriate ritual, prescribing and interpreting human life events, and articulating myth, doctrine, and ethics—all of this in a context of crisis and change.

The black church currently is faced with a serious crisis of gender relations. More than any other African-descended group in the New World, the black communities and churches in the United States have been shaped by the status and agency of women. The current assertive prominence of women as clergy and educational leaders in the "churches of what's happening now" is rooted in the leadership of earlier generations of women. Some of the current women clergy have come to the revitalized Baptist and Methodist churches from the Sanctified Church, where earlier generations of Baptist and Methodist women found room for their gifts and voices in the face of discrimination and lost skirmishes over the pulpit. This special religious history and women's ability to maintain autonomous religious and secular organizations have existed alongside their auxiliary and backbone service to the church, service resulting in a womanist infrastructure securing the organizational integrity of churches and other black-led associations. This womanist infrastructure finds itself facing an emergent militant black manhood that is highly ambivalent about the importance of the church's women's history.

The black church "of what's happening now" claims connection with and responsibility to the new urban poor, those left behind by the recessions of the 1970s and 1980s and the deindustrialization of the American economy. The issues of poverty, youth education, and black families, along with the new ways in which institutional and interpersonal racism assaults the lives of black Americans, remain central to the "mighty causes . . . calling" the black church. According to Andrew Billingsley (1992), "the Black Church is at the leading edge of the African American community's push to influence the future of its families" (349). The successful response of clergy in the Greater Boston area to the problems of youth violence, the rapid organization of relief through South Central Los Angeles churches during the 1992 disaster, and the high visibility of black churches in southern California as the cutting edge for ethnic diversity within congregations point to the potential of the black church as it faces the twenty-first century.

In the most critical moments of African American life and history, the most defensible and most helpful institution was the black church. There is every reason to conclude that it will continue to be one of the most potent forces for positive social change in a setting of continued social inequality. The ability of black churches to adapt to changing circumstances and the increased self-confidence that the professionalized laity and mobilized women bring to the institution mean that black churches can be increasingly assertive in their engagements with public policy. Success in addressing social problems will require that black churches maintain their independence from white intrusion and control, and resist the white hegemony of anti-feminist backlash and conservative biblicism. The historical role of black churches in creating a globalized Pentecostalism currently provides a context for black people to negotiate relationships with newer black and brown communities in the United States from Africa, Latin America, and the Caribbean.

Overall, the black church appears to be persisting in its tradition of adapting to social change at the same time that it pursues the "dual agenda" of civil justice and socioeconomic equality, the "mighty causes" that continue to call. Both the revival and reclamation of tradition across denominational lines and the invention of new ways of worship demonstrate that the diversity and unity of the black church still create spaces where black Americans and their allies may "choose your seat and sit down." Adaptation guarantees that there is still "plenty good room."

Notes

1. Wording depends upon Lovell (1972, 280).

2. The phrase "the church of what's happening now" comes from a recently rapidly growing black church in New England that would not be considered a megachurch simply because its members number too few (under 3000), but it has experienced the rapid growth of the larger churches.

3. Several doctor of ministry programs, modeled on the Martin Luther King Fellows Program of Colgate Rochester Divinity School, provide very direct mentoring for these newer pastors by nationally respected pastors of the prominent older black churches. One such mentor was the late Reverend Dr. Samuel Dewitt Proctor, pastor emeritus of the Abyssinia Baptist Church in New York City, an early megachurch with a membership of over 10,000 during the 1950s.

4. "Sanctified Church" is an indigenous African American term that denotes historically and predominantly black Holiness and Pentecostal denominations and congregations. The term is used by both members of these churches and nonmembers.

5. And When the Revolution Came, from How I Got Ovah, by Carolyn M. Rodgers. Copyright © 1986, 1969, 1970, 1971, 1972, 1973, 1975 by Carolyn M. Rodgers. Used by permission of Doubleday, a division of Bantam Doubleday Dell Publishing Group, Inc.

6. The entire leadership of the Student Nonviolent Coordinating Committee was present at Malcolm X's funeral in 1965 (King 1987). That segment of civil rights leadership often questioned the tactics of nonviolence and their Christian and philosophical underpinnings.

7. Emphasis in the original.

8. Two national organizations, the National Convention of Gospel Choirs and Choruses and the Gospel Music Workshops of America, have very large youth departments. Since most young people in black churches join or socialize with the junior, youth, or young-adult choirs, the choirs function as age-graded features of the churches' social organization, fostering a solidarity within generational cohorts and at the same time providing essential socialization in the folk traditions of the church. These choirs are also the conduits into the churches of more recent trends in contemporary gospel music. It is in these settings where every kind of musical skill is often encouraged.

9. The spelling of "seditty" varies across African American dictionaries. Geneva Smitherman spells it "sadiddy" and defines it as "snooty, uppity-acting, [and otherwise putting on airs]" (Smitherman 1994, s.v. "sadiddy").

References

Ammerman, Nancy Tatom. 1987. *Bible Believers: Fundamentalists in the Modern World*. New Brunswick, NJ: Rutgers University Press.

Andrews, William L., ed. 1986. *Sisters of the Spirit: Three Black Women's Autobiographies of the Nineteenth Century*. Bloomington: Indiana University Press.

Banks, Adelle M. 1997. Megachurches at the Epicenter of African-American Middle Class. *Religion News Service*, 13 May.

Barnett, Evelyn Brooks. 1978. Nannie Helen Burroughs and the Education of Black Women. In *The Afro-American*

Woman: Struggles and Images, ed. Sharon Harley and Rosalyn Terborg-Penn. Port Washington, NY: Kennikat Press.

Billingsley, Andrew. 1992. Climbing Jacob's Ladder: The Enduring Legacy of African-American Families. New York: Simon & Schuster.

Browne, Irene. 1997. The Black-White Gap in Labor Force Participation Among Women Heading Households. American Sociological Review 62(2):236-52.

Cade, Toni. 1970. The Black Woman: An Anthology. New York: New American Library.

Caldwell, Deborah Kovach. 1997. More Than Worship: Black Megachurches Offer Broad Ministries to Burgeoning Middle Class. Dallas Morning News, 11 May.

Carmichael, Stokely and Charles V. Hamilton. 1967. Black Power: The Politics of Liberation in America. New York: Random House.

Collier-Thomas, Bettye. 1997. Daughters of Thunder: Black Women Preachers and Their Sermons, 1850-1979. San Francisco: Jossey-Bass.

Cornelius, Janet Duitsman. 1991. When I Can Read My Title Clear: Literacy, Slavery, and Religion in the Antebellum South. Columbia: University of South Carolina Press.

Deloria, Vine. 1970. We Talk, You Listen: New Tribes, New Turf. New York: Dell.

Dodson, Jualyne E. and Cheryl Townsend Gilkes. 1986. Something Within: Social Change and Collective Endurance in the Sacred World of Black Christian Women. In Women and Religion in America, ed. Rosemary Radford Ruether and Rosemary Skinner Keller. Vol. 3, The Twentieth Century. San Francisco: Harper & Row.

Du Bois, W.E.B. [1924] 1975. The Gift of Black Folk. Millwood, NY: Kraus-Thomson Organization.

———. 1980. Prayers for Dark People. Ed. Herbert Aptheker. Amherst: University of Massachusetts Press.

Durkheim, Emile. 1995. The Elementary Forms of Religious Life. Trans. Karen E. Fields. New York: Free Press.

Flake, Margaret Elaine McCollins. 1995. Preaching Healing to Hurting Women: A Womanist Hermeneutical Approach to Ministry to African American Women. D. Min. thesis, United Theological Seminary.

Frazier, E. Franklin. 1957. The Black Bourgeoisie: The Rise of a New Middle Class. Glencoe, IL: Free Press.

———. [1963] 1974. The Negro Church in America. New York: Schocken Books.

Giddings, Paula. 1984. When and Where I Enter: The Impact of Black Women on Race and Sex in America. New York: William Morrow.

Gilkes, Cheryl Townsend. 1980. The Black Church as a Therapeutic Community: Areas of Suggested Research into the Black Religious Experience. Journal of the Interdenominational Theological Center 8(1):29-44.

———. 1984. Race Relations, Afro-American Church History, and the Contradiction of the Sanctified Church. Bunting Institute, Radcliffe College. Manuscript.

———. 1987. "Some Mother's Son and Some Father's Daughter": Gender and Biblical Language in Afro-Christian Worship Tradition. In Shaping New Vision: Gender and Values in American Culture, ed. Clarissa Atkinson, Constance H. Buchanan, and Margaret Miles. Ann Arbor, MI: UMI Research Press.

———. 1989. Mother to the Motherless, Father to the Fatherless: Power, Gender, and Community in an Afrocentric Biblical Tradition. Semeia: An Experimental Journal for Biblical Criticism 47:57-85.

——. 1990. "Liberated to Work Like Dogs!": Labeling Black Women and Their Work. In *The Experience and Meaning of Work for Women*, ed. Nia Lane Chester and Hildy Grossman. Hillsdale, NJ: Lawrence Erlbaum Associates.

——. 1993. "If It Wasn't for the Women . . .": African American Women, Community Work, and Social Change. In *Women of Color in U.S. Society*, ed. Maxine Baca Zinn and Bonnie Thornton Dill. Philadelphia: Temple University Press.

——. 1994. Mis-Readings for Justice: The Bible and the African American Cultural Imagination. Society for the Scientific Study of Religion. Manuscript.

——. 1995. The Storm and the Light: Church, Family, Work, and Social Crisis in the African-American Experience. In *Work, Family, and Religion in Contemporary Society*, ed. Nancy Tatom Ammerman and Wade Clark Roof. New York: Routledge.

Glazer, Nathan. 1973. The Issue of Cultural Pluralism in America Today. In *White Ethnics: Their Life in Working-Class America*, ed. Joseph A. Ryan. Englewood Cliffs, NJ: Prentice Hall.

Glenn, Norval D. 1977. The Religion of Blacks in the United States: Some Recent Trends and Current Characteristics. *American Journal of Sociology* 83(2):443-51.

Golden, Marita. 1995. *Saving Our Sons: Raising Black Children in a Turbulent World*. New York: Doubleday.

Hall, Prathia LauraAnn. 1997. The Religious and Social Consciousness of African American Baptist Women. Ph.D. diss., Princeton Seminary.

Hamilton, Dona Cooper and Charles V. Hamilton. 1997. *The Dual Agenda: The African American Struggle for Civil and Economic Equality*. New York: Columbia University Press.

Harris, Hamil R. 1997. Growing in Glory: . . . the Generation of the Megachurch. *Emerge: Black America's News Magazine*, 6 Apr., 48-53.

Hatch, Nathan O. 1989. *The Democratization of American Christianity*. New Haven, CT: Yale University Press.

Haygood, Will. 1998. Keeping the Faith. *American Legacy: A Celebration of African American History and Culture* 3(4):23-30.

Higginbotham, Evelyn Brooks. 1993. *Righteous Discontent: The Women's Movement in the Black Baptist Church, 1880-1920*. Cambridge, MA: Harvard University Press.

Hill, Robert B. 1997. *The Strengths of African American Families: Twenty-Five Years Later*. Washington, DC: R and B.

Holloway, Joseph E., ed. 1990. *Africanisms in American Culture*. Bloomington: Indiana University Press.

Killian, Lewis M. 1975. *The Impossible Revolution Phase 2: Black Power and the American Dream*. New York: Random House.

King, Mary. 1987. *Freedom Song: A Personal Story of the 1960s Civil Rights Movement*. New York: William Morrow.

Knowles, Louis L. and Kenneth Prewitt. 1969. *Institutional Racism in America*. Englewood Cliffs, NJ: Prentice Hall.

Landry, Bart. 1987. *The New Black Middle Class*. Berkeley: University of California Press.

Lawrence, Beverly Hall. 1996. *Reviving the Spirit: A Generation of African Americans Goes Home to Church*. New York: Grove Press.

Lee, Spike with Ralph Wiley. 1992. *By Any Means Necessary: The Trials and Tribulations of the Making of Malcolm X*. New York: Hyperion.

Lincoln, C. Eric. 1973. *The Black Muslims in America*. Boston: Beacon Press.

——. 1974. *The Black Church Since Frazier*. New York: Schocken Books.

Lincoln, C. Eric and Lawrence H. Mamiya. 1990. *The Black Church in* the African American Experience. Durham, NC: Duke University Press.

Litwack, Leon F. 1979. Been in the Storm So Long: The Aftermath of Slavery. New York: Vintage Books.

Lovell, John, Jr. 1972. Black Song: The Forge and the Flame, the Story of How the Afro-American Spiritual Was Hammered Out. New York: Macmillan.

Malcolm X and Alex Haley. 1964. The Autobiography of Malcolm X. New York: Grove Press.

Mason, Charles Harrison. 1969. Is It Right for the Saints of God to Dance. In History and Formative Years of the Church of God in Christ, with Excerpts from the Life and Works of Its Founder, Bishop C. H. Mason, ed. German O. Ross, J. O. Patterson, and Julia Mason Atkins. Memphis, TN: Church of God in Christ Publishing House.

McAdam, Doug. 1984. Freedom Summer. New York: Oxford University Press.

McKenzie, Vashti M. 1996. Not Without a Struggle: Leadership Development for African American Women in Ministry. Cleveland, OH: United Church Press.

Morris, Aldon. 1984. The Origins of the Civil Rights Movement: Black Communities Organizing for Change. New York: Free Press.

Papanek, Hanna. 1973. Men, Women, and Work: Reflections on the Two-Person Career. In Changing Women in a Changing Society, ed. Joan Huber. Chicago: University of Chicago Press.

Parker, Gwendlyn M. 1997. Trespassing: My Sojourn in the Halls of White Privilege. Boston: Houghton Mifflin.

Patterson, Orlando. 1995. The Crisis of Gender Relations Among African Americans. In Race, Gender, and Power in America: The Legacy of the Hill-Thomas Hearings, ed. Anita Faye Hill and Emma Coleman Jordan. New York: Oxford University Press.

Raboteau, Albert J. 1978. Slave Religion: The Invisible Institution in the Ante-

bellum South. New York: Oxford University Press.

Rodgers, Carolyn. 1976. and when the revolution came. In how i got ovah: new and selected poems. Garden City, NY: Doubleday.

Roof, Wade Clark. 1993. A Generation of Seekers: The Spiritual Journeys of the Baby Boom Generation. San Francisco: HarperCollins.

Smitherman, Geneva. 1994. Black Talk: Words and Phrases from the Hood to the Amen Corner. New York: Houghton Mifflin.

Taylor, Clarence. 1994. The Black Churches of Brooklyn. New York: Columbia University Press.

Thumma, Scott Lee. 1996. The Kingdom, the Power, and the Glory: The Megachurch in Modern American Society. Ph.D. diss., Emory University.

Trescott, Jacqueline. 1997. Spiritual Reawakenings: Finding Refuge in Books and Retreats. Emerge: Black America's News Magazine, 6 Apr., 54-59.

Vanzant, Iyanla. 1996. The Spirit of a Man: A Vision of Transformation for Black Men and the Women Who Love Them. San Francisco: HarperCollins.

Walker, Alice. 1983. Womanist. In In Search of Our Mothers' Gardens: Womanist Prose. San Diego, CA: Harcourt Brace Jovanovich.

Washington, Joseph R., Jr. 1973. Black Sects and Cults. Garden City, NY: Doubleday, Anchor Books.

White, Deborah Gray. 1985. Aren't I a Woman: Female Slaves in the Plantation South. New York: W. W. Norton.

Wiggins, Daphne C. 1997. "Where Somebody Knows My Name": A Social and Cultural Analysis of Church Attendance Among African American Women. Ph.D. diss., Emory University.

Wilhelm, Sidney M. 1971. Who Needs the Negro? Garden City, NY: Doubleday.

Wills, David W. 1997. The Central Themes of American Religious History: Pluralism, Puritanism, and the Encounter of Black and White. In *African-American Religion: Interpretive Essays in History and Culture*, ed. Timothy E. Fulop and Albert J. Raboteau. New York: Routledge.

Wilmore, Gayraud S. and James H. Cone. 1980. *Black Theology: A Documentary History, 1966-1979*. Maryknoll, NY: Orbis Books.

Wilson, William Julius. 1973. *Power, Racism, and Privilege: Race Relations in Theoretical and Sociohistorical Perspectives*. New York: Macmillan.

———. 1978. *The Declining Significance of Race: Blacks and Changing American Institutions*. Chicago: University of Chicago Press.

———. 1987. *The Truly Disadvantaged: The Inner City, the Underclass, and Public Policy*. Chicago: University of Chicago Press.

Rome and American Catholics

By MICHELE DILLON

ABSTRACT: This article considers the paradox evidenced by American Catholics' simultaneous rejection of papal teaching and their enduring commitment to Rome. This issue is explored by focusing on one group of apparently anomalous Catholics, members of the Women's Ordination Conference (WOC), who contest Vatican opposition to women priests. It is suggested that the legitimation narratives that WOC members use to validate their identity as Catholics committed to a doctrinal stance denounced by Rome illuminate one of the mechanisms that enable Catholics in general to maintain their religious identity while disagreeing with papal teaching. Derived from their lived knowledge of Catholicism, WOC respondents claim the authority to interpret doctrine and use that interpretive autonomy to offer doctrinally grounded reasons in favor of change. Empowered by Catholicism to reflexively critique church doctrine and practices, WOC members both validate their particularized interpretations of Catholicism and maintain communion with the church's more universal community of memory.

Michele Dillon is an associate professor of sociology at Yale University. She is the author of Reason, Faith, and Power: Redrawing the Boundaries of Catholic Identity *(forthcoming) and* Debating Divorce: Moral Conflict in Ireland *(1993).*

TO talk about the significance of Rome for American Catholics is invariably to talk not about the Rome of Bernini's sculptures or Raphael's frescoes, although these and other great works of art are appreciated by Americans. Rather, in the encoded everyday language of Catholicism in America, Rome signifies the Vatican and, more specifically, the pope and the bureaucratic apparatus that provides the administrative and ideological infrastructure to the exercise of the papacy. This Rome is as complex and multifaceted as any Renaissance sculpture or fresco, and what it means defies easy classification.

American Catholics themselves also defy simple categorization. Catholics compose 26 percent of the American population and, given the denominational divisions within Protestantism, constitute the largest single denomination in America. They are comparatively more religiously involved than either American Protestants or European Catholics, with 51 percent of them reporting weekly church attendance (Gallup 1994). European Catholics, with the exception of those in Ireland, show significantly lower rates of church attendance.

While American Catholics demonstrate their commitment to the Catholic doctrinal and communal tradition by their church attendance and participation in the sacraments, their disposition toward Rome is more ambiguous. As several national studies document (for example, D'Antonio et al. 1996, 43-64; Gallup 1994, 142-48), substantial majorities of American Catholics reject official church teaching on contraception, di-

vorce, abortion, homosexuality, the death penalty, economic redistribution, women's ordination, and celibacy for priests. Dissatisfaction with church teaching is further underscored by the proliferation of pro-change groups in the church who are committed to various projects of institutional transformation.

On the other hand, it is evident that, while challenging the relevance of papal teaching to the practical context of their everyday lives, American Catholics also celebrate the pope. For instance, during John Paul's American visit in the fall of 1995, over 100,000 people attended his Central Park Mass, 85,000 people attended his Giants Stadium Mass, and 60,000 people attended his Mass in Camden Yards (Foley and Avato 1997, 32-33). These are impressive numbers. American Catholics are also financially generous to the pope. For example, in the 1992 annual Peter's Pence collection, held in dioceses around the world to raise papal revenue, American Catholics contributed the most, giving $23 million of the $67 million raised. That same year, 3000 Americans mailed unsolicited financial donations to the pope (Reese 1996, 224-25).

While it would be naive to read too much into any of these numbers, they do nonetheless lend support to the notion that, as headlined by the *Washington Post*, American Catholics "love the messenger, [but] not [the] message" (Goodstein and Morin 1995). In this article, I will argue that this paradox can be understood by appreciating how Catholics' doctrinal interpretive authority allows them to selectively reject Rome's teaching and simultaneously affirm their connection with the Catholic doctrinal tradition.

CATHOLIC ANOMALIES

The ambiguity of American Catholics' relation with Rome derives in part from the historical, cultural, and political context of American Catholicism. As an immigrant church in a hegemonically Protestant society, American Catholics historically relied on their connection with Rome to give them a sense of collective identity against their cultural marginality. At the same time, especially in the domains of politics and national security, Catholics have had to distance themselves from Rome against charges that their first loyalty was not to America and its nationalist, democratic, and constitutional values. All religions are suspect to the degree that they articulate ethics that transcend the strategic interests of any one nation (Bellah et al. 1991, 181-82). Catholicism is comparatively more suspect in this regard because of its claims to universal communal ethics and its cross-national presence as a global church.

To be a Roman Catholic, therefore, in America's pluralist denominational society, where the very notion of denominationalism challenges the idea of a universal church or universal theology (Ahlstrom 1972, 381), cannot be easy. To imply, however, that American Catholics' dissent from Rome, including the progressivism of American Catholic theologians, might evince a desire to create an autonomous American Catholicism largely independent of Rome (cf. Cuneo 1997,

29) would, in my judgment, be a mischaracterization of the situation. It is not only American Catholics who reject papal teaching; substantial numbers of Irish, German, and Polish Catholics also disagree with the church's stance on sexuality, abortion, women's ordination, and matters of church governance. It is also the case that progressive theologians are not distinctive to America but are prominent and visible in these other countries, too.

Rather than tending toward the schismatic creation of an autonomous national Catholicism, American Catholics' disposition toward Rome crystallizes some of the doctrinal interpretive tensions contained more broadly in the Catholic tradition. This is not to suggest that American Catholics' relation with Rome is not unique. In fact, what makes the American Catholic case so interesting is that, despite the strong voluntaristic strand in American religion and the pluralism of the options it offers Americans who wish to be religiously involved, so many Catholics who disagree with Rome choose to continue to be Catholic.

This anomaly becomes even more striking when attention is focused on those Catholics whose identity is objectively marginalized by the Vatican. Among other groups, substantial numbers of gay and lesbian Catholics and Catholics who are pro-choice on abortion choose to stay Catholic even though the Vatican has been quite clear in stating that these are contradictory identities. Similarly, advocates of women's ordination choose to remain within the church, notwithstanding Rome's declaration that the inadmissibility of women to the priesthood is a settled question to be held as part of the deposit of faith. In a time, therefore, when there is a cultural premium on the celebration of individual choices and unique personal identities, the practice of Catholicism by people whose identity aspirations and differences are delegitimated by the church presents as an interesting social phenomenon by which to mark the end of the so-called American century and its accent on individual autonomy.

The enduring commitment to the church by Catholics who reject the doctrinal stances of Rome on various issues also raises important theoretical questions. From the perspective of the religious economy model (for example, Finke and Stark 1992; Iannaccone 1992), which is the dominant thesis explaining the vitality of religion in America, the behavior of American Catholics is hard to explain. The religious economy model emphasizes a supply-side approach to understanding religious participation. It argues that, with so many different denominations (or firms) competing to maximize their appeal to distinct market segments, successful religions are the ones that respond to the demands of their current and potential consumers, thus neutralizing the tendency of dissatisfied customers to switch to alternative firms.

Catholics who, for instance, are divorced, gay or lesbian, pro-choice, or committed to women's ordination have many options in the American religious landscape that would appear on the surface, at least, to be more attuned to their particularized identities and lifestyle situations.

Why, then, in such a pluralist religious economy, do Catholics act as if the church were, in fact, a monopoly church? Why do they maintain their links with Rome rather than switch denomination or establish a new religious identity independent of Rome?

In this article, I will argue that American Catholics are able to stay Catholic and to celebrate the pope while selectively rejecting Rome's teaching because, in many instances, they exercise doctrinal interpretive authority. To illustrate how this mechanism works in practice, I will draw on survey data I have gathered from a representative random sample ($N = 214$) of members of the Women's Ordination Conference (WOC), a group of religiously involved American Catholics who oppose the church's ban on women priests and who therefore occupy an identity delegitimated by Rome.[1]

In sociology, there is a long theoretical tradition, starting with Karl Marx and developed more recently by some feminist theorists (for example, Smith 1990), that the standpoint of those who are objectively marginalized in social and institutional relations gives them a perspective that facilitates their recognition of the processes that reproduce power-based inequalities. While there is always the possibility that people who are on the margins can distort or misrecognize institutional processes, it is nonetheless the case that those who occupy objectively conflicting identities confront in a more immediate way the dilemmas that stem from the pluralism of their self-identity (cf. Calhoun 1995, 185-87).

WOC respondents' simultaneous commitment to Catholicism and to women's ordination makes them self-conscious carriers of a plural identity. For them, the contestation of doctrine is a proactive, collectively engaged institutional project. As Catholics who have mobilized to achieve institutional transformation, they may differ in important ways from their coreligionists who, while rejecting Rome's teaching, do not collectively and publicly challenge it. Nonetheless, the mechanisms that enable those who are objectively marginalized to subvert the primacy of Rome's interpretive authority will likely illuminate what many other Catholics do in an attenuated and implicit way.

Similar to American and European Catholics as a whole (Greeley and Hout 1996), not only do WOC respondents disagree with Rome's opposition to women priests, but a majority of them also disagree with the church's teaching on issues of sexuality and abortion. It is also the case that while WOC respondents are unequivocal in their rejection of Rome's authority to settle the question of women's ordination, they, too, similar to other Catholics, selectively value papal pronouncements on discrete sociomoral and ethical issues.

The vast majority of the WOC Catholics I surveyed (82 percent) said that they think of the church not in terms of the church hierarchy but as the people of God. But, while articulating a democratic communal model of church, they believe that it is important for the church to have a pope. In WOC respondents' views, the pope's role should be to provide moral leadership that is informed by responsiveness to diverse voices and openness to new ideas. Pointing to the value that WOC respondents invest in the pope as a global public symbol of Catholicism, several of them identified John Paul II's various visits to the United States and elsewhere and his statements on human rights and social justice as sources of pride in their Catholicism. WOC respondents therefore appreciate the voice of Rome while rejecting the validity of the Vatican's understanding of Catholic doctrine on women's ordination.

CONTESTING DOCTRINE

In articulating a contrary stance to Rome, WOC respondents' narratives demonstrate the intertwined connection between the source of their interpretive authority and the validity of the alternative interpretations they offer to legitimate women's ordination. Although it is artificial to separate these entangled processes in the arguments articulated by the respondents, I do so for analytical reasons. What WOC respondents do is, first, use their own lived experiences of Catholicism and their practical knowledge of Catholic doctrine to claim the authority to interpret doctrine. Second, in exercising their interpretive autonomy, it is doctrine rather than nondoctrinal, cultural reasons that WOC respondents use to justify their claims for a change in official church teaching and practice. In this regard, they use Catholic doctrine in a self-reflexive way, using doctrine to critique doctrine and thus making it a source of institutional transformation. Let me illustrate this process as evidenced in WOC respondents' narratives on women's ordination.

Several of the WOC respondents found the authority to contest church doctrine by linking their emancipatory project to what they underscored as the exemplary activism personified by Christ on behalf of equality and justice. As expressed by one of these WOC respondents, "Basically I experience Jesus in the New Testament as being with the causes—standing with all who are on the journey for truth. I believe in equality and justice and I hope for the dawning of the day when both women and married priests experience fullness within Catholicism." Another of these respondents wrote:

To me, being a Catholic means to participate in the Church established by Jesus. Jesus always seemed to espouse the dignity of humankind. To realize that dignity, all people need to be afforded the opportunity to follow their calling, to utilize their individual gifts and talents given to them by their creator. To deny that dignity to half of humankind does not fulfill the example set by Jesus to be Catholic.

Respondents also drew on the theology of liberation and equality embodied in the redemptive narrative of Christ's life to highlight how church practices deviate from the values that are foundational to the church's identity. One of these respondents stated, "I experience the gospel as a call to the liberation of all people. The theology and anthropology which underlie the non-ordination of women is faulty and not pointing to our identity as the sons and daughters of God,

as brothers and sisters of Jesus." Another stated, "If Christianity teaches that all are redeemed in Jesus Christ, then it is a contradiction to exclude women in the full ministry. It is a denial of redemption. Either Jesus is savior of all or what we believe is false."

Other respondents emphasized their investment in and attachment to Catholicism and its ethics of justice. These respondents in large part saw their activism as compelled by their moral obligation to redeem the church from the errors it commits in straying from the higher values inspired by the Jesus narrative. One middle-aged man summarized the views of many of his WOC peers stating, "Equality, fairness, evenhandedness—all are values that the Catholic Church has and does espouse. These are good mature values—human, humane, and person-enhancing. Preaching equality and practicing it in actuality *must* go together, or else it's just words" (emphasis in original). Another WOC respondent stated:

Catholicism is important to me because it has provided the framework in which I could exercise my belief in God and in the life and work of Jesus. I need the church to show the way to live justly. I wish it would begin with following more closely the message of Jesus.

As construed by WOC respondents, therefore, the rejection of Rome's understanding of women's ordination is compelled by their alternative understanding of Catholicism. Their experience of Catholicism is one that requires Catholics to commit themselves to working toward making the church a more just community. Respondents' doctrinal knowledge demands the dismantling rather than the maintenance of exclusionary boundaries. Thus they cannot be Catholic without being involved in contesting the inegalitarian institutional practices legitimated by the Vatican.

WOC respondents' advocacy for an inclusive church is driven by what they perceive as the contradictions between the higher meanings in Catholicism and the church's contemporary practices. On the one hand, respondents have a firsthand everyday knowledge of the church's institutional routines that exclude and discriminate, such as the celebration of the Mass by male priests only. At the same time, they derive a contrasting knowledge from the scriptural narratives of inclusivity and justice celebrated in church liturgy and selectively actualized in the church's social justice activities. In short, it is the perceived inconsistencies that respondents witness in the church between theory and practice that oblige them to challenge the doctrine that is offered as the rationale for maintaining inequality.

In contesting Rome's view of Catholicism, the vast majority of WOC respondents use reasons from the Catholic doctrinal tradition to validate their claims for an inclusive church.[2] Underscoring the hold of the Christocentric paradigm for Catholics who disagree with Rome, the relevance of the redemptive meanings of Christ's life practices was a theme evident in the narratives of almost two-thirds (64 percent) of the WOC respondents. Whereas official church arguments defend the exclusivity of a male-only priesthood by pointing to the single act of Jesus in choosing only men as apostles, WOC respondents focus on the social dimensions and relational meanings of Christ's life as a whole. For them, narrative accounts of Christ's life lead to an alternative theological interpretation that illuminates an inclusive rather than a discriminatory Jesus whose exemplary practices model equality. One WOC respondent argued, "If we take to heart Jesus' words about equality, we must be willing to look at institutions and our individual lives and be willing to *live* accordingly" (emphasis in original). Another argued, "Jesus, I don't think, would have wanted to be exclusive. He wanted the Good News given to everyone and by everyone who believed it."

Respondents' narratives also stressed the universalism rather than the maleness of Christ's humanity, and they pointed to the theological implications that flow from the church's exclusion of women from symbolizing Christ as priests. One woman who is a pastoral counselor stated, "If the most important thing about Christ is maleness, are women saved? The Vatican's Christology is warmed-over misogyny-androcentric daydreaming."

Other WOC respondents argued: "Christ died for all mankind. . . . To be fully committed to Christian redemption we must include everyone, male and female. In a practical sense, it would humanize the Church." "The universality of Catholicism must reflect the universality of gifts, given by God to be used for the good of all. The ordination of women will demonstrate the universality of God's call, without distinction or human-ordered restrictions. The more complete image of Jesus, the Incarnate One, will be made manifest when women assume the overt and visible role of priest/shepherd."

As seen by these respondents, a church that claims to be universal and inclusive of all humanity undermines its foundational ethics by institutionalizing what respondents construe to be arbitrary, gender-based boundaries of exclusion. Several other WOC respondents were explicit in framing women's ordination as an issue of institutional credibility for a church grounded in Christ-embodied ethics of justice and equality. They stated:

I believe women reflect something of God as do men. The Church should be in the forefront of creating an equal place for women. I think oppression of any type (bigotry against women, non-Caucasians, the poor, gays and lesbians) has to be eradicated. That's part of the Gospel message and has to be the mission of the Church.

I feel that the Catholic Church should be a leader in justice issues. I feel that the ordination of women is a justice issue and therefore the Catholic Church should act justly and ordain women. I think women are discriminated against in this issue despite the fact that the Church says that this is not discrimination. I can't believe that Jesus would discriminate in this way. If Jesus did select only men for ordination, it was because it was the norm for the times; it isn't now.

We have to accord human rights and equality to all if we are truly Christian. Patriarchy, domination of any one, discrimination of all kinds are all irreconcil-

able with Christianity. If Catholics are truly followers of Christ, we can't do it.

I don't believe we can say one thing or have a vision of reaching out to embrace all, yet put up boundaries or limitations on people and how they minister within the community. I believe that goes against the innate nature of the church and the reality of the Gospel.

The WOC respondents' arguments that have been presented provide a powerful set of counterclaims against the Vatican's position on the ordination of women. It is strikingly evident that, although these Catholics disagree with Rome, they are strongly connected with the Catholic doctrinal and institutional tradition as a whole. This tradition, moreover, as the respondents' remarks underscored, is multidimensional and rich in the plurality of meanings that it contains. Maintaining a legitimate Catholic identity therefore, as many Catholic theologians would validate, transcends the disposition taken toward papal teaching on any specific doctrinal question.

WOC respondents' challenge to Rome's interpretive authority reflects appreciation of the fact that doctrinal interpretations, like other forms of knowledge, are socially grounded. In other words, they are contingent on the specific historical, cultural, and institutional contexts in which they are expressed. Rather than seeing the papacy as a divinely prescribed institution, these Catholics regard the church hierarchy's authority—rightfully, as many historical and theological accounts would suggest—as one but not the sole paradigm in the church's doctrinal tradition (cf. Sanks 1974;

Tierney 1971). WOC respondents thus see doctrinal interpretive authority as diffuse and fluid rather than concentrated in Rome, notwithstanding Rome's systematic efforts, particularly since the Middle Ages, to consolidate the supremacy of its interpretive power.

COMMUNAL AUTHORITY IN THE CATHOLIC TRADITION

The more democratic and reasoned understanding of doctrinal authority demonstrated by WOC respondents is faithful to important and distinctive strands in the Catholic tradition. Historically reconstructed biblical accounts of the early church present a model of organizational equality in which authority and leadership alternate between members to illuminate a church constituted as a "discipleship of equals" (Schussler Fiorenza [1983] 1994). This contemporary view accords with standard Catholic theological accounts stressing the communal bases of Catholic identity. Writing before Vatican II, for example, the late French theologian Yves Congar argued that "it is the visible, organized body of Christians that is the Body of Christ. There is nothing in [Scripture] to suggest a dissociation between a community of faithful . . . and the system . . . of dogmas, sacraments, powers and ministries exercised under apostolical authority" ([1957] 1965, 33).

WOC respondents' critical disposition toward Vatican pronouncements on women's ordination is also legitimated by the distinctive emphasis in the Catholic theological tradition on the coupling of faith and reason (McCool 1977) and the expectation that church teaching should make sense. Assent to the church hierarchy's teaching therefore is not based on blind faith but is seen as a cognitive act of reasoned judgment (Sullivan 1983). Since the church's establishment of theology as an intellectual discipline in the medieval university (Boyle 1985), theologians' professional role in developing an understanding of faith formalized the idea that doctrinal knowledge is accessible to those outside the church hierarchy.

More recently, at the Second Vatican Council (1962-65), the church hierarchy itself articulated a vision of a reflexive, deliberative, and communal church in which disagreements are resolved by reasoned dialogue and where, as explicated by the council, "no one is allowed . . . to appropriate the Church's authority for his opinion" (Abbott 1966, 244). Vatican II, moreover, exhorted the laity to take responsibility for collectively transforming unjust institutional practices, including contradictions within the church, and it provided the symbolic resources with which to legitimate the construction of a more pluralist and inclusive church.

MAINTAINING CATHOLIC IDENTITY

Against the backdrop provided by these strands in the church's tradition, and the lived reality of their own experiences of Catholicism, WOC respondents and other Catholics who disagree with Rome are empowered to make doctrine a site of what Steven Seidman (1994) would call "contested knowledge." Yet, as demonstrated by WOC respondents, the autonomous doctrinal meanings produced are reflexively grounded in Catholicism. WOC respondents' claims for women's equality are not driven by American cultural discourses of individual or group rights (Bellah et al. 1985; Glendon 1991) or by a postmodern ethos that anything goes. It is significant, rather, that it is Catholicism that gives Catholics both the authority to participate in the interpretation of doctrine and the tools to use that interpretive autonomy in ways that serve their emancipatory agendas. Thus, in demonstrating their autonomy from Rome, WOC respondents simultaneously evidence engaged participation in and commitment to the Catholic tradition.

Rather than construing their disagreement with the Vatican as a reason to leave the church, respondents' particularized interpretive engagement with the church's doctrine allows them to keep the Catholic "community of memory" alive (cf. Bellah et al. 1985, 153). They exploit the reflexivity and multiple doctrinal meanings in the church's tradition to argue for the actualization of equality in contemporary church practices. Rather than leave the church, "contradictory" Catholics are consequently able to remain Catholic without abandoning their quest for inclusivity. For those who contest Rome's interpretive authority, Catholicism thus continues to act as an obligatory moral, doctrinal, and communal tradition instead of being relegated to a past that is no longer relevant (cf. Bellah et al. 1985).

In this reading it is somewhat reductionist to suggest that the disjuncture between Catholics' understanding of doctrine and that offered by Rome is, as Mark Chaves (1994) argues, evidence that "there is little effective religious authority" among American Catholics (769). Moving beyond a narrow understanding of authority as the prerogative of those who hold formal office, it is evident that Catholicism continues to have meaningful authority for its adherents. As highlighted by the data in this article, even in a hierarchical religious organization the production of doctrine is not confined to the church hierarchy alone but is, in part, a communally diffused and reflexively engaged interpretive process. Catholics can disagree with Rome and stay Catholic because they know that the Catholic tradition, while encompassing Rome, is larger than the papacy. Equally important, it provides them with the symbolic resources with which to validate their multiple identities and construct what they construe to be a more Christ-like inclusive and participative church.

Therefore, although living in a pluralist religious economy, Catholics' interpretive differences with Rome do not necessarily lead to religious switching or the formation of new particularized subcultures or sects that are severed from a historically continuous tradition. The religious economy model (Finke and Stark 1992), with its emphasis on religious segmentation, may thus be more Protestant than Catholic in its explanatory assumptions. Although the supply-side religious economy model affirms the autonomy of believers to switch to different producers, it gives little agency to the auton-

omy of consumers to reflexively produce doctrine themselves from within
a doctrinally differentiated tradition
in ways that fit with their own life
contexts.[3]

In sum, although in theory people
are free to switch identities, it is evident that in practice the voluntarism
of religious identity is constrained by
sentimental and reasoned attachments to specific doctrinal and communal traditions. This constrained
voluntarism may be particularly pronounced for Catholics since their collective memory reminds them that
their genealogy is entwined with a
historically continuous church rather
than a history of sectlike divisions.
There is a disposition therefore to stay,
rather than to leave, and to work
toward transformation from within
the tradition.

Catholics' doctrinal reflexivity
thus maintains the universality of
the Catholic community and the link
with Rome. The practical understanding of universality held, however, is not one in which differences
are denied. As highlighted by the le-
gitimating arguments used by WOC
respondents to contest papal teaching, the vision of universality presented is one in which pluralism is
constitutive of, rather than negated
as a threat to, communal solidarity.
Accordingly, for these Catholics the
church's unity is not threatened by
the interpretive differences between
Catholics and Rome in mapping the
boundaries and meanings of Catholic
identity. Overall, as underscored by
their own holding of multiple identities, committed Catholics who disagree with Rome demonstrate that
participation in a universal commu-

nity does not demand adherence to a
dominant, uniform identity.

On the verge of a new century, the
demands of living in a global moral
community require us to bridge the
excesses of both individualism and
community (Etzioni 1997). American
Catholics' relation with Rome points
to the possibility that particularized
differences and more universal communal attachments can be held together. Rather than thinking that the
regeneration of moral community requires a qualified diversity (cf. Etzioni 1997, 197), it may be in fact that,
as suggested by Catholics' reflexive
engagement with their doctrinal tradition, for a community to be vibrant
and vital, it must not disqualify diversity but recognize and integrate
differences.

Notes

1. The WOC data are based on narratives
written by respondents in response to open-
ended questions in a mailed, self-administered
questionnaire probing the reasons for their
commitment to women's ordination. The larger
study from which these data are drawn includes ethnographic research with gay and
lesbian Catholics active in the Boston chapter
of Dignity/U.S.A., a national organization of
gay and lesbian Catholics; a survey of regional
volunteer activists for Catholics for a Free
Choice; and in-depth interviews with professional Catholic theologians. The points discussed in this article are documented in
greater substantive and statistical detail in
Dillon (forthcoming).

2. Respondents' reflexive reasoning engaged both Catholic theological principles and
the church's social teaching on women. In addition, themes of power were also evident.
These overlapping themes are elaborated in
Dillon (forthcoming, chap. 5).

3. Although Iannaccone (1995) recognizes
religion as a collective production process, he
does not explore the interpretive dynamics of

religion as a cultural commodity whose meanings are contextually dependent.

References

Abbott, Walter, ed. 1966. *The Documents of Vatican II*. New York: Herder & Herder.

Ahlstrom, Sydney. 1972. *A Religious History of the American People*. New Haven, CT: Yale University Press.

Bellah, Robert N., Richard Madsen, William M. Sullivan, Ann Swidler, and Steven M. Tipton. 1985. *Habits of the Heart: Individualism and Commitment in American Life*. Berkeley: University of California Press.

———. 1991. *The Good Society*. New York: Knopf.

Boyle, John. 1985. The Academy and Church Teaching Authority: Current Issues. *CTSA Proceedings* 40:172-80.

Calhoun, Craig. 1995. *Critical Social Theory: Culture, History and the Challenge of Difference*. Cambridge, MA: Basil Blackwell.

Chaves, Mark. 1994. Secularization as Declining Religious Authority. *Social Forces* 72:749-74.

Congar, Yves. [1957] 1965. *Lay People in the Church*. Westminster, MD: Newman Press.

Cuneo, Michael. 1997. *The Smoke of Satan: Conservative and Traditionalist Dissent in Contemporary American Catholicism*. New York: Oxford University Press.

D'Antonio, William, James Davidson, Dean Hoge, and Ruth Wallace. 1996. *Laity, American and Catholic: Transforming the Church*. Kansas City, MO: Sheed & Ward.

Dillon, Michele. Forthcoming. *Reason, Faith, and Power: Redrawing the Boundaries of Catholic Identity*. New York: Cambridge University Press.

Etzioni, Amitai. 1997. *The New Golden Rule*. New York: Basic Books.

Finke, Roger and Rodney Stark. 1992. *The Churching of America: Winners and Losers in Our Religious Economy*. New Brunswick, NJ: Rutgers University Press.

Foley, Felician and Rose Avato. 1997. *1997 Catholic Almanac*. Huntington, IN: Our Sunday Visitor.

Gallup, George. 1994. *The Gallup Poll 1993*. Wilmington, DE: Scholarly Resources.

Glendon, Mary Ann. 1991. *Rights Talk*. New York: Free Press.

Goodstein, Laura and Richard Morin. 1995. Love the Messenger, Not His Message. *Washington Post*, 9-15 Oct., 37.

Greeley, Andrew and Michael Hout. 1996. Survey Finds Catholics Want More Say. *National Catholic Reporter*, 14 June.

Iannaccone, Lawrence. 1992. Sacrifice and Stigma: Reducing Free-Riding in Cults, Communes, and Other Collectives. *Journal of Political Economy* 100:271-91.

———. 1995. Risk, Rationality, and Religious Portfolios. *Economic Inquiry* 33:285-95.

McCool, Gerald. 1977. *Catholic Theology in the Nineteenth Century: The Quest for a Unitary Method*. New York: Seabury Press.

Reese, Thomas. 1996. *Inside the Vatican: The Politics and Organization of the Catholic Church*. Cambridge, MA: Harvard University Press.

Sanks, T. Howland. 1974. *Authority in the Church: A Study in Changing Paradigms*. Missoula, MT: Scholars' Press.

Schussler Fiorenza, Elisabeth. [1983] 1994. *In Memory of Her: A Feminist Theological Reconstruction of Christian Origins*. New York: Crossroad.

Seidman, Steven. 1994. *Contested Knowledge: Social Theory in the Postmodern Era*. Cambridge, MA: Basil Blackwell.

Smith, Dorothy. 1990. *The Conceptual Practices of Power*. Boston: Northeastern University Press.

Sullivan, Francis A. 1983. *Magisterium: Teaching Authority in the Catholic Church*. New York: Paulist Press.

Tierney, Brian. 1971. Origins of Papal Infallibility. *Journal of Ecumenical Studies* 8:841-64.

ANNALS, *AAPSS*, **558**, July 1998

The Reweaving of Catholic
Spiritual and Institutional Life

By MARY JOHNSON

ABSTRACT: As we prepare to cross the bridge to the twenty-first century and to a new millennium, there is much analysis of the state of Catholicism in the United States. While the number of Catholics continues to increase, much of the analysis continues to focus on institutional decline, particularly of the priesthood and religious life and institutions dependent on them, such as schools and parishes. However, another phenomenon, more difficult to measure but equally alive in Catholic culture, is that of a spiritual resurgence. While there is clear evidence that there is a disjuncture between religion and spirituality in the thinking and behavior of some in the society, this article speculates about Catholicism in the United States in the twenty-first century as a spiritual-institutional church that weaves spiritualities through institutions in new, and old, ways. New tools will be needed for the analysis of the construction of spiritual cultures within and outside of Catholic institutions and the responses of generational cohorts to elements of those cultures.

Mary Johnson S.N.D. de N. is an associate professor of sociology at Emmanuel College in Boston. She is currently conducting a national study of post–Vatican II recruits to U.S. Catholic religious orders of women and is also part of a research team engaged in a national study of Catholics in their twenties and thirties.

IF one were to describe the mood of Catholics in the United States at the end of the twentieth century, it could be said that the mood is, at the same time, exultant, uncertain, and despairing. The complexity of the mood is due to the complexity of Catholicism, the largest social organization in the world. On one level, Catholicism is fundamentally an institution of institutions. Within each institution are structures and cultures animated by various teachings and spiritualities. Individual Catholics live some or most of their lives within some of these institutions. The state of the institution in question often determines the mood of the respondent.

One could say that Catholics today are exulting in the sense of mission—the response to the needs of the world demanded by the Second Vatican Council—manifested in tens of thousands of Catholic institutions, great and small, rich and poor, new and old, urban, rural, suburban, and inner-city. But, at the same time, Catholics are uncertain about the future of some institutions that have dotted the Catholic landscape, served as instruments of mission, or constituted visible and identifiable dimensions of the Catholic identity for generations. Catholics are despairing about the lack of access to certain institutions by certain segments of the population, and the disparity of wealth and resources between other institutions.

Much discussion in recent years has focused on declining numbers of institutions and declining numbers in institutions. But to define the situation in institutional terms alone, or in terms of numerical decline alone,

ignores what is probably the most compelling phenomenon alive in U.S. Catholicism today as the church prepares to cross the bridge to the new century. It is also the phenomenon with the capacity to effect the most far-reaching consequences for Catholic institutions, those of mission and of community.

In speculating on the church of the new century, I see that phenomenon as the shift from an institutional church of the twentieth century to a spiritual-institutional church of the twenty-first century. While so many Catholics and others in the society speak of being spiritual on the individual level, they sometimes ignore or even seem to want to jettison the thousands of institutions that constitute the Catholic character. Such attitudes minimize the significant contribution that these institutions have made to the church and the wider society of the United States during this century. The task of the twenty-first century will be to minimize neither the spiritual nor the institutional but to meld them in new ways, which will be marked by a deeper and broader prayerfulness and simplicity, a more pronounced communal impulse, and a greater and more consistent commitment to issues raised by the social teachings of the church.

The sociological distinction between institution and spirit was found most recently by Wade Clark Roof in his 1993 national study of baby boomers (those born between 1946 and 1964). In sum, spirit had to do with the varied and multiple quests for meaning that many in that generation embarked upon and with which they continue to be engaged. Institution had to do with those structures—congregations and parishes among them but certainly not limited to them—in which some in that generation are involved and from which some in that generation draw meaning.

But in the Catholic case, will the dichotomies between spirit and institution, and between spirituality and religion, actually be false dichotomies in the new century? Is the question for the twenty-first century really, What of spirituality and religion, spirit and institution?

Obviously, neither the distinctions between the two nor the melding of the two is neat and clean. That is the challenge, because somewhere therein lies the seedbed for whole new social arrangements in a church comprising thousands of institutions. The spiritual transformation of those institutions will be the story of the new century. For now, we turn to an appraisal of these institutions at the end of the current century.

DEMOGRAPHICS

While there are conflicting reports of the exact number of Catholics in the total U.S. population, the proportion is about 25 percent (Greeley 1991). Church officials now use the figure of 61 million as the number of U.S. Catholics (*Official Catholic Directory* 1997, 2069).

These 61 million move within and outside of an array of Catholic institutions at various times in their lives. A look at the array is provided by the *Official Catholic Directory*.

Institutions

Catholics today may be members of or attend one or more of the 19,677 parishes or 3051 missions. They may be employed by or served by one of the 590 Catholic hospitals, which served over 61 million patients last year.

In regard to education, they may attend, work in, or send their children to one of the 6822 parish or diocesan elementary schools or 343 private elementary schools, which together serve over 2 million children. On the secondary level, they may be involved with one of the 794 parish or diocesan high schools or 563 private high schools, which together serve well over a half million students. They may be involved in Catholic higher education, which is composed of 241 colleges and universities, which serve 690,826 students. These figures do not include the over 6000 pastoral centers, health care centers, specialized homes, residential care settings for children, day care and extended day care centers, and special centers for social services, which serve over 24 million people in total.

This quick sketch does not include other institutions that have also been considered core pieces of Catholic identity, namely, the priesthood and religious life. The numerical decline of priests and sisters has been well documented (Schoenherr 1993; Wittberg 1994; Ebaugh 1993; Nygren and Ukeritis 1993). The causes, consequences, and significance of the decline continue to provoke discussion, and attempts to recruit are now under way in some areas.

THE CATHOLIC RECLAMATION

I predict that the twenty-first century will be marked by a Catholic reclamation of spiritualities, prayer forms, traditions, practices, and artifacts from previous centuries, which will be woven into existing institutions and which will become foundational for new institutions. These spiritual forms will be informed by the new and old ethnic traditions that will represent people of color, who will greatly compose the U.S. Catholic church of the next century. While some would argue that some of these forms have been reproduced and reintroduced of late by a reactionary minority for the purposes of undermining the initiatives of the Second Vatican Council, in the next century they will be coupled with social movements, communal enterprises, and mission responses for the purpose of unleashing spiritual energies to undergird, ground, and animate initiatives for mission and community. This reclamation will involve a movement from private to public, and from individual to communal, spiritualities.

COMPONENTS OF SPIRITUAL CAPITAL

While Catholics of the next century will be involved in ecumenical and interfaith efforts of all types and will be influenced by theologies inspired by the new science, boundaries will be maintained that will ensure the creation of distinctly Catholic elements of the spiritual capital that will be used in the transformation of the cultures of institutions. Examples of these elements follow.

Saints

While a focus on angels has marked the waning years of the twentieth century, saints of all ages, backgrounds, and lifestyles will be lifted up as sources of wisdom and as guides for thinking and behavior in the twenty-first. New saints will be proclaimed. Dorothy Day, the founder of the Catholic Worker Movement, and Pope John XXIII will join their company. Old saints will be turned to again and linked to significant social movements. Saint Francis of Assisi, for example, will be seen as an animator of the environmental movement.

Mystics will be embraced again for their countercultural message to the society. A recent example of this is the proclamation of Saint Thérèse of Lisieux as a doctor of the church, only the third woman in history to be so designated. She joins an elite class of scholarly saints, Catherine of Siena and Teresa of Avila among them. Thérèse, who died at the age of 24, is the youngest person to be named a doctor of the church. Her autobiography, *Story of a Soul* (Clarke 1996), has been translated into more than 40 languages, with millions of copies sold. Her embrace of suffering has made her, "in an age of anxiety such as ours, . . . a saint for those of us plagued by fear of suffering or death" (Kreilkamp 1997, 2).

Symbols

Symbols are constitutive elements of Catholicism. The new century will see the reintroduction of old symbols and the introduction of new ones. The old symbols will be imbued with new meanings in response to the fundamental need to find paths to contemplation in new, and sometimes inhospitable, social contexts. The new symbols will arise from the need to make concrete and visible the spiritual forms of the multitude of new ethnic Catholics. Attention will be paid to the question of which symbols will transcend all divisions and speak to all people. The example of the reclamation of two old symbols, the labyrinth and the rosary, follows.

The use of the labyrinth and its introduction in several Catholic institutions is being discussed at the present time. The person responsible for bringing the labyrinth to the attention of religious and secular institutions of all types is Dr. Lauren Artress, canon for special ministries at Grace Cathedral, the Episcopal cathedral of San Francisco. Within the last couple of years she has instituted the Labyrinth Project, a project that originated in her own experience of discovering the labyrinth, "an ancient mystical tool . . . which had dropped out of human awareness more than 350 years ago" (Artress 1995, xi).

The labyrinth in Grace Cathedral, presented in 1991, is modeled on the Chartres labyrinth. Located in the thirteenth-century Gothic Chartres Cathedral in the Plain of Beauce in France, the Chartres labyrinth was laid in the floor of the cathedral around 1220. It is approximately 42 feet in diameter. The labyrinth is an archetype found in all religious traditions; the Chartres labyrinth is the only one remaining from the thirteenth century.

Within the Christian mystical tradition, walking the labyrinth reintroduces the walking meditation. Walking the path of the labyrinth involves three stages: purgation, illumination, and union. Literature in Grace Cathedral describes the stages as follows: "Purgation is a releasing, a letting go of the details of your life. This is an act of shedding thoughts and emotions. It quiets and empties the mind." Illumination occurs "when you reach the center. Stay there as long as you like. It is a place of meditation and prayer. Receive what is there for you to receive." Union is "joining God, your Higher Power or the healing forces at work in the world. Each time you walk the labyrinth you become more empowered to find and do the work you feel your soul reaching for."

The goal of the Labyrinth Project is to build labyrinths in schools, hospitals, jails, and other institutions across the country. The sites of the various labyrinths are being linked in a national database. The project is anticipating gathering people at sites of labyrinths across the world on New Year's Eve in 1999.

The rosary is a second symbol being reclaimed. The rosary comprises prayer beads that are accompanied by various prayers, the Hail Mary being the most frequent. The purpose of praying the rosary is to meditate on events in the life of Christ. The use of prayer beads in many traditions is being examined currently. People of widely varying religious heritage have used beads or counters to guide and sustain their prayer for centuries. Madeleine L'Engle wrote, "To use beads with a prayer,

Indian or Moslem or Christian, is to enflesh the words, make thought tangible" (quoted in Hastings 1993, 5).

The rosary is being used and reclaimed by many people for various reasons. It is being reclaimed at the time of a major resurgence of interest in Mary, the mother of Jesus, a resurgence that will continue into and increase in the next century.

The following is an example of the rosary as a symbol intersecting with a social movement, namely, the recent feminist interpretation of the mysteries, the events in Christ's life. In the traditional recitation of the rosary, 15 events are divided into three mysteries: joyful, glorious, and sorrowful. The following is the traditional naming and interpretation of the sorrowful mysteries.

— the Agony in the Garden: Jesus confronts the fear of death and accepts the will of God;
— the Scourging at the Pillar: Jesus endures torture and is stripped of every vestige of humanity;
— the Crowning with Thorns: Jesus' divine kingship is mocked;
— the Carrying of the Cross: Jesus bears the burden of all our pain; and
— the Crucifixion and Death of Jesus (Weber 1995, 17).

After listing the traditional interpretations of the mysteries, Weber provides this interpretation of what she calls mysteries of sorrow, of women experiencing transformation:

— the Agony in the Garden: the mystery of fear; we transform the death of our dreams;
— the Scourging at the Pillar: the mystery of emptiness; we transform violence, abuse, and the desecration of beauty;
— the Crowning with Thorns: the mystery of despair; we transform social systems and the abuse of power.
— the Carrying of the Cross: the mystery of unknowing; we transform the masculine within ourselves and in our sons; and
— the Crucifixion: the mystery of death; we are transformed by death and all that overwhelms us (Weber 1995, 18).

Symbols will continue to be imbued with new meanings by groups who are marginalized in the church and in the society. The challenge for some will be to look beyond the old symbol to find the new meaning.

Teachings

The social teachings of the church, called the best-kept secret of the church, will no longer be secret. The body of teachings, which begin with Pope Leo XIII's 1891 encyclical, *Rerum Novarum* (*On the Condition of the Working Classes*), includes social encyclicals from subsequent popes and deals with a myriad of social issues affecting the world.

The teachings on personal morality that received emphasis in this century will be analyzed in light of the social teachings. Again, there will not be a dichotomy between personal and social but a new synthesis wherein the teachings on personal morality will be interpreted within the context of the social teachings.

Structures

Because the emphasis placed on spiritual health in the next century will equal the one on physical health and fitness today, there will exist within Catholic institutions time and space for silence, chant, and prayer of various sorts, particularly meditation. Individual and communal prayer time will be available.

Parishes, institutions whose primary function is to serve the sacramental needs of their members, will exist alongside a wide array of spiritual centers. The sacrament of reconciliation will be reclaimed and highlighted since the need to forgive and be forgiven as individuals and groups will be seen as essential for spiritual health. Since parishes will be able to respond to only some of the spiritual needs of their members, spiritual centers will be opened to meet people's needs. Monks and nuns from monasteries will be available to provide training in spiritual practices and prayer. Monasteries will, again, be centers of learning and culture. Lay people will lead many of the spiritual centers and will focus on the spiritual needs of people from youngsters to the elderly, in all lifestyles. Religious orders will be able to articulate and disseminate the meaning and significance of their particular spiritual gifts.

CLASHES AND COHORTS

This exercise has provided a unique opportunity to speculate about the future of one of the most powerful institutions in the United States. How much of the foregoing will come true, only time will tell. But if some of what is speculated does come true, it will be due, in some measure, to the transmission of values to new generational cohorts.

Some demographers divide U.S. society today into six dominant cohorts: the depression cohort, born between 1912 and 1921; the World War II cohort, born between 1922 and 1927; the postwar cohort, born between 1928 and 1945; the boomers I cohort, born from 1946 to 1954; the boomers II cohort, born 1955 to 1965; and the Generation X cohort, born 1984 to 1994 (Meredith and Schewe 1994). Since each cohort has its own culture, the obvious question for us is, Which elements of the spiritual-institutional church of the twenty-first century will provoke cultural clashes of cohorts?

As time goes on, the importance of the Second Vatican Council as the most significant shaping influence for the postwar cohort and for some in the older baby-boom cohort will be eclipsed by new religious and social forces that will have shaped younger cohorts. The survival of some institutions will depend upon navigating the cultural clashes of certain cohorts and creating meaning systems that transcend cohort lines.

In the midst of the new religious economy, the perception of the value placed on various elements of religious capital by different cohorts will be fascinating to observe. The tussles between cohorts will be even more exciting to watch.

A case in point is a recent incident at Georgetown University. Some students, who compose a group made up of the tail end of Generation X and the beginning of a new cohort already labeled Generation Dot Com by some pundits, demanded that crucifixes be placed in classrooms as an indicator of the Catholic identity of the university. The crucifixes had been removed after the Second Vatican Council. After a yearlong university-wide debate, Georgetown president Father Leo O'Donovan, a Jesuit, said the school would accede to the wishes of the students who "have held rallies, circulated petitions, and secured funding to pay the cost of returning to the tradition of hanging crucifixes in classrooms" (Ribadeneira 1998). It is conceivable that the members of the generational cohort that took the crucifixes down when they were young are now the ones being asked by the young to put them back up.

An analysis of Catholic culture in the United States in the new century will demand taking seriously elements of the culture—symbols, saints, structures, and teachings—that hold different values for different cohorts. The test for twenty-first century U.S. Catholicism, which will be conducted in each of its myriad institutions, is whether the creation of new spiritual and institutional alignments will retain the older generational cohorts and serve as recruitment incentives for newer generational cohorts. As the decades pass, it will be fascinating to observe which of the institutions that have the capacity to be multigenerational will actually meld their institutional-spiritual resources in such a way that they give witness to a multigenerational way of being the church.

References

Artress, Lauren. 1995. *Walking a Sacred Path: Rediscovering the Labyrinth as a Spiritual Tool.* New York: Riverhead Books.

Clarke, John, ed. 1996. *Story of a Soul: The Autobiography of St. Thérèse of Lisieux.* 3d ed. Washington, DC: ICS.

Ebaugh, Helen Rose Fuchs. 1993. *Women in the Vanishing Cloister: Organizational Decline in Catholic Religious Orders in the United States.* New Brunswick, NJ: Rutgers University Press.

Greeley, Andrew M. 1991. The Demography of American Catholics: 1965-1990. In *Religion and the Social Order: Vatican II and U.S. Catholicism,* ed. Helen Rose Ebaugh. Greenwich, CT: JAI Press.

Hastings, Joanna. 1993. *The Rosary: Prayer for All Seasons.* Collegeville, MN: Liturgical Press.

Kreilkamp, H. D. 1997. "Little Flower" a Likely Doctor of Church for an Age of Anxiety. *National Catholic Reporter,* 24 Oct.

Meredith, Geoffrey and Charles Schewe. 1994. The Power of Cohorts. *American Demographics* 12(Dec.):22-31.

Nygren, David and Miriam Ukeritis. 1993. *The Future of Religious Orders in the United States: Transformation and Commitment.* Westport, CT: Praeger.

Official Catholic Directory. 1997. New Providence, NJ: P. J. Kenedy.

Ribadeneira, Diego. 1998. Georgetown to Go Way of the Cross Amid a Widespread Debate, a Decision to Be Catholic. *Boston Globe,* 24 Feb.

Roof, Wade Clark. 1993. *A Generation of Seekers: The Spiritual Journeys of the Baby Boom Generation.* San Francisco, CA: HarperSanFrancisco.

Schoenherr, Richard. 1993. *Full Pews, Empty Altars: Demographics of the*

Priest Shortage in U.S. Catholic Dioceses. Madison: University of Wisconsin Press.

Weber, Christin Lore. 1995. *Circle of Mysteries: The Women's Rosary Book.* St. Paul, MN: Yes International.

Wittberg, Patricia. 1994. *The Rise and Fall of Catholic Religious Orders: A Social Movement Perspective.* Albany: State University of New York Press.

ANNALS, *AAPSS*, 558, July 1998

The Symbol and the Stone: Jerusalem at the Millennium

By ROGER FRIEDLAND and RICHARD HECHT

ABSTRACT: This article explores the relationship between sacrality and sovereignty, between symbolic and material realities in Jerusalem's politics from the Six Day War of 1967 to the present and as Jerusalem moves toward the millennium. It begins with the Israeli efforts to separate the city's sacred places from political solutions and how this affects religious traditions and their communities in the city. It takes up the growing symbolic importance of Jerusalem for American evangelical Christians, then how the city functions as a ritual theater for Israeli and Palestinian politics, and, finally, how the city is doubly cleaved: between communities at the level of politics and within each community around the relationship between the political order and the religious order, especially since the signing of the Oslo accords and the defeat in 1993 of Jerusalem's longtime liberal mayor, Teddy Kollek, and his replacement by center-right Likud mayor Ehud Olmert.

Roger Friedland is professor of religious studies and sociology and Richard Hecht is professor of religious studies at the University of California at Santa Barbara.

IN early June of 1867, Mark Twain, then a relatively unknown newspaper correspondent and a professional humorist, joined a group of 150 Americans on a grand tour of Europe, Egypt, and the Holy Land on board the *Quaker City*. The tour had been organized by the Reverend Henry Ward Beecher's Plymouth Church, although the minister withdrew before the ship's departure. The itinerary included stops in Tangier, Marseilles, Paris, Genoa, Milan, Venice, Florence, Rome, Naples, Athens, Constantinople, Antioch, Beirut, Jerusalem, Alexandria, and Cairo.

When Twain and seven of his traveling companions reached Jerusalem more than three months later, their first glimpse of the city was from its northern heights. His first thought at seeing the city gleaming in the sun was that it was so small. "Why," he wrote, "it was no larger than an American village of four thousand inhabitants, and no larger than an ordinary Syrian city of thirty thousand. Jerusalem numbers only fourteen thousand people." To give his readers back home an idea of how small Jerusalem was in comparison to the symbolic Jerusalem of religious memory, he wrote that a "fast walker could go outside the walls of Jerusalem and walk entirely around the city in an hour." His description of the city's inhabitants reflected all the prejudices of the nineteenth century. The city's poverty and dirt were indicators of Muslim rule; lepers, cripples, and the blind assailed the visitor at every step appealing for alms; and the numbers of "maimed, malformed, and diseased humanity" suggested the immediate expectation that the angel of the Lord would heal this wretched multitude by stirring the waters of Bethesda. For Twain, "Jerusalem is mournful, and dreary, and lifeless. I would not desire to live here" ([1869] 1899, 2:326).

Twain, of course, published his account of the grand tour eastward as *The Innocents Abroad or The New Pilgrims' Progress* in 1869, and it quickly became one of the most popular American guidebooks to the Holy Land of the second half of the century, selling 67,000 copies during its first year alone. Not only would Americans buy the book in record numbers, but almost every other American writer on the Holy Land after Twain would echo his tone. Romantic travelers and scholars had given a completely false portrait of the Holy Land and Jerusalem. The Holy Land and its holy city were arid, squalid, boring, and depressing. The contradiction between Jerusalem the symbol and Jerusalem the city was fully exposed in *The Innocents Abroad* and the descriptions that followed it, making it easier, as one traveler observed, "to feel that Christ was born in New England than in Judea" (Shepherd 1987, 175).

Today Jerusalem is a vital world city and center with a population nearing 600,000 and projected to reach more than 800,000 in the next twenty years. While the nineteenth-century visitors, like Mark Twain, often commented on the city's relative smallness, it is now a sprawling metropolis whose farthest boundary is more than 10 kilometers from the same walls of the Old City that Twain thought he could walk around in an hour. The Old City itself is approximately 1 square kilometer and constitutes less than 1 percent of the total space of the holy city at the end of the twentieth century.

Despite, however, its urban and demographic transformations and the changes in sovereignty that have taken place over the course of the last century, Jerusalem remains an urban reliquary riven by ancient hatreds, its stones sedimented with blood and memory. It is a real city but also a contested symbol. It is the foundational site of nationhood, claimed by both Israel and Palestine, and invested with extraordinary power and memory for communities far removed from it. In the present article, we will discuss some aspects of the city as both symbol and stone, the Jerusalem of the religious and American imagination, and the real politics of the city in which America will continue to be involved with both Israelis and Palestinians as we come to the end of one century and the beginning of another.

SEPARATING
THE SACRED

Ever since the signing of the Oslo accords in 1993 by Prime Minister Yitzhak Rabin and Palestine Liberation Organization (PLO) Chairman Yasir Arafat, the Israelis have sought to separate the city's sacred sites from the struggle over its sovereignty. The Israelis have never been comfortable being the umpire in the often nasty, and sometimes bloody, fights between the Armenian Orthodox, Greek Orthodox, White and Red Russian Orthodox, Greek and Latin Catholics, Syrian Jacobites, Ethiopians, and Egyptian Copts over their respective rights to space and time in the city's Christian shrines. The Israelis are more than willing to cede sovereign powers to a council of Christianities over the sites where Pontius Pilate ordered the execution of Jesus as "King of the Jews," where he was buried and triumphed over death, where Mary was entombed, where Jesus ascended after the 40 days of post-resurrection appearances to his followers, and where he was born in Bethlehem.

Pope John Paul II, too, has now made it clear that the Holy See is willing to separate sacrality from sovereignty. In its 1993 fundamental agreement with Israel establishing reciprocal diplomatic relations, the Holy See made an extraordinary ecumenical concession in promising to respect the Status Quo in the Holy Places, that labyrinthine compilation of decrees and agreements allocating time and space among the competing Christian communities in their sacred places. The Catholics thereby agreed to remain in a very disadvantaged position vis-à-vis the Greek Orthodox and the Armenians. Because of the Status Quo, for example, in the Church of the Holy Sepulcher, the Catholics must celebrate their Easter New Fire ritual of lighting the paschal candles and blessing the baptismal waters very early on Saturday morning, not at midnight between Holy Saturday and Easter Sunday as everywhere else in the world. Moreover, they cannot celebrate the Easter Sunday mass at the traditional site of the burial chamber of Jesus but are confined to the adjacent Chapel of St. Mary. While in the past, the Latins, as the Catholics are known in Jerusalem, had used the influence of the colonial powers to alter their disadvantaged situation or played the bargaining chip of promises to rebuild most of the holy places in exchange for a more equitable division of time and space within them, the Vatican's position now seems to be that an unprecedented emphasis upon ecumenicism will gain them what power and money could not. Michel Sabbah, who became the Latin patriarch of Jerusalem in 1987, told us in a 1996 interview that much of this ecumenicism is focused on preparations for the Christian jubilee, which will mark 2000 years of Christian history. Despite the fractious relations between Catholic and Greek Orthodox Christians in Jerusalem and elsewhere in the past and present, Monsignor Sabbah believes that ecumenicism in Jerusalem can achieve much because, irrespective of their theological differences, Palestinian Catholics like him and Palestinian Greek Orthodox Christians share, as he put it, a similar "Arabic culture."

On the other hand, although the Vatican has not yet talked officially with Israel about Jerusalem, the Holy See has initialed a second set of agreements with Israel that will grant it rights to buy and sell properties anywhere in Israel, which as far as Israel is concerned includes Jerusalem, not as a civil right but as a treaty obligation between two sovereign powers. Even though the Latins constitute only about one-quarter of Jerusalem's Christian population, as the only world religion which has a sovereign personality, the Latin church will be in a privileged position. While the Holy See wants whatever Christian authority is recognized in Jerusalem to locate its sources in international law, as opposed to Israeli national codes, there are strong indications that the Holy See will not make the progress of its negotiations with Israel over its future status in Jerusalem conditional upon a particular resolution of the Palestinians' sovereign claims in the city. Just as Egyptian President Sadat separated the Sinai from the Palestinian question, the Holy See is ready to separate the status of Jerusalem as the Savior's city from its status as a Palestinian capital.

Here we offer two hypotheses that might explain the Vatican's diplomatic initiative—some might even describe it as a desperate initiative—which seemingly disregards the national aspirations of the Palestinians. First, it is ecumenicism itself that is motivating a deal with Israel. The Christian jubilee, which will begin in 1999, will bring millions of pilgrims to Jerusalem. Jerusalem is the critical node in which the Vatican must have a presence, the place where it can play its ecumenical strategy of being the center of the Christian world, and play it there because it cannot be played from Rome. Christians outside Catholicism deny Rome, but they cannot deny Jerusalem. It is in Jerusalem that it can be a broker between different Christianities. It is through Jerusalem that it, as the only diplomatic interlocutor, can guarantee the rights of the Christianities in the city's holy sites. The second hypothesis is that ecumenicism is the means by which the Vatican can reenter the Middle

East diplomatic game, in which it has become almost irrelevant. It is through Jerusalem that the Vatican might become a broker between Jews and Muslims in Israel and Palestine and also between Christians and Muslims in other Middle Eastern regimes.

There is substantial evidence, however, that the Christianities on the ground in Jerusalem do not want the Vatican involved in the final-status negotiations and that global ecumenical groups are also opposed to the Vatican's self-perceived role. Indeed, the local Christianities are being radicalized. In June 1996, 11 Christian leaders from Jerusalem, Lebanon, Egypt, and Syria joined seven Muslim clerics from Jerusalem, Lebanon, Syria, Egypt, and the gulf region to sign an urgent appeal addressed to the world, expressing their demand that all of Jerusalem, not just the Old City, or East Jerusalem, be the capital of a Palestinian state. In part, the militancy of Arab Christians is the result of their increasing sense of vulnerability as a minority within an emergent nation-state that is, from their perspective, steadily moving toward radical Islam. In the late spring of 1996, there were reports circulating among Palestinian Christians that their co-religionists were being tortured in Bethlehem by the Palestinian National Authority's police.

For believing Muslims, Jerusalem's fall to the Prophet's armies proved the superiority of their faith to that of their Abrahamic predecessors. Inside the Dome of the Rock, the magnificent structure marking the place from which the Prophet Muhammad was believed to have as-cended to heaven, the beautiful calligraphy is directed specifically against the divinity of Jesus and Christian trinitarian speculation (Grabar 1996; Rosen-Ayalon 1989). Jerusalem's surrender treaty in 638 C.E., the Pact of Umar, provided the template for Islam's relations with Jews and Christians as tolerated minorities with circumscribed civil rights. There is a pervasive impulse, grounded in centuries of Islamic doctrine and almost continuous Islamic rule of Jerusalem from 638 to 1099 and from 1187 to 1917, to recapture the city. Jewish sovereignty here is more than a stain on Arab honor; it is a challenge to Islamic belief.

Palestinian nationalism is tied to Jerusalem in a way that Zionism is not. Pre-state Jerusalem was dominated by non-Zionist or anti-Zionist Jews from the old Yishuv[1] who came to Zion to pray and wait for the advent of the Messiah, indeed to prompt him on his way. Most were discomfited, if not horrified, at the modern Jewish nationalist project. The great Zionist leaders expressed deep antipathy for the city. It seemingly expressed everything they were opposed to; they were creating a new Jew, building a new Jewish society, and establishing a new Jewish polity, free from the weaknesses of the past (Elon 1989). Before 1948, the pioneering, socialist Zionists were not a powerful force in Zion itself. The British administered all of Palestine from Jerusalem and this drew the Zionists to the city, hoping that proximity to the British center of mandatory Palestine would confer authority upon their institutions. The World Zionist Organization and the Jewish Agency relocated offices there, but the Histadrut remained in Tel Aviv (Hertzberg 1996). The World Zionist Organization and the Jewish Agency built some institutions in Jerusalem, such as the Hebrew University, in conjunction with other Zionist groups but controlled comparatively little land in the city. This was in great part due to the ideology of pioneering Zionism, which gave little or no emphasis to Jerusalem.

In contrast, the Palestinian nation was led into battle against British and Jewish colonization from al-Quds ("the Holy," the Arabic name for Jerusalem). It was from here that the Palestinians were galvanized as a nation by Haj Amin al-Husayni, the Grand Mufti of Jerusalem, Palestine's highest Islamic officer, through pilgrimage and orchestrated conflict with revisionist Zionists over ritual rights at the Western Wall. Yasir Arafat claims to have been born in the Arab neighborhood that once abutted the Western Wall, a neighborhood razed immediately after the Six Day War of 1967 to make way for the present enormous plaza that forms an Israeli national shrine. The Grand Mufti's nephew, Faisal Husayni, whose family supplied many of Jerusalem's Arab mayors, now leads the Palestinian struggle for the city.

While Western commentators sharply distinguish between the PLO's secular nationalism and the theocratic impulses of the Muslim Brotherhood and its young offshoot, Hamas, Islam suffuses all Palestinian nationalism. Arafat got his start as a soldier fighting with volunteers from the Muslim Brotherhood in the 1948 war. His nom de guerre, Abu Ammar ("father of Ammar"), refers to Ammar ibn Yasir, one of the Prophet's companions, a fighter from a poor family whose members were tortured for their faith. The Palestinian flag is modeled on the Prophet's banner kept by the Husayni family in the Dome of the Rock. "Fatah," the name of a faction of the PLO, is a classical word from the Qur'an that means "to open" or "to conquer," referring to Islamic conquest of infidel lands. "Ours is the obligation of jihad," declared Fatah's very first official communiqué on 1 January 1965. Paralleling events from the 1930s, one of the Palestinian Authority's very first postage stamps issued in 1995 showed the Dome of the Rock as the symbol of Palestinian nationhood.

The Israelis are struggling to denationalize the *haram al-sharif*, the platform upon which Solomon's and Herod's temples once stood, now the site of the Dome of the Rock and the al-Aqsa mosque. In this they are making common cause with the larger Islamic world, including some of its most powerful states, such as Saudi Arabia and Kuwait, which do not trust Arafat's Palestinian Authority as a guardian of this Islamic site and who have little love left for Arafat, who supported Saddam Hussein, their mortal enemy, in the gulf war. By granting the world's Islamic community control over the *haram*, the Israelis hope to counter the Palestinian nationalist significance of this site and thereby, de facto, to garner some Islamic support for Israeli sovereignty elsewhere in the city.

The Israelis' first move was toward the Jordanians. In the summer of 1988 and after nine months of the

Palestinian uprising, or *intifada*, King Hussein abdicated all claims to the West Bank. At least this is what he did publicly on radio and television. In reality, he continued to maintain the Jerusalem *waqf*, or religious trust, of which the *haram* is an integral part, and the network of mosques, schools, and Islamic courts that it controls throughout the West Bank. King Hussein's family are descendants of the ancient guardians of the holy places of Mecca and Medina; today only the symbolism of Jerusalem remains theirs. In the 1994 peace treaty with Jordan, at Jordan's insistence, Yitzhak Rabin wrote the section promising to give Jordan's "historical role" in administering Jerusalem's Islamic sites "high priority" in future negotiations with the Palestinians. At present, there are, in fact, two muftis in Jerusalem, one beholden to the Palestinians and one, shunned by the Palestinians, representing King Hussein and his family.

Controlling Jerusalem's Islamic center is critical to Arafat not only because Islam is genetic to Palestinian nationalism but also because it is such a potent instrument for his Islamic opponents. While the Muslim Brothers were severely repressed in Nasser's Egypt and subsequently supported by the Central Intelligence Agency, Jordan's King Hussein made common cause with them as a strategic ally against his Palestinian nationalist and revolutionary socialist enemies. In return, he granted them hegemony in Jerusalem's Islamic institutions. Over the years, the Muslim Brotherhood has gained diffuse powers in Palestine's Islamic institutions as its members have become

prayer leaders, preachers, religious court judges, teachers, and distributors of *zakat*, or charity, funds. Israel repeatedly repressed cross-local Palestinian political institutions in the West Bank and Gaza. In so doing, the Israelis had the tacit support of the Jordanians, who saw these institutions as inimical to their efforts to control the West Bank, and the PLO, which feared that these institutions might become the mechanisms for an independent Palestinian voice. Only the mosques remained. They became one of the most important networks by which political communication and mobilization across geographic and political space could be accomplished. Jerusalem has been known as a bastion of support for Fatah. Indeed, some Israeli analysts referred to the city as "Fatah Town." But, by the end of the 1980s, Jerusalem had also become a critical node of strength for the Islamicists. In 1993, for example, when the Palestinians held Chamber of Commerce elections throughout the territories, the elections were put off in Jerusalem for fear that Hamas would win. As in Iran, the Palestinian merchant class has strong affinities with radical Islam. Jordan still looks to the Islamicists as a counterweight to the PLO. Jordan's toleration of the Muslim Brotherhood and Hamas did not stop after its peace accord with Israel, even after Hamas's suicide bombers murdered scores of Israelis. Tens of millions of dollars continued to flow through Amman to the West Bank and Gaza. Hamas has not been banned in Jordan and continues its radio broadcasts from the Jordanian capital. Arafat desperately wants a position in Jerusalem, and the *haram* in particular, if nothing else, to counter the Islamic threat to his rule.

JERUSALEM IN THE AMERICAN EVANGELICAL IMAGINATION

By the beginning of the 1980s, almost all of the Protestant evangelical ministries in the United States had taken up the cause of Israel. The television and radio programming, direct-mail campaigns, and outreach ministries of Pat Robertson, Jerry Falwell, Oral Roberts, Jimmy Swaggart, Jim and Tammy Bakker, and Mike Evans, being only the most prominent, all featured the state of Israel, Jerusalem, and the Jews as important components in their religious world-views. All led tour groups to Israel and Jerusalem, featuring seminars on the Bible in situ. They crisscrossed the state looking for the traces of patriarchs and matriarchs, for David and Solomon, the prophets, and Jesus and his disciples. They and the members of their tours listened to Israeli archaeologists and Middle Eastern specialists and spoke with Israeli politicians and prime ministers. Each tour attempted to demonstrate Israel's role in the continuing unfolding of God's plan, the progress of salvation, in which they, or the members of and contributors to their ministries, were playing a direct role.

Each of these major evangelists read the history of our century regarding the Jews and the Jewish nationalist movement, Zionism, in a similar way. Zionism had brought the Jews back to their ancestral land under divine providence, fulfilling the prophecies of both the Hebrew Bible and the New Testament. It was this providence that explained the foundation of the modern Jewish state and its defeat of overwhelmingly more powerful Arab forces in 1948; the stunning victory of the Six Day War in 1967, in which Israel reclaimed East Jerusalem and, most important, the Old City with its Jewish, Muslim, and Christian holy places, and defeated the Jordanians on the West Bank of the Jordan, the Syrians on the Golan Heights, and the Egyptians in the Sinai; and Israel's narrow escape from military disaster in the 1973 Yom Kippur War. The flourishing of the Jewish people in their homeland and their seeming miraculous military victories were the concrete demonstrations that the end times were near, the Second Coming of the Risen Christ was at hand, and the ultimate and final victory over the powers of evil was already beginning.

But while all seven evangelists featured this similar message, there was considerable differentiation between them as they sought their own unique message and niche within the ever expanding evangelical audience. Pat Robertson, for example, adapted his ministry to the daily television news with an evangelical twist, including feature stories and the talk-show guest format in his Christian Broadcasting Network, the 700 Club, and the PTL ministry. Economics forced each to quickly adapt to the new information technologies and to find a distinctive voice and message.

In this competition for the evangelical audience, Mike Evans, based in Bedford, Texas, emerged in the second half of the 1980s as the distinctive voice on Israel and Jerusalem. In many respects, his ministry, like those of the others, was involved in numerous projects, including prayer in the public schools and support for the anti-abortion movement, that were common themes on the evangelical agenda. For example, in December 1984, Evans mailed his supporters a calendar for the new year entitled *Partners in Prophecy '85— Partner Devotional Guide* (Evans 1984b), which was intended to provide his followers with a day-by-day series of biblical texts for meditation, a division of the entire Bible so that they would read the entire text in the coming year, and weekly ideas or themes through which they would join him as partners in prayer. For example, the prayer request for 1-6 April was the following: "This is a fast day. Let's all fast and believe God that every precious partner of this ministry would experience an answer to their most important unspoken request." For July, the prayer request was "I want you to bind the powers of darkness with me coming against those who are in mental hospitals—that Jesus would free them in HIS name and they would go and tell of the freedom found in Christ." *Partners in Prophecy* also included various photographs of the Evans ministry in action. For January, there was a photograph of Evans shaking the hand of President Ronald Reagan with the following comment:

President Reagan invited Jim Bakker, Jimmy Swaggart, Jerry Falwell, myself and a few others to meet with him in private. I will never forget what he told us. The President expressed the belief that America was on the verge of a spiritual awakening. And I believe it with all my heart. God is raising up people like you and me in intercessory prayer and love to prepare the world for the King of Kings and the Lord of Lords.

Another photograph, for August, showed the evangelist surrounded by a circle of his followers bowed in prayer. Here the captioned narrative read:

More than 2,000 people responded to the altar call, but the most amazing thing was that as we went into the counseling ten, the convicting power of the Holy Spirit fell like a mighty roar. The weeping and travailing was so strong that I had to wait for over one hour to even talk. As I stood in amazement, 200 homosexuals came to the front, crying and repenting and praying for deliverance.

The calendar also contained personal testimonies, in Evans's voice, of the power of God in his own family. For March, there was a picture of his wife, Carolyn, with the following brief narrative: "Carolyn, my lovely wife, stood at the platform with some of the most prominent Christian women in America, in Washington, D.C., making the official presentation for the Christian Woman of the Year Award to Ruth Gramm [the wife of Texas Senator Phil Gramm]." With tears in his eyes, Evans watched his wife among these prominent people, knowing that she shunned the public world for the maintenance of a Christian home. But he also drew a lesson from this event: "Isn't that just like the Amazing grace of our God . . . how He takes individuals who do not seek positions of honor and blesses them abundantly."

This calendar also contained the narrative of his specialized mission for the Jews, Israel, and Jerusalem.

For November, there was a photograph of Evans seated in an armchair, with his wife standing behind him. He wrote that they were married in November 1969, and, one month later, he left his Bible school in his third year to begin his ministry. The first year, the newlyweds lived in a house with one room to themselves, sharing the house with 22 men who had been in and out of prison but whom he had led to Jesus. The Evanses' purpose was to train these former convicts "in the ways of the Lord." Further, he wrote:

I will never forget those early years when we began this ministry. We sold our furniture and were sick with the flu and had only one mattress in the entire apartment. Many criticized me and told me I was a fool. Six ministers prayed over me and asked God to tell me to repent of my "delusion" for believing that God was going to touch Israel. Another person came up to me and said, "You are so foolish to think that Christians really care about Israel and the Jewish people. They really don't." How I thank God that I didn't listen to those people at that time, and how I thank God that he has sent friends into our lives like you who believe in us and are standing with us. No matter what pressures you are under, remember, God is on your side.

According to this brief narrative of Evans's early ministry, Israel and the Jews became increasingly a part of his career and his activities. His direct-mail campaigns and his use of television from 1985 through 1989 suggested that. In 1986, he distributed to his mailing list the Chick tract *Support Your Local Jew* (Chick n.d.), which provides a cartoon historicization of God's promise to Abraham that those who bless him and his

descendants would be blessed by God and those who curse Abraham's family would be similarly cursed.

In the first blocks of the cartoon, the wonders of ancient Egypt are depicted: "Egypt . . . the Envy of the world! No nation could touch her for wealth, military power, agriculture and science. In architecture Egypt had no rivals. At that time Egypt was the most powerful nation on this earth. She made one mistake . . . Egypt did not support her local Jew." In the last of these initial depictions, an Egyptian taskmaster is shown beating a Hebrew slave, with the verses from Exodus 1:13-14 in the bottom register. The narrative proceeds with the Ten Plagues, culminating with the destruction of Pharaoh's army at the Red Sea. The final picture shows a modern Egyptian tour guide in front of the broken remnants of Egypt's glorious past. "Today," Chick's narrative continues, "Egyptian tourist guides can only boast about her glorious past. Egypt is now a backward nation, full of memories, relying on others for aid . . . Egypt is still the enemy of Israel." The cartoon narrative continues through the Greeks and the Romans, then the rise of the Nazis and Germany's punishment, division of the nation in which, according to Chick, "one-half is now under Communist slavery."

Moreover, Chick continues, the curse is still in effect today. Here we see an emaciated African clutching a famine-withered child on her lap. "The following African nations have TWO things in common," Chick states, and the cartoon lists Niger, Ethiopia, Upper Volta, Mali, Kenya,

Nigeria, Dahomey, Senegal, and Chad. The first thing that these nations have in common, according to Chick, is that "they were caught up in the terrible famine caused by the expanding Sahara desert." The second is that "they had all broken diplomatic relationship with Israel."

Of course, the Chick cartoon tract was another rendering of millenarian and apocalyptic symbolism that ran deep in the American evangelical community. This symbolism stretches back to the nineteenth century and reaches other popular representations, such as the immensely popular Hal Lindsey's *Late Great Planet Earth* (1970) or Tim LaHaye's *Coming Peace in the Middle East* (1984).

Evans's ministry called upon his supporters to contribute to a number of projects that directly involved Jews. He developed a program to support the emigration of Russian Jews. The program first emerged as a direct-mail campaign and then a syndicated one-hour television special shown on evangelical stations with the title *Let My People Go*, which was accompanied by frequent "Prophetic Update Reports." From 1984 to 1989, he published a monthly newsletter, *Middle East News Alert*, which focused on his missions to Israel and his understanding of the dangers facing the Jews, the Israelis, and the Americans. He also became a supporter of Operation Moses, which brought Ethiopian Jews to Israel. Many of these campaigns carried a sense of utmost urgency. For example, one of the newsletters from 1984 carried the following message:

An Urgent Appeal. Over 7,000 Ethiopian Jews are in the country, but with malnutrition, malaria, intestinal parasites, dysentery, skin diseases, tuberculosis and even typhoid. We have received an urgent appeal to immediately help these dear people. I will be leaving immediately to take a love gift in the name of our Lord. Anything you send would be greatly appreciated.

In some cases, his appeals contained stories reprinted from the *Jerusalem Post*, and he coined new names for his campaigns. He labeled his campaign to support Ethiopian Jews "Operation Ezekiel 37," named after the section in the Bible in which the prophet Ezekiel speaks of how the children of Israel would be brought from the nations to their own land. In other cases, he raised funds for the Jewish Children's Rehabilitation Center in Jerusalem, a center that, he proudly noted time and again, served the needs of both Jews and Arabs.

Evans's most extensive campaign, however, was his JerUSAlem DC project. This campaign exemplified the classic millenarian or premillennialist temporal consciousness. The Jews, Israel, and Jerusalem were viewed as the visible signs of the immanent end of time and final battle with the satanic forces arrayed against God and the now returning Christ. In one of his letters in 1985 addressed to his prayer partners, he described just getting off the telephone with a "senior advisor" to former Prime Minister Begin. He wrote that

the Israelis have urgently appealed to me to encourage Bible-believers to pray for them. . . . I have mailed letters out to hundreds of thousands asking them to stand by Israel so that God can bless us. I have also spent over $25,000 utilizing the media to encourage prayer for Israel and for divine intervention against the demonic terrorism problem. If it is possible—I know I am asking a lot, but this is a great need—could you send an extra love gift to help us pay these bills? Your sacrificial gift would mean so very much to me.

While the letter was reproduced in a typed format, he also included a handwritten postscript to his readers: "Rush this letter back to me with your generous donation. Together we will stand by Israel and see God's mighty hand move in her behalf."

The JerUSAlem DC campaign also featured free bumper stickers and replicas of the "Proclamation of JerU-SAlem DC" accompanied by a gold stick-on seal that would be sent with the supporter's own name to both the president of the United States and the prime minister of Israel. As part of the campaign, Evans marketed a book and a television special. Central to the campaign was the discovery in the very name "Jerusalem" its not too secret relationship to the United States. Jerusalem and the United States were linked symbolically and in the world of real politics by the appearance of the letters "usa" in the middle of the city's name. The letters "dc" were also significant. As Evans pointed out, they stood for "David's capital," which Jerusalem was, and, simultaneously, for the capital of the United States, thereby conjuring the relationship between Jerusalem and Washington. This relationship was not left unexploited by the cover of his

calendar, which showed a rainbow connecting the Capitol and Jerusalem's Dome of the Rock with Israeli flags flying in front of it (Evans 1984a).

There were suspicions that Christian evangelicals were not confining their activity to fund-raising for charitable organizations and prayers for Israel, Jews, and Jerusalem. In the early 1980s, two Jewish organizations began serious efforts to mobilize various constituencies around the Temple Mount. One of them, the Faithful of the Temple Mount, was organized in 1982 with the express purpose of having Israeli sovereignty extended over the Temple Mount. In the wake of the Six Day War, the Knesset had voted its approval of the Law for the Preservation of the Holy Places, which put Jewish, Christian, and Muslim holy places under the direct supervision of their respective religious communities. The Temple Mount was in a very real sense the last and only piece of real estate outside direct Israeli sovereignty. The Faithful of the Temple Mount successfully pushed this issue onto the Israeli national scene, and their political activities around the mount sparked a number of violent confrontations between Israelis and Palestinians well into the early 1990s.

The second organization, Yeshivat Ataret-Cohanim, began as a yeshiva of the same name that had been founded in the 1930s by the then chief rabbi of Palestine and one of the century's most important religious nationalists, Avraham Yitzhak Ha-Cohen Kook. This institution had originally trained men who were born into the priestly lineage, which had the responsibility of implementing the religious laws regarding the Temple's sacrificial rituals. In the 1980s, the renewed Yeshivat Ataret-Cohanim included individuals who could not make such claims to the priestly lineage but were only interested in studying the laws pertaining to sacrifice. In many respects, this yeshiva was an extension of the growing religious nationalist movement within Israel and the effort to settle the West Bank and Gaza Strip as part of a divinely ordained return to the heartland of biblical Israel. During the end of the 1980s and throughout the 1990s, Yeshivat Ataret-Cohanim expanded its operations to include the buying and renovation of Arab homes in the Old City of Jerusalem on the periphery of the Jewish quarter or in the heart of both the Christian and Muslim quarters. These efforts to reclaim all of the Old City for Jews were directly related to the messianic or millenarian vision of the settlement movement.

There was a series of efforts to bring American Christian evangelicals into the project. Both the evangelicals and the two Jewish groups were united in their views that the current time period was the entrance to the messianic era, although they differed in terms of the end of that process. For the evangelicals, the return of Jesus would signal the conversion of the Jews. For the Jewish messianists of the Faithful of the Temple Mount and Yeshivat Ataret-Cohanim, this end time would be signaled by the building of the Third Temple and the reinstitution of sacrificial worship. A shared sense of time

produced a common political goal. There was speculation that a number of wealthy evangelicals funneled moneys to both organizations. The first chairman of the Faithful of the Temple Mount, Stanley Goldfoot, also organized the Jerusalem Temple Foundation, whose board of directors was made up of himself and five prominent evangelicals.

The chairman of the board of the Jerusalem Temple Foundation was Terry Risenhoover, an Oklahoma oil man and land speculator, who had attempted to dig for oil in Israel and had set up a West Coast branch of the foundation in Malibu, California. Risenhoover described himself as a classical Southern Baptist whom God had stirred up to prepare for the Messiah's Second Coming. Risenhoover apparently gave Goldfoot a gift of $50,000 to establish a headquarters in Jerusalem for the foundation, but Goldfoot determined that it was not the appropriate time for such a move, believing that his group might be seen as another Christian effort to evangelize the Jews. On a visit to Jerusalem, Risenhoover was guided around the city by Jewish activists engaged in the effort to repeal the Knesset's 1967 law giving the Muslims control over the Temple Mount. He was introduced to key Knesset members who advocated this position. Risenhoover was subsequently arrested, tried, and found guilty of selling phony oil leases; he served his sentence in the federal penitentiary in Norman, Oklahoma.

Another prominent figure on the board was the Reverend Chuck Smith of the Calvary Chapel in Costa Mesa, California, who sent a Cadillac to pick up Goldfoot at the Los Angeles International Airport when he addressed Smith's congregation of 3000 on the activities of the Jerusalem Temple Foundation. As Louis Rapoport wrote in the *Jerusalem Post*, Goldfoot told the appreciative audience that "Jerusalem is not truly liberated yet—its heart is still under alien control. There is no freedom of worship on the Temple Mount, not for Jews and not for the Christians . . . the Waqf employs thugs who will prevent you from praying there" (Rapoport 1984). Goldfoot was angered by the revelation of his contacts with the evangelicals in the United States and fired off an angry letter to the editor of the *Jerusalem Post* accusing Rapoport of "misrepresentation, intentional 'errors' and personal affronts (not only with regard to myself but also maligning others in Israel and the United States)" (Goldfoot 1984).

While Goldfoot might have had second thoughts about his evangelical friends, however, they were more than willing to participate in projects aimed at rebuilding the Temple. The Reverend Jim DeLoach of Houston, Texas, and another board member were quoted as saying that "we know there was gentile involvement in the financing and building of both the First and Second Temples. So why not the Third?" (Rapoport 1984). DeLoach, according to Rapoport's article, distributed a prospectus written by the board outlining the foundation's contemplated projects, including financial support for Yeshivat Ataret-Cohanim, where the rituals of the Temple were being studied in "preparation for the construction of the Third Temple in Jerusalem." The Reverend Jan Willem van der Hoeven, the spokesman for the Christian Embassy in Jerusalem, one of the most prominent evangelical groups in the city, indicated that he was most disturbed by the ambivalence of the Israelis themselves toward the Temple Mount. "The Israelis are too goyified," he said (Rapoport 1984).

It is almost a certainty that these understandings and possible political activities among American evangelicals will multiply as the city moves closer to the millennium of 2000.

BACK TO
THE CENTER

Today it appears as though Labor has delivered the PLO to the Camp David accords, which the PLO rejected nearly 20 years ago. But there are three major differences between the Oslo accords and the accords hammered out by President Jimmy Carter with Prime Minister Menachem Begin and President Anwar Sadat. First, Camp David was fashioned over the heads of the Palestinians. The Oslo accords have the direct involvement of Arafat and the Palestinian National Authority. Second, Camp David promised only limited autonomy for the Palestinians. Oslo implied the establishment of a Palestinian state at the end of the process. Third, Jerusalem was on the table in the Oslo accords in the sense that the third stage of the process would resolve the issues of the refugees, the settlements, and the city that both Palestinians and Israelis claimed as their capital. Now, two of three major differences have been eliminated. A former general in the Israel Defense

Forces, Benjamin ben-Eliezer, who was nicknamed "Fuad" by his troops and "the Bulldozing Builder" by the settlers while he held the portfolio of construction in the Rabin-Peres government, was heard to ask a Jewish settler about what was in the Oslo II agreements. "A lot of committees," came the reply. "Excellent!" ben-Eliezer exclaimed, "We can slow this up for years."

President Clinton concluded his memorial speech at the funeral of Yitzhak Rabin by saying, "Shalom, chaver." In the tortuous months following the assassination, this phrase, "Shalom, chaver," gave many Israelis solace, and it became one of the slogans Labor returned to over and over again in the election campaign. After Peres's defeat, we heard a new goodbye: "Shalom, shalom" ("Farewell, peace").

Without a state, without a post in Jerusalem, Arafat's position will become weaker and weaker. He will be forced to be more dependent on repression as the mechanism for his rule. Ifrach Zilberman, a scholar at the Hebrew University's Truman Institute and one of the most astute students of the religious culture and politics of the Palestinians, suggested to us in May 1996 that Arafat appears more and more as the classic embodiment of the ra'is ("head" or "chief"), which goes back to pre-Islamic times as one of the terms for a tribal chieftain. The ra'is is the head of the polity and his power is determined by his ability to replicate himself throughout his community. This may be done by sheer physical force and power or through the economy of patronage. Arafat uses both and is the classic

Islamic ruler. Since his return to Gaza, he has set up nine separate intelligence services. "Palestinians are fearful," Zilberman commented, "because he watches everything." Arafat has spent little time in the last two years in the West Bank, and many argue that he chose to center his operations in Gaza, where he can operate easily as a dictator, given the predominance of refugees and the consequent importance of political parties. This situation differs from that on the West Bank, where civil society is more developed and people are more able to resist Arafat's demands because of the extensive power of the great Palestinian families.

Arafat's leadership depends on his ability to deliver economically and politically while repressing all significant opposition. Hamas has always maintained that Arafat would never obtain a state. Now they appear to have been proven correct. If Arafat cannot produce what all Palestinians consider the bare minimum, Arafat's only possibility is to use these four or more years of the Netanyahu government to develop a new society, the real infrastructure of a state waiting to be birthed, and a new economy. But with Hamas's return to terror and perhaps new political and even military power to challenge the Palestinian Authority and to carry out terrorism inside Israel, the climate for investment, whether by private firms or international agencies, is not particularly propitious.

Right after Dr. Baruch Goldstein murdered Muslims praying in the al-Ibrahimiya mosque in Hebron—a mosque that contains the tombs of

Abraham and Sarah, Isaac and Re-becca—a substantial portion of the Labor government's cabinet supported removing all Jews from the city of Abraham. Although the government backed away from this idea, religious Zionists, mindful that they may not be able to sustain popular Israeli sup-port for their settlements in Nablus or Hebron, have increasingly cen-tered their attention on Jerusalem as the most productive battlefield to stop territorial partition. There is a pervasive and primordial Israeli con-sensus on undivided Israeli sover-eignty over Jerusalem, which Netan-yahu exploited to the fullest to defeat Peres.

Between the National Religious Party, United Torah Jewry, and Shas, the religious parties captured 23 seats in the New Knesset, 7 more than they held in 1992. They did not wait long before exercising their new power to assert the primacy of Jeru-salem's sanctity. In early July, the National Religious Party's transpor-tation minister, Yitzhak Levy, or-dered the closure of Jerusalem's Bar Ilan Street for 10 hours on Shabbat and holidays on a trial basis for four months. Bar Ilan Street is one of the major east-west thoroughfares on the northern side of the city, and it cuts through the most densely populated *haredi* sections of Jerusalem. While the High Court temporarily set the minister's order aside and asked that he show cause, there were almost immediate confrontations between the *haredim* (Orthodox Jews who deny the state theological legitimacy) and the secularists at the major in-tersections along the road. The con-frontations quickly grew, with as many as 150,000 people squaring off with nasty rhetoric, pushing and shoving, and throwing rocks on every Shabbat during July and August. *Haredi* wall posters proclaimed, "We will give our lives for [Shabbat]" and "The Torah faithful will shake the world. The sound of their cries will echo around the globe, wherever there are Jews" (Greenberg 1996). The mounted police were forced to wade into the crowds of *haredim* and secularists, and water canons were used to disperse the demonstrators. It was an ugly scene in which secular drivers screamed, "Dogs! Garbage!" at the *haredim*, who responded with chants of "Nazi" against the police. For many, it was reminiscent of the protracted struggle to control the road linking Ramot to central Jerusa-lem in the late 1970s and early 1980s.

Some initially thought the confron-tations were simply about whether the secularists who live in the north-ern reaches of Jerusalem would be able to cross the city on Shabbat and religious holidays. This may have been the case with earlier confronta-tions on the Ramot road. But in the ensuing decade, new roads were built that connected the area of French Hill, in the north, to the central city, as well as new highways that linked northern Jerusalem directly to the coastal plain and Tel Aviv and also to the western city at the Givat Shaul western entrance. Closing Bar Ilan for 10 hours or for all of Shabbat would not cut the city in two or create a major inconvenience for the secu-larists who wanted to drive for what-ever purpose. This was simply another battle between the Jews over the na-ture of the holy city. Ornan Yekutieli, now in his second term as a Meretz city councilman, described the conflict precisely in this way: "We are not only fighting for Bar Ilan Street. Jerusalem is our face to the world. The question is whether it will be the face of Los Angeles, Paris, London and other Western cities, or whether it will be Tehran. The religious want to take steps toward Tehran and further from the world I want to belong to" (Miller 1996).

Within the first weeks of the election, Netanyahu's government increased pressure on the Palestinians in Jerusalem by threatening to close down the New Orient House. Many Palestinians commented that the New Orient House would be the first litmus test for the Netanyahu government's commitment to the peace process. For some, the New Orient House was also the fuse that could ignite what they called a "second *intifada*." During the campaign, Netanyahu had argued that the New Orient House was serving as a base for the Palestinian National Authority's activities in the city. He charged that Peres was not being strict enough with Palestinians on the stipulations of the Oslo accords, which confined such activity to the areas under Palestinian authority. The event that triggered the Israeli threat was the planned diplomatic visit in July of Hervé de Charette, the French foreign minister. Israel's pressure was sufficient to cause de Charette to cancel his visit a few short days before it was to take place (Makovsky 1996). The New Orient House remained a problem, however. Ziad Abu Zayyad, a longtime Fatah activist and an elected member to the Palestinian

Legislative Council from Jerusalem, indicated in an interview that while the peace process was not based on the New Orient House, the closure of the house would be "interpreted as a negative step by the Israeli government. And if it comes at this time, [when] there is a standstill in the peace process, it may constitute the death blow to the process." Israel expanded its demands to include three other offices—the Palestinian Central Bureau of Statistics branch office, the Higher Islamic Council, and Higher Education Minister Hanan Ashrawi's personal office. Arafat fired back that in the Oslo discussions, Israel had agreed to "accept and respect the Palestinian institutions in Jerusalem." Hasan Tahboub, the Palestinian Authority's Islamic and religious affairs minister, immediately responded that the Higher Islamic Council had been created in 1967, was not an office of the Palestinian National Authority, and clearly fell under the preexisting institutions that Israel had pledged to respect. Faisal Husayni noted that the New Orient House had been operating as the headquarters of the Palestinian peace delegations before the PLO and Israel signed the Oslo accords and added that, ironically, the New Orient House began its operations during the Likud-led government of Yitzhak Shamir.

The issue of the New Orient House was momentarily defused when Chairman Arafat agreed in his meeting with Foreign Minister David Levy in July 1996 to halt any political activity there (Jehl 1996). Internal Security Minister Avigdor Kahalani reiterated the Israeli position in speaking to the Knesset as Levy met with Arafat. The situation intensified once again when Hattem Abdel Khader, who had been elected to the Palestinian Legislative Council in January, announced that he would open an office, the living room of his home, for his constituency in Bet Hanina in northern Jerusalem. Kahalani reached a compromise with Abdel Khader in which he indicated that no political activity would be initiated from this office. This was not strong enough for Netanyahu, who immediately told the internal security minister to close the office. The cabinet communiqué quoted Netanyahu as saying, "I gave an unequivocal directive to the Minister of Public Security to close the office of Hattem Abdul Khader. . . . In the wake of the warning order, the police [were] charged with preventing activity at the office, period. I gave clear directives on this matter, and I request the Public Security Minister to [see to it] that these directives be carried out."

The *haram al-sharif* is the symbolic center of the Palestinian nation in a way that the Temple Mount is not for the Israelis. Most Israelis see the unbuilt Temple, in fact, as a potential theocratic challenge to the democratic foundations of their national state. Israelis are forbidden by the ruling of the Chief Rabbinate from entering the compound and by Israeli law from even praying there. For most Zionists, rebuilding the Temple is either something they would rather not contemplate or a project best left to God. Jerusalem's former mayor, Teddy Kollek, often declared that he would not mind if, one day, an Arab flag flew from the ramparts of the

haram. In contrast, the defense of Israeli sovereignty over, and the expansion of Jewish ritual rights regarding, the *haram* has become a rallying cry for large portions of the religious Zionist community. After the Oslo accords were signed, when Arafat announced he intended to lead a pilgrimage of a million of his fellow Palestinians to the *haram*, Jewish settlement leaders announced they would be able to bring hundreds of thousands of Israelis into the streets to stop him. In this, they had the energetic support of the new Likud mayor, Ehud Olmert, who declared that he would have Arafat arrested if he tried to enter his city. More radical religious Zionists, whether from Gush Emunim or from Meir Kahane's Kach and its successors, have repeatedly looked to profanation, if not destruction, of its sites as an apocalyptic tactic to stop the peace process.

On both sides of the city, the struggle against splitting sovereignty will lead to efforts to define the conflict as a religious war, to build the Jewish and the Islamic sanctity of Jerusalem, and for each group to profane the sacred sites of the other. Ever since the *intifada* began in late 1987, Hamas has struck repeatedly in Jerusalem using knives and, now, human martyrs wired with explosive charges. As the peace process moves into its final stages, the city invites carnage. Without an agreement on Jerusalem that is acceptable to the Palestinians, those Islamic forces that oppose the peace process will likely be victorious. Such an agreement, however, risks pushing radical religious Zionist Israelis toward violent resistance at the center, in Zion.

Note

1. The old Yishuv comprises the Jews who settled in Palestine before Zionism, most of whom were very religious.

References

Chick, *Support Your Local Jew*. Chino, CA: Chick, n.d.

Elon, Amos. 1989. *Jerusalem: City of Mirrors*. Boston: Little, Brown.

Evans, Mike. 1984a. *JerUSAlem DC*. Bedford, TX: Bedford Books and Mike Evans Ministries.

———. 1984b. *Partners in Prophecy '85—Partner Devotional Guide*. Bedford, TX: Mike Evans Ministries.

Goldfoot, Stanley, 1984. Letter to the Editor. *Jerusalem Post*, 3 July.

Grabar, Oleg. 1996. *The Shape of the Holy: Early Islamic Jerusalem*. Princeton, NJ: Princeton University Press.

Greenberg, Joel. 1996. Jerusalem Road Is Secular-Religious Battleground. *New York Times*, 15 July.

Hertzberg, Arthur. 1996. Jerusalem and Zionism. In *City of the Great King: Jerusalem from David to the Present*, ed. Nitza Rosovsky. Cambridge, MA: Harvard University Press.

Jehl, Douglas. 1996. Likud Hard-Liner, in a First, Sees Arafat. *New York Times*, 24 July.

LaHaye, Tim. 1984. *The Coming Peace in the Middle East*. Grand Rapids, MI: Zondervan.

Lindsey, Hal, with C. C. Carlson. 1970. *The Late Great Planet Earth*. Grand Rapids, MI: Zondervan.

Makovsky, David. 1996. French FM Won't Visit Orient House. *Jerusalem Post*, 23 July.

Miller, Marjorie. 1996. "Sabbath War" Flares in Holy City. *Los Angeles Times*, 26 July.

Rapoport, Louis. 1984. The Temple Mount Connection. *Jerusalem Post*, 15 June.

Rosen-Ayalon, Miriam. 1989. *The Early Islamic Monuments of al-Haram al-Sharif: An Iconographic Study*. Qedem: Monographs of the Institute of Archaeology of the Hebrew University of Jerusalem, vol. 28. Jerusalem: Magnes Press.

Shepherd, Naomi. 1987. *The Zealous Intruders*. San Francisco: Harper & Row.

Twain, Mark. [1869] 1899. *The Innocents Abroad or the New Pilgrims' Progress Being Some Account of the Steamship Quaker City's Pleasure Excursion to Europe and the Holy Land*. New York: Harper & Brothers.

ANNALS, *AAPSS*, **558**, July 1998

The Latino Religious Resurgence

By ANTHONY M. STEVENS-ARROYO

ABSTRACT: The study of religion among Latinos and Latinas has often suffered from unstated sociological premises. Sometimes it was approached as an anachronistic religious expression doomed to assimilation; at other times, it was viewed in a romantic light as folk customs without importance to religion in the United States. This article views religion among Latinos and Latinas as part of a more general social history of the United States. The acceptance of Latino religious expression as a uniquely American one entails a rejection of manifest destiny and other key premises of U.S. culture, including assimilation. Explained here are the internal migration of Latinos to urban centers in the 1950s and how the response of churches prepared for the emergence of autonomous forms of Latino religion within the major denominations. Current population trends are described, and three key areas for further research are profiled.

Anthony M. Stevens-Arroyo is professor of Puerto Rican and Latino studies at Brooklyn College. He is author of the award-winning Prophets Denied Honor *(1981), recently described as "a landmark of Catholic literature." A frequent contributor to both academic publications and journals of opinion, he served as general editor of four books of the Program for the Analysis of Religion Among Latinas/os (1994-95).*

THE study of religion necessarily involves a study of the milieu in which religion functions. Religion among Latinos and Latinas today[1] has been shaped by manifest destiny. More than a century ago, in the wars with Mexico (1846-48) and Spain (1898), the U.S. public acted upon their perceptions as presented in newspapers and as preached from pulpits. As recapitulated in *Our America*, the 1891 book by Josiah Strong, an evangelical preacher, it was God's will that the United States expand into Latin America in order to impose the Protestant values of "the Anglo-Saxon race" upon "Romanism, Spanish ignorance and superstition" (Silva Gotay 1994). The nineteenth-century marriage between Calvinist predestination and jingoist greed resulted in a nationalistic providentialism that justified base political and economic policies with religious fervor. The premise that invasion and conquest were not only permissible violations of international law but somehow beneficial favors to the conquered has wormed its way into the core of how most citizens of the United States view their relationship with Latinos born in this country. In an 1898 issue of *The Annals* of the American Academy of Political and Social Science, H. H. Powers mixed religion with politics when he claimed a war to take colonies was "a revelation rather than a revolution" (cited in Nagel 1971, 323-24). At the end of the century, as at its midpoint during the Mexican-American War, manifest destiny legitimated military conquest.

But while the acquisition in 1898 of a tropical island with strategic advantages, like the earlier annexation, in 1848, of huge tracts of land with invaluable agricultural capacity and mineral resources, was the event celebrated in public view, a problematic effect was the incorporation of the native Spanish-speaking residents of the colonies. When the United States annexed these territories, the Spanish-speaking residents there became "Latinos and Latinas"—persons of Latin American heritage who were born and raised in the United States, since they could no longer claim a foreign country as homeland. Viewed in the sharp light cast by these historical events, the origin of the Latino presence is unique in comparison with all other ethnic population groups, save the Native Americans. It was not immigration of the Spanish-speaking to the United States that initially placed Latinos and Latinas under the Stars and Stripes; rather, military invasion hoisted the U.S. flag over the Latino homelands. Texas, the Southwest, California, and Puerto Rico are "conquered America" (Acuña 1972; Maldonado Denis [1969] 1972).

The treaties of peace allowed the conquered lands to be viewed as a free bounty for those who spoke English. Thousands of wagon trains of English-speaking settlers poured into the conquered Mexican territories. The new settlers, even where they were a numerical minority in comparison with the original inhabitants, became the ruling class of the invaded lands. This was a civil invasion: its arms were new laws of banking, real estate, compulsory education, and language proficiency in English. With these weapons, the English-speaking immigrants marginalized the Spanish-speaking residents, much as the force of arms earlier had subdued the Mexican and Spanish soldiers (Weber 1992; Griswold del Castillo 1979).

Civil religion complemented the vision of U.S. culture offered by Frederick Jackson Turner in an 1891 article (Nagel 1971, 263-66). The "spirit that struggled against wilderness" was the true essence of the American character for Turner. Manifest destiny contributed a religious component to the conquest and the struggle, because Latino religion, with its myriad Catholic devotions and processions, was by analogy a "wilderness" destined for attack and elimination. These ideas were carried over to Puerto Rico, which became the testing ground for a coordinated effort in the Comity Agreements of 1900 and 1902 to "remove the island and its inhabitants from Romanism and superstition" as quickly as possible (Moore 1969).

It is no surprise that manifest destiny legitimated the ascendancy of Protestants and Protestantism over the existing Latino culture and its social institutions. What is ironic is the role that U.S. Catholicism played in the same process. Offered the opportunity to assume a role as the religious vehicle for nationalist sentiment, Catholicism tended instead to "Americanize" the Latino population no less than Protestantism did (Stevens-Arroyo 1995a; Silva Gotay 1994). Texas, New Mexico, and California at midcentury, just like Puerto Rico at the end of the period, were not seen as destined to become pockets of Catholic nationalism as in a conquered Poland or Ireland. Like many

of their Protestant counterparts, the Catholic bishops viewed the Latino homelands as areas requiring missionary work, even though Catholicism had been in Puerto Rico since 1511, longer than anywhere else in the hemisphere.

These efforts, like most human endeavors, met with mixed success. The reaction at the grass roots to such ecclesiastical impositions formed the core of what can be called "Latino religion." Because it was protected over the course of a century and a half from secular interventions, religion provided a space for Latino consciousness that was not readily available in education, law, or politics. Much as some sociologists developed the notion of internal colonialism to distinguish the annexation of Latino homelands from U.S. interventions in Latin America (Bailey and Flores 1973; Barrera 1974), I have coined the term "pious colonialism" to describe the practices of churches that used the gospel as a tool of Americanization (Stevens-Arroyo 1995a, 1995b).

FROM MISSIONARY TO REVOLUTIONARY

Beginning in 1921 with the publication of his first important book, Hubert Eugene Bolton developed a view of the Southwest as "borderlands" that refuted some of the premises of Turner's frontier thesis. In Bolton's perception, the borderlands were not so much battlefields where the English-speaking values inevitably triumphed but stew pots where each element flavored the others (Weber 1992, 353-55). Bolton's influence, although principally focused on the field of history, prepared the way for twentieth-century sociological study of Latinos.

Interest in the transition of a society as it confronted modernization spurred an effort to study Puerto Rico in the years immediately after World War II. The plans of the insular regime to open the island to investment and a manufacturing economy presented social science with a unique opportunity. Combining history, sociology, and anthropological case studies of typical towns in each of the significant agricultural regions of Puerto Rico, *The People of Puerto Rico* provided a cohesive interpretation of one of the Latino homelands (Steward et al. 1956). A little more than two decades later, Leo Grebler, Joan Moore, and Ralph Guzmán undertook a similar multidisciplinary study, *The Mexican-American People* (1970).

These two major works in empirical science stand as classics in a genre that studied Puerto Ricans on the island and the people of Mexican heritage in Texas, the Southwest, and California. But while these two masterworks studied the two largest Latino population groups in situ, there was a need to examine what happened to Latinos when they migrated to U.S. cities. In the metropolis of New York, the mass migration of Puerto Ricans in the period 1946-64 provoked sociological interest. C. Wright Mills produced *The Puerto Rican Journey* (1950) with Clarence Senior and Rose Kohn Goldsen. Together with Oscar Handlin's *Uprooted* (1951) and *Newcomers* (1959), this work reflected a new sensitivity to cultural persistence and questioned presumptions about assimilation. Latino urban migration came to be treated in much the same way that Bolton's notion of borderlands had approached Mexican Americans. When Nathan Glazer and Daniel P. Moynihan published *Beyond the Melting Pot* in 1963, the thesis that Latinos and others needed to hold on to vestiges of traditional culture had become the reigning sociological interpretation of urban ethnic groups. Metaphors like the "stew pot" or "mosaic of individual cultures" were embraced by sociology not only as the paradigm for the Latino presence but as the explanation for much of immigrant accommodation among Euro-American groups as well. Now accommodation by both sides was preferred to the unilateral surrender by newcomers connoted by assimilation.

While some sociologists bemoaned that culture was often fodder for capitalist progress and inevitable secularization, others saw religion as a saving grace. Will Herberg popularized the idea that civil religion provided a shelter for immigrants between the backwardness of traditions and the secularization of society. In his influential *Protestant, Catholic, Jew* (1955), Herberg argued that while the immigrants were changed by the American experience, they also managed to transform their religious institutions into unifying forces for social cohesion as Americans with common bonds.

The stew-pot metaphor was transferred to the religious experiences of Latinos and greatly influenced the missionary efforts of the churches, Protestant and Catholic. Assimilation was no longer a prerequisite for church attentions. Policy was formed on the basis of this social science, and innovations such as training large numbers of Irish Catholic clergy to speak Spanish and to provide social services in neighborhood churches were the results (Fitzpatrick 1995). Specialized cultural training schools taught non-Latino church personnel what life was like in the Latino homelands so that adjustments could be made when the Latinos arrived in the big cities (Díaz-Stevens 1993a). The harsh contours of manifest destiny had been replaced by a gentler, kinder notion of Americanization through religion. One finds in the work of the late Fordham Jesuit Joseph P. Fitzpatrick a chronicle of this enlightened approach, which altered the missionary effort among Latinos, presaging the end of pious colonialism. Many parishes, reported Fitzpatrick, no longer rejected linguistic and ethnic groups from the English-speaking segment but integrated two or more diverse groups under the roof of a single religious institution (Fitzpatrick 1971). Assimilation into U.S. society was inevitable, but the Catholic church could sweeten the process by providing a religious environment with vestiges of the homeland customs and language (Fitzpatrick 1987).

Changes in church policies during the 1950s and 1960s had an effect on Latino religion. Steward's study of Puerto Rico in 1948 (Steward et al. 1956) had approached traditional religion as folklore and predicted the eclipse of the island's Catholicism in the face of modernization. Twenty years later, however, this was not the conclusion of Grebler, Moore, and Guzmán's study (1970), which was undertaken after the United Farm Workers (UFW) under César Chávez had organized its strike in 1965. One member of the research team, Patrick McNamara, was able to include in his report the response of clergy to *la causa*, as the struggle of the UFW came to be known. His insightful observations (McNamara 1970) and subsequent analysis (McNamara 1973) suggested that Latino activism had an ally in the Catholic religion. Along with the long-standing progressive social activism of liberal Protestantism, the leadership of the Catholic church had chosen to advocate a Latino political cause.

LATINO INTERNAL
MIGRATION

The success of these ecclesiastical initiatives seemed to produce contradictory effects. By the time that Grebler and his colleagues' work was published in 1970, Latino Catholics no longer espoused the integration championed by their advocates among Catholic liberals. Instead, the cry was for native Latino and Latina leaders to replace the Euro-Americans in posts from the episcopate to local parish leadership. The Latino and Latina Catholic leaders used militant demonstrations to apply pressure on the hierarchy and force adoption of these measures (Stevens-Arroyo 1980, 123-33). An appropriate summary of the seismic shift in attitudes toward what was required for the study of Latinos among sociologists is rendered by Patrick McNamara (1995). Commitment and solidarity with Latino causes was valued, and it was expected to be a quality possessed almost exclusively by Latino and Latina scholars. In other works (Stevens-Arroyo 1994; Díaz-Stevens and Stevens-Arroyo 1998), I call this "cultural idiosyncrasy." It was a type of Latino religious separatism that developed in parallel with social movements of the radical 1960s and 1970s. Carrying the argument of Mario García (1989) to this new generation, it could be suggested that the cohort of religious leaders who came of age after 1967 tended to repeat in ecclesiastical terms the demands made in secular society by political and educational leaders. Cultural idiosyncrasy stipulated that only Latinos could understand or represent Latinos. When repeated in a church context, this message had a revolutionary impact on Catholics and Protestants alike. Although many of the ideas espoused by Latino leaders were similar to those of previous generations (García 1989; Stevens-Arroyo 1980, 77-96), the seeds fell on more fertile soil. The institutions had to listen to Latino leaders in ways that they had not done before because rising numbers threatened the status quo. Latinos demanded "de-Americanization" of the American churches (Stevens-Arroyo 1995b).

In my opinion, the mid-twentieth-century urban migration of Latinos and Latinas ought to be seen as one of the significant internal migrations of U.S. history. Admittedly, internal migration to urban centers was not confined to the 1950s. Nonetheless, the major influx of this internal migration began during the economic boom after World War II (Stevens-Arroyo and Díaz Ramírez 1982). Latinos from Texas, the Southwest, and

Puerto Rico, who already were citizens, migrated in huge numbers to urban centers. This migration of Latinos and Latinas is as much an internal migration as the push to the frontier by Euro-Americans in the nineteenth century. Just as the image of the wagon train winding its way to the West is ingrained as a symbol in the U.S. cultural psyche, this migration of Latinos and Latinas to urban centers has created a cultural awareness that is deep and lasting among Latinos and Latinas (Díaz-Stevens 1993a).[2] The Latino internal migrations may come to rank in importance with the Okie migration to California described in John Steinbeck's *Grapes of Wrath* and the migration from the postbellum South that is being reconstructed by serious scholars of the African American experience. To the core Latino communities formed during the post–World War II internal migrations have been added today's explosive international migrations, so that these core communities experience both continuity and renewal.

THE SPANISH LANGUAGE IN THE CHURCHES

Grasping the nature of the Latino internal migration until 1964 helps explain why the churches preserved Latino culture and the Spanish language rather than eliminate them. Unlike earlier internal migrations of Okies and African Americans from the southern states, Latinos and Latinas spoke a language other than English. Many Latinos are bilingual: while proficient in Spanish, they also speak English. There is a trend among

Latino social scientists to view the persistence of the Spanish language as the battlefield of resistance to imperialism (Flores 1993). Rather than blame the schools for "not teaching English properly" or accuse the students of lacking sufficient intelligence to understand English, it is possible to see the persistence of the Spanish language as a badge of social identity (Stevens-Arroyo and Díaz-Stevens 1993a). As long as a person can speak Spanish, he or she is usually considered by peers to have preserved a Latino cultural heritage (Stevens-Arroyo 1994).

It is through the Spanish language that religion provided an identity for Latinos and Latinas and helped them form communities in the urban centers during the post–World War II migrations. The church was where Spanish was employed to talk about life's most important duties; where an elevated diction was enjoyed; where congregants sang traditional hymns in the tongue of the motherland. Catholics still attended masses said in Latin, but all other services, like those of the Protestant and Pentecostal congregations, were in Spanish. Baptisms, weddings, and funerals, like Christmas, First Communions, and Good Friday, were special occasions when even the lax and fallen-away were brought together as family (Stevens-Arroyo and Díaz-Stevens 1993b). These church services forged a communitarian awareness of being Latino in the big city, even though uprooted from the traditionally agricultural societies of the homelands (Díaz-Stevens 1993b).

On this basis, we can separate the period of church attentions to the internal migration until 1967 from what has since occurred (Stevens-Arroyo and Díaz Ramírez 1982; Rodríguez 1989). This periodization is based on the singular importance to Latino religion of the decree by the Second Vatican Council of the Catholic church to provide the liturgy in the vernacular, that is, in the common language of the people. In most countries of the Catholic world, this simply meant the abandonment of Latin as a liturgical language for the official tongue of that country. But in the United States, the decree was interpreted to mean that the Spanish-speaking parishioners should have services in Spanish—which was their vernacular—rather than in English. By fiat, the United States became a bilingual—and even multilingual—country in ecclesiastical terms.

This drastic change in Catholic liturgy occurred at a time of major political and social changes in the United States. The Civil Rights Act of 1964 outlawed voter restrictions based on language as well as those that erected racial barriers. The War on Poverty legislation that began in 1965 provided government funds to community agencies run by Latinos and Latinas. The Immigration and Nationality Act of 1965 permitted a huge shift in Western Hemisphere migrations that brought new immigrants from Latin America. Finally, the Bilingual Education Act of 1967 established Spanish as a language of instruction in the public schools.

THE LATINO RELIGIOUS
RESURGENCE

Taken as a whole, these laws of government and church radically restructured religion among Latinos and Latinas in the United States, in ways as striking as those described by Robert Wuthnow (1988) for other Americans in religion. A new mentality emerged among the cohort of Latino and Latina leaders who came of age during the 1960s. During the period that began in 1967, when the strike of the UFW came into national prominence, there was a Latino religious resurgence (Díaz-Stevens and Stevens-Arroyo 1998). The resurgence brought a remarkable growth spurt for Latino religious organizations, ending as church leadership in the 1980s codified new policies on cultural and linguistic autonomy for Latinos. The Latino resurgence was one of many social movements by peoples of color that challenged the U.S. vision of itself and the historical role of religion. These movements shook the confidence in a civil religion capable of embracing the experiences of all Americans (Bellah 1975).

A restructured Latino religion animates the institutions that today serve not only the children from the internal migrants of the 1950s and 1960s but also the Latin American immigrants of the 1980s and 1990s. The restructuring seems to have changed the trajectory of the immigrants' entry into U.S. society. The Spanish language is maintained not only in church services but also in bilingual education, national television networks that transmit in the Spanish language, an active cultural expression among Latinos, commercial services that cater to Spanish-speaking clientele, and a professional leadership among Latinos in public and civic agencies (Stevens-Arroyo

1994). Church policies have been redesigned not to Americanize, as before, but to preserve Latino identity.

There is now a symbiosis between Latinos and incoming Latin Americans: the greater the number of Spanish-speaking persons, the greater the need for professionals trained to serve them in commercial, public, and educational agencies. Latinos with university training are likely to identify with the Spanish-speaking newcomers because that identification increases job opportunities and social advancement. At the same time, the children of Latin Americans born in the United States become Latinos and Latinas. Intermarriage between the nationality groups may make the Latino identity stronger than any particular national one. For instance, the child of a Puerto Rican father and a Dominican mother is neither wholly Puerto Rican nor wholly Dominican and is likely to prefer "Latino" as a cultural tag.

DEMOGRAPHIC TRENDS

Demographic growth is the result of new births and immigration. Latino birthrates are higher than in the general U.S. population and are the principal reason for yearly increases in the number of Latinos. When Puerto Ricans on the island are included, nearly 70 percent of Latinos in 1990 were born as U.S. citizens: the majority of us are not immigrants (Enchautegui 1995, 6; Moore 1994, 9 passim). But although the Latino, or U.S.-born, population is more than twice as large as the immigrant, or foreign-born, population, it is not evenly distributed. As a result, in some areas, such as San Diego and New York City, the foreign-born Latin Americans outnumber the Latinos; elsewhere, the conditions may be reversed. Sunseri reports that nearly 95 percent of New Mexican respondents to his questionnaire came from families that had been living in New Mexico between 1840 and 1865 (Sunseri 1979, 44-46).

The combination of high birthrates and heavy immigration has produced an explosion in the Latino presence in the United States (Moore 1994). From 1970 to 1990, the number of Latinos in the United States doubled. The 1997 report of the U.S. Bureau of the Census states that by 2010, Latinos will be more numerous in the United States than African Americans. By 2020, there are expected to be 47 million Latinos, or nearly 15 percent of the total U.S. population; by 2050, there will be 95 million Latinos, or 25 percent of the people in the country (U.S. Bureau of the Census 1997; Seelye 1997). Moreover, the high birthrates and lower median age for the Latino population—not immigration—constitute the principal factors for demographic growth. In other words, even if tomorrow the borders with Latin America were closed, Latino population growth would still outstrip Euro-American and African American rates of increase, although not by as much.

The projected growth in the number of Latinos and Latinas is greatly influenced by the relative youth of the population. The difference in the percentages under the age of 18 is striking: only 23 percent of Euro-Americans (whites) as compared to 35 percent of Latinos. The 1990 census shows that Latino families are larger; they are younger; they have more children; and they are growing at a dramatically faster rate (53 percent) than the non-Latino population (7 percent).

LATINOS IN POVERTY

The rapid growth of the Latino population, and differences between the foreign- and native-born are not the only challenges faced by the churches. Another is financial well-being. Latinos and Latinas are poor and becoming poorer, especially compared to other demographic groups. This can be seen in income and poverty statistics. From 1992 to 1995, both African Americans and Euro-Americans showed increases in median family income (10 percent and 2 percent, respectively) (Baugher and Lamison-White 1996), while median income for Latinos dropped 7 percent (Baugher and Lamison-White 1996; Goldberg 1997). Between 1993 and 1995, income increased by 4 percent in African American households but decreased 5 percent for Latino households (Baugher and Lamison-White 1996). From 1974 to 1995, the number of African American families living in poverty grew 44 percent; the number of Euro-American families in poverty grew 49 percent; but the number of Latino families in poverty grew by 222 percent (Díaz-Stevens and Stevens-Arroyo 1998). Thus, in 1998, Latinos stand as a statistically poorer group than African Americans and Euro-Americans, and their position is likely to worsen in the next decade.

Poverty is often attributable to single-parent households. It is alarming, then, that even among Latino families with both parents living under the same roof, the poverty growth rate increased 189 percent between 1974 and 1995. That is a dramatically higher pace than for Euro-American families with two parents, for whom the rate of increase was a much more modest 30 percent. Strikingly, African American families with both parents increased their income between 1974 and 1995, making for a negative poverty growth rate (−28 percent). Keeping the family together will not by itself end Latino poverty. The group of married people worst off in 1992 were the Mexican Americans, having overtaken the endemic levels of Puerto Rican families.

Enchautegui (1995, 13) points out that, even with comparable levels of unemployment, Latinos have a proportionally lower participation in welfare and food-stamp programs than either Euro-Americans or African Americans. It might be expected that churches will encourage Latinos and Latinas to enroll in the dwindling number of government programs that benefit the poor, although the current climate in Washington makes this an uncertain remedy for poverty. In contrast to other groups, the Latino wage earner receives less pay, has more children to feed, and is less likely to have a spouse who brings home an additional paycheck (although tending to have a third worker in the household). As Moore has pointed out (1994; Moore and Pinderhughes 1993), poverty in the Latino barrio is long-standing and many of the char-

acteristics of the black underclass described by Harvard scholar William Julius Wilson (1987) do not apply to Latinos and Latinas.

In sum, the indicators of poverty point in the direction of a widening gap between Latinos and the general population. With minimal progress on the educational front and almost no promise of governmental intervention in the form of welfare or similar programs, the prospects of alleviating poverty seem dim. In this environment, religion as a road to empowerment, and church institutions as tools for community organizing, become indispensable factors for improvement for the Latino future (Stevens-Arroyo 1997).

INSTITUTIONAL CHANGES

The religious institution most profoundly altered by the Latino presence in the United States has been the Catholic church. Despite intense efforts at the Protestantization of Latinos throughout the nineteenth century and into the first third of the twentieth century, 65 percent of Latinos identify as Catholic (Kosmin and Lachman 1993). Because so many Latinos and Latinas are Catholic, many Latino cultural traits and traditional customs have sprung from Catholicism. Social science is fortunate that Latinos and Latinas have begun to examine the contemporary transformation of U.S. religious institutions by the encounter with Latinos. As in so many other disciplines, scholars are no longer content with analyzing what the institutions have done for Latinos but are investigating what Latinos and Latinas have done for the institution. A key study in the genre is the prize-winning *Oxcart Catholicism on Fifth Avenue* by Ana María Díaz-Stevens (1993a).

Díaz-Stevens's masterful analysis points out that many of the pastoral policies affecting Puerto Rican Catholics in New York were instituted out of necessity. For instance, there were few native clergy, so lay persons were encouraged to assume tasks within the Spanish-speaking segments of the church that had been ordinarily restricted to priests and religious sisters. Archdiocesan resources were assigned to movements and associations with the expectation of evangelizing Spanish-speaking migrants who were not practicing the faith. These measures created a Puerto Rican lay leadership that transcended control by individual pastors. But as Díaz-Stevens concludes, these initiatives, undertaken in the 1950s as temporary measures to respond to a missionary condition, by the 1980s had become the ordinary circumstances of all of New York's Catholics. The Euro-American church is now learning how to practice a clergy-poor Catholicism and how to create lay-led movements for evangelization to take up the slack created by the dearth of priests and religious sisters—experiences that are part of the Latino patrimony.

With the dramatic rise in numbers nationwide, Latinos are destined to become the majority of Catholics in the United States. Although existing church counts are not very reliable, it is safe to say that Latinos already outnumber the Irish Americans and the Italian Americans, respectively. By 2010, they will likely outnumber both groups combined. The eminent historian at the University of Notre Dame, Jay P. Dolan, predicts that Latinos will transform the Catholic church as dramatically in the twenty-first century as the Irish did during the nineteenth (Dolan 1992).

Nor is the impact of Latinos restricted to Catholicism. Major Protestant denominations in urban areas now include multiethnic congregations that include Latinos. Without Latino members, some of these city churches would be forced to close their doors. Pentecostalism has had a vigorous Latino membership virtually from its beginnings in Azuza Street in California in the first years of this century (Díaz-Stevens and Stevens-Arroyo 1998, 112-14). The 1991 National Survey of Religious Identification (Kosmin 1991) found that 3 percent of Latinos profess membership in a Pentecostal church. When added to evangelical and fundamentalist churches like the Assemblies of God, Southern Baptists, and Jehovah's Witnesses, as much as 13 percent of Latinos and Latinas—or half of all the Latinos who are not Catholics—belong to these denominations. Because such congregations are frequently small (with fewer than 300 members each), the number of these churches mushroomed from 1970 to 1990, along with the doubling of the Latino population. The leadership supplied by these churches represents a force more potent than membership numbers alone. There is evidence that as Latino Pentecostalism has flexed its muscles within denominational circles, it has moved in the direction of maintaining Latino culture and language. This trend is very similar to the Catholic experience and might indicate that denominational loyalties are less important than cultural ones (Stevens-Arroyo and Cadena 1995).

FURTHER RESEARCH

In conclusion, I would like to highlight areas for further research and investigation into the patterns of Latino religion. First, has the manifest destiny that seeped into U.S. civil religion now been replaced with a multicultural, multilingual model for religion in the United States? Will religion among Latinos be presented as the first and original Christianity in this country, as much an icon as the Pilgrims at Plymouth Rock? Any church efforts to correct current mythology would rank with the antislavery crusades of the mid-nineteenth century. The preservation, resistance, and eventual resurgence of Latino religion as a major actor on the American stage was not the result of Latin American immigration, just as the achievements of former slaves is not the consequence of immigration from Africa. The challenge to the sociology of religion is to incorporate the Latino experience as an American one without advocating that a single experience or expression will ever be able to accommodate the country's pluralism.

A second area for research is into the role of religious tradition as a modernizing force. Edward Shils (1981) has treated this issue extensively in a theoretical examination of the premises of secularization that have long underpinned Weberian and Durkheimian approaches to the sociology of religion. I would suggest that Latino religion offers specific examples of this ability to build from tradition modernizing social movements and organizations capable of pursuing group interests in a complex society. Perhaps most important, the Latino resurgence is a combination of various nationality groups, such as the Mexicans, Puerto Ricans, and Cubans (Stevens-Arroyo 1994). It remains to be seen if this tendency will produce separatist tensions as in conflicted parts of the world or if, instead, religion will integrate both Latinos and Euro-Americans (Barrera 1988; Díaz-Stevens and Stevens-Arroyo 1998).

Finally, the sociology of religion in the United States will have to cast an eye upon syncretism. Although the term "syncretism" conjures notions of an illicit mixture of Christianity with paganism or superstition, religious expression is constantly influenced by contact with other faiths. Today, culture as much as dogma assumes religious importance. The appearance of new religions among Latinos is a phenomenon of U.S. religious syncretism. For example, the African-derived Latino religions such as Santería are a phenomenon particular to the United States, where various nationality groups have encountered each other (Stevens-Arroyo and Pérez y Mena 1995). These mixtures have received considerable input from New Age and Afro-centered movements, so that today Santería can no longer be considered a religion practiced exclusively by Latinos. Moreover, it influences contemporary Catholic devotions, particularly among Caribbean peoples (Tweed

1996). I suspect that sociologists interested in these general trends will discover that religious syncretism in the United States is a part of the public role of religion in changing societies (Casanova 1994). Perhaps it will be possible to revisit the statement written a century ago in the pages of *The Annals* and state that Latino religion has provided both a "revelation" and a "revolution" (Powers, cited in Nagel 1971, 323-24).

Notes

1. A social science subfield focused on this topic has been developed through the efforts of the Program for the Analysis of Religion Among Latinas/os, which has been generously funded by the Lilly Endowment and the Pew Charitable Trusts.

2. The sociological importance of Latino literature about the migration experience needs to be explored systematically. See Díaz-Stevens (1996) for an important essay on this source for sociological reflection on Latino religion.

References

Acuña, Rodolfo. 1972. *Occupied America*. San Francisco: Canfield Press.

Bailey, Ronald and Guillermo V. Flores. 1973. Internal Colonialism and Racial Minorities. In *Structures of Dependency*, ed. Frank Bonilla and Robert Girling. Palo Alto, CA: Nairobi Press.

Barrera, Mario. 1974. The Barrio as an Internal Colony. In *La Causa Política: A Chicano Politics Reader*, ed. F. Chris Garcia. Notre Dame, IN: University of Notre Dame Press. First published in *Urban Affairs Annual Reviews* 6:465-98 (1972).

———. 1988. *Beyond Aztlán*. Notre Dame, IN: University of Notre Dame Press.

Baugher, Eleanor and Leatha Lamison-White. 1996. *Poverty in the United States: 1995*. Current Population Re-

ports, P60-194. Washington, DC: Department of Commerce, Bureau of the Census.

Bellah, Robert N. 1975. *The Broken Covenant: American Civil Religion in a Time of Trial*. New York: Seabury Press.

Casanova, José. 1994. *Public Religions in the Modern World*. Chicago: University of Chicago Press.

Díaz-Stevens, Ana María. 1993a. *Oxcart Catholicism on Fifth Avenue*. Notre Dame, IN: University of Notre Dame Press.

———. 1993b. The Saving Grace: The Matriarchal Core of Latino Catholicism. *Latino Studies Journal* 4(3):60-78.

———. 1996. In the Image and Likeness of God: Literature as Theological Reflection. In *Hispanic/Latino Theology: Challenge and Promise*, ed. Ada María Isasi-Díaz and Fernando F. Segovia. Minneapolis, MN: Fortress Press.

Díaz-Stevens, Ana María and Anthony M. Stevens-Arroyo. 1998. *Recognizing the Latino Resurgence in U.S. Religion: The Emmaus Paradigm*. Boulder, CO: Westview Press.

Dolan, Jay P. 1992. *The American Catholic Experience*. Notre Dame, IN: Notre Dame University Press.

Enchautegui, María E. 1995. *Policy Implications of Latino Poverty*. Washington, DC: Urban Institute.

Fitzpatrick, Joseph P. 1971. *Puerto Rican Americans: The Meaning of Migration to the Mainland*. Englewood Cliffs, NJ: Prentice Hall.

———. 1987. *One Church, Many Cultures*. Kansas City, MO: Sheed & Ward.

———. 1995. The Dilemma of Social Research and Social Policy: The Puerto Rican Case, 1953-1993. In *Old Masks, New Faces: Religion and Latino Identities*, ed. Anthony M. Stevens-Arroyo and Gilbert R. Cadenas. Program for the Analysis of Religion Among Latinas/os, vol. 2. New York: Bildner Center Books.

Flores, Juan. 1993. *Divided Borders: Essays on Puerto Rican Identity*. Houston, TX: Arte Público Press.

García, Mario T. 1989. *Mexican Americans: Leadership, Ideology and Identity, 1930-1960*. New Haven, CT: Yale University Press.

Glazer, Nathan and Daniel P. Moynihan. 1963. *Beyond the Melting Pot: The Negroes, Puerto Ricans, Jews, Italians and Irish of New York City*. Cambridge, MA: MIT Press.

Goldberg, Carey. 1997. Hispanic Households Struggle as Poorest of the Poor in U.S. *New York Times*, 30 Jan.

Grebler, Leo, Joan Moore, and Ralph Guzmán, eds. 1970. *The Mexican-American People*. New York: Macmillan, Free Press.

Griswold del Castillo, Richard. 1979. *The Los Angeles Barrio, 1850-1890: A Social History*. Berkeley: University of California Press.

Handlin, Oscar. 1951. *The Uprooted*. Boston: Little, Brown.

———. 1959. *The Newcomers*. Cambridge, MA: Harvard University Press.

Herberg, Will. 1955. *Protestant, Catholic, Jew*. Garden City, NY: Doubleday.

Kosmin, Barry A. 1991. *The National Survey of Religious Identification, 1989-1990*. New York: City University of New York.

Kosmin, Barry A. and Seymour P. Lachman. 1993. *One Nation Under God: Religion in Contemporary American Society*. New York: Harmony Books.

Maldonado Denis, Manuel. [1969] 1972. *Puerto Rico: Una interpretación histórico-social*. Mexico: Siglo Ventiuno. Translated as *Puerto Rico: A Socio-Historic Interpretation*. New York: Vintage Books.

McNamara, Patrick Hayes. 1970. Dynamics of the Catholic Church from Pastoral to Social Concerns. In *The Mexican-American People*, ed. Leo Grebler, Joan Moore, and Ralph Guzmán. New York: Macmillan, Free Press.

———. 1973. Catholicism, Assimilation and the Chicano Movement: Los Angeles as a Case Study. In *Chicanos and Native Americans*, ed. Rudolfo de la Garza, Z. Anthony Kruszewski, and Tomás A. Arciniega. Englewood Cliffs, NJ: Prentice Hall.

———. 1995. Assumptions, Theories and Methods in the Study of Latino Religion After 25 Years. In *Old Masks, New Faces: Religion and Latino Identities*, ed. Anthony M. Stevens-Arroyo and Gilbert R. Cadena. Program for the Analysis of Religion Among Latinas/os, vol. 2. New York: Bildner Center Books.

Mills, C. Wright, Clarence Senior, and Rose Kohn Goldsen. 1950. *The Puerto Rican Journey*. New York: Harper & Row.

Moore, Donald T. 1969. *Puerto Rico para Cristo*. Cuernavaca: CIDOC Sondeos.

Moore, Joan. 1994. The Social Fabric of the Hispanic Community Since 1965. In *Hispanic Catholic Culture in the U.S.: Issues and Concerns*, ed. Jay Dolan and Allan Figueroa Deck. Notre Dame, IN: University of Notre Dame Press.

Moore, Joan and Raquel Pinderhughes. 1993. *In the Barrios: Latinos and the Underclass Debate*. New York: Russell Sage.

Nagel, Paul C. 1971. *This Sacred Trust: American Nationality, 1798-1898*. New York: Oxford University Press.

Rodríguez, Clara E. 1989. *Puerto Ricans Born in the U.S.A.* Boston, MA: Unwin Hyman.

Seelye, Katherine Q. 1997. The New U.S.: Grayer and More Hispanic. *New York Times*, 27 Mar.

Shils, Edward. 1981. *Tradition*. Chicago: University of Chicago Press.

Silva Gotay, Samuel. 1994. The Ideological Dimensions of Popular Religiosity and Cultural Identity in Puerto Rico. In *An Enduring Flame: Studies of Latino Popular Religiosity*, ed. Anthony M. Stevens-Arroyo and Ana Maria Díaz-Stevens. Program for the Analysis of Religion Among Latinas/os, vol. 1. New York: Bildner Center Books.

Stevens-Arroyo, Antonio M. 1980. *Prophets Denied Honor*. Maryknoll, NY: Orbis Books.

Stevens-Arroyo, Anthony M. 1994. The Emergence of a Social Identity Among Latino Catholics: An Appraisal. In *Hispanic Catholic Culture in the U.S.: Issues and Concerns*, ed. Jay Dolan and Allan Figueroa Deck. Notre Dame, IN: University of Notre Dame Press.

———. 1995a. Latino Catholicism and the Eye of the Beholder: Notes Towards a New Sociological Paradigm. *Latino Studies Journal* 6(2):22-55.

———. 1995b. Il programma latino: Deamericanizzare e recattolicizzare il cattolicesimo americano. *Religioni e società: Revista di scienze sociali della religione* 21(10):10-29.

———. 1997. Building a New Public Realm: Moral Responsibility and Religious Commitment in the City. In *The City and the World*, ed. Alberto Vourvoulias-Bush and Margaret Crahan. New York: Council on Foreign Relations Press.

Stevens-Arroyo, Anthony M. and Gilbert R. Cadena, eds. 1995. *Old Masks, New Faces: Religion and Latino Identities*. Program for the Analysis of Religion Among Latinas/os, vol. 2. New York: Bildner Center Books.

Stevens-Arroyo, Anthony M. and Ana María Díaz Ramírez. 1982. Puerto Ricans in the United States. In *The Minority Report*. 2d ed. Ed. Gary and Rosalind Dworkin. New York: Holt Rinehart & Winston.

Stevens-Arroyo, Anthony M. and Ana María Díaz-Stevens. 1993a. Latino Church and Schools as Urban Battlegrounds. In *Urban Schooling in America*, ed. Stanley Rothstein. Westport, CT: Greenwood Press.

———. 1993b. Religious Faith and Institutions in the Forging of Latino Identities. In *Handbook for Hispanic Cultures in the United States*, ed. Felix Padilla. Houston, TX: Arte Publico Press.

Stevens-Arroyo, Anthony M. and Andrés I. Pérez y Mena, eds. 1995. *Enigmatic Powers: Syncretism with African and Indigenous Peoples' Religions Among Latinos*. Program for the Analysis of Religion Among Latinas/os. New York: Bildner Center Books.

Steward, Julian, Robert A. Manners, Eric R. Wolf, Elena Padilla Seda, Sidney W. Mintz, and Raymond L. Scheele. 1956. *The People of Puerto Rico*. Urbana: University of Illinois Press.

Sunseri, Alvin R. 1979. *Seeds of Discord: New Mexico in the Aftermath of the American Conquest. 1846-1861*. Chicago: Nelson Hall.

Tweed, Thomas A. 1996. Identity and Authority at a Cuban Shrine in Miami: Santería, Catholicism, and Struggles for Religious Identity. *Journal of Hispanic/Latino Theology* 4(1):27-48.

U.S. Bureau of the Census. 1997. *Demographic State of the Nation: 1997*. Series P23-193. Washington, DC: Government Printing Office. Mar.

Weber, David J. 1992. *The Spanish Frontier in North America*. New Haven, CT: Yale University Press.

Wilson, William Julius. 1987. *The Truly Disadvantaged*. Chicago: University of Chicago Press.

Wuthnow, Robert. 1988. *The Restructuring of American Religion: Society and Faith Since World War II*. Princeton, NJ: Princeton University Press.

ANNALS, *AAPSS*, **558**, July 1998

Asian Indian and Pakistani Religions in the United States

By RAYMOND BRADY WILLIAMS

ABSTRACT: American religion is the product of immigration, and the change made in the U.S. immigration law in 1965 continues to affect American society, culture, and religion profoundly. Immigrants from India and Pakistan were admitted in significant numbers for the first time as a result of that change. The number of Asian Indian and Pakistani residents more than doubled between the 1980 and 1990 censuses, and this immigration continues apace. Adherents of all the religions of the Indian subcontinent—including Hindus, Sikhs, Jains, Muslims, and Christians—are now at home in America, creating a new religious landscape and requiring new religious adaptations to pluralism in America. New modes of rapid communication and modern mobility create transnational communities and networks that intimately link the United States with India and Pakistan and instigate transformations in all three countries—in America most of all.

Raymond Brady Williams is LaFollette Distinguished Professor in the Humanities and professor of religion at Wabash College. His books on recent immigration include A New Face of Hinduism *(1984);* Religions of Immigrants from India and Pakistan *(1988); and* Christian Pluralism in the United States: The Indian Immigrant Experience *(1996). He is the founding director of the Wabash Center for Teaching and Learning in Theology and Religion and founding editor of* Teaching Theology and Religion.

INDIA and the United States share some characteristics that provide the environment for the flowering of religious faith and devotion. India and the United States are the world's largest democracies, in which religious freedom is a part of basic civil rights. The constitution of each establishes a secular government that permits religions to develop as they will within the restraints of civic order. Both countries incorporate a large number of ethnic, social, and religious groups for whom religion is an important and primary marker of individual and group identity. The constellation of characteristics combined with contemporary migrations of peoples provides the framework for the development of modern multicultural and multireligious societies in both India and the United States—and a set of transnational religious networks between them.

India and the United States are, by some measures, the most religious countries in the world, which is surprising. Citizens of these countries share high levels of various markers of religiosity: self-identification with religious groups, participation in individual and group religious activities, and affirmations of belief in God. Religions shape much of the calendar, cultural affairs, and negotiations of political power in both countries. Difference extends beyond dichotomies of First World, of which the United States is exemplary, and developing world, in which the Indian subcontinent has been a prominent member since independence. The majority religion in India is an indigenous religion—or constellation of religious systems—that was designated as Hinduism, whereas adherents of indigenous religious systems in the United States form a small minority. The Indian subcontinent is a mother of religions—as is the Middle East, which gave birth to the Abrahamic religions of Judaism, Christianity, and Islam—but the Indian subcontinent conceived a family of religions significantly different from the Abrahamic tradition: Buddhism, Hinduism, Sikhism, and Jainism. Through the centuries, other religions entered India with conquerors and migrants, including those with missionary zeal, such as Muslims and Christians, but these religions did not displace the indigenous ones. The United States is the primary receiver of the people and religions of the world, at first various forms of Christianity and, more recently, most of the other religions of the world, and all these virtually replaced indigenous religions.

The United States is permanently and firmly linked with the countries of the Indian subcontinent by the new immigrants who accepted the opportunities provided by the changes in immigration laws since 1965 to establish their families and their religions in a new land. In the new transnational context, South Asian religions are becoming world religions in new ways, resulting in significant changes in India and Pakistan. More important, however, is the fact that new religions are finding their place in the United States with increasing numbers of adherents, thereby changing the American religious landscape.

IMMIGRATION FROM INDIA AND PAKISTAN TO THE UNITED STATES

A commonly told story of American immigration is about the open door to European peoples that resulted in the designation of the United States as the country of immigrants symbolized by the Statue of Liberty. Not all peoples of the world participated in these early migrations, however, and the history has been like a swinging door as people from the Indian subcontinent and other Asian countries have ventured toward America. Although the first immigrants from the Indian subcontinent entered in 1820, it was not until the beginning of this century that more than 275 persons immigrated from South Asia in a single decade (INS 1982, 2-1). Punjabi farmers moved from western Canada into Washington, Oregon, and California to escape the aftermath of an anti-Oriental riot in Vancouver on 7 September 1907, eventually establishing a thriving farming community in California. They were denied the opportunity for citizenship in 1923 by a decision of the U.S. Supreme Court that South Asians, who had previously been treated as Caucasians, were not "free white persons" under the law. They were defined as Asian under immigration and naturalization procedures.

As Asians, they were excluded by a series of laws culminating in the Immigration Act of 1924, which codified the "Asiatic Barred Zone," placed the first permanent limitation on immigration, and established a "national origins" quota system. The door was effectively closed to Asians. From 1820 to 1960, a total of only 13,607 persons emigrated from the Indian subcontinent, and an unrecorded number of these departed (INS 1982, 2-4). The 1924 act had the effect of dramatically reducing the total number of immigrants from all countries, so that the previous levels of immigration were not reached again until 1989.

The years between 1925 and 1965 were a peculiar period of American history when there was a major lull in immigration. Because of a variety of special circumstances during that period, which included the passage of restrictive laws, the Great Depression, and World War II, many fewer people immigrated to the United States than before or since. Indeed, in some years during the lull, more people left the United States than entered as immigrants. This lull had profound effects on developments in American culture and religion. A rather homogenized religious-cultural synthesis of Christianity, Judaism, and Enlightenment deism shaped what was called the Judeo-Christian tradition that underlay much of mid-century educational, political, and religious rhetoric. Ecumenical movements of all sorts thrived during this period, when successive generations of immigrant families passed through a common experience of Americanization undisturbed by the arrival of new immigrants on the scene. The growth and influence of the ecumenical movement among Protestants, the homogenization of ethnic groups, the shape of American general education, and the general placidity of the 1950s could be attributed, in part, to the lull in immigration. Second and third generations of immigrant families were learning to get along, after a fashion, and the results of their negotiation provided the context for the development of the civil rights movement in which African Americans demanded their place at the negotiating table.

All that dramatically changed when the Immigration and Nationality Act of 1965 was passed in the emotional aftermath of the assassination of President John F. Kennedy, along with several other bills that he had proposed to the Congress. By setting a nondiscriminatory quota for immigrants from every country, the act reopened the doors to immigrants, especially those from Asia and from other places who had previously been systematically excluded. The number of immigrants increased rapidly. In 1991, some 1.8 million persons were granted permanent resident status, the highest total ever recorded (INS 1991, 12, 18). The places of origin of immigrants shifted from Europe to Asia, so that, for the period of 1981-90, nearly 50 percent of those naturalized as citizens had been born in Asia. Those born in South Asia contribute to the growth in immigration, with 57,448 gaining admission in 1993 (India 44,121; Pakistan 8927; Bangladesh 3291; and Sri Lanka 1109). The number from India has dropped slightly (40,121 in 1993; 34,921 in 1994; and 34,748 in 1995), and the number from Pakistan has grown slightly, to 9774 in 1995 (INS 1995, tab. 5).

Those arriving in the first decade after passage of the 1965 law were part of the brain drain, not "Your tired, your poor/Your huddled masses yearning to breathe free," as earlier immigrants were described by words enshrined on the Statue of Liberty. Rather, they were the physicians, engineers, scientists, nurses, and computer specialists needed in the growing American economy.

South Asian immigrants in the 1970s were among the best educated, most professionally advanced, and most successful of any immigrant group, and the income of Asian Indians recorded in the 1980 census ranked second highest among ethnic groups in the country. However, a major shift has taken place from the 1970s and early 1980s, when a majority of immigrants qualified by meeting professional and educational criteria, to the current situation, in which a large majority qualify on the basis of family reunification.

The growth of the South Asian community in the United States has been dramatic, up from 371,630 persons, as recorded in the 1980 census, to 919,626 in 1990. Specifically, those from India increased by 815,447, or 125.6 percent, in the decade; those from Pakistan, by 81,371, or 415.3 percent; those from Bangladesh, by 11,838, or 800.9 percent; and those from Sri Lanka, by 10,970, or 275.3 percent. These percentages reflect the fact that Pakistanis and Bangladeshis were relatively slower at moving through the open door in the 1970s but arrived in somewhat greater numbers in the 1980s.

The most important fact about the new immigration is that it continues unabated. Even though the number of immigrants changes year by year and new regulations revise the preference categories slightly, the door remains open, and new immigrants from South Asia arrive every year in large numbers both to join the established communities and religious groups and to transform them. They will continue to do so for the foreseeable future, reinforcing the special defining characteristic of the United States as a country of immigrants.

IMMIGRANT RELIGIONS AND RELIGIOUS PLURALISM IN THE UNITED STATES

Because the Indian subcontinent is such a fertile place for religions, immigrants bring and establish several religions and regional forms of religions from India and Pakistan previously relatively absent from the American religious landscape: for example, Hinduism in several regional forms, Sikhism, Jainism, Syro-Malabar Catholicism, Orthodox Christianity, and both Sunni and Shi'a forms of South Asian Islam. Together immigrants from India and Pakistan introduce the most diverse and active new ingredients into American religious pluralism of any immigrant group. Since 1957 the U.S. government has observed a congressional prohibition against maintaining records of religious affiliation on immigrants and American citizens, so reliable governmental statistics on the number of adherents of these religions are lacking. Nevertheless, their presence is revealed by the many temples, gurdwaras, mosques, and churches they have constructed and by the many new religious festivals and rituals they have introduced. Diana Eck's Pluralism Project at Harvard University demonstrates that one can study the world's religions in any major U.S. metropolitan

area; it is certainly the case that one can study in America all the major religions of the Indian subcontinent, without traveling to South Asia.

Hindus

The survival of Hinduism in India through the turmoil of several invasions and conquests results in part from its strong links to the home, where both mothers and fathers are religious specialists for the family. Home shrines are more central to the lives of most Hindus than temples are, and life-cycle and other family-based rituals are fundamental to personal identity. This home-based strategy serves Hindus well in India, where Hindus form the religious majority, and it proves effective also in the United States, where Hindus are a very small minority. The new immigrants of the brain drain came to the United States as individuals, brought personal ritual objects for home shrines, and practiced privately at home. Then they engaged in more elaborate religious activities after bringing spouses and families to join them. As they became financially secure, they established homes throughout metropolitan areas and in many towns and cities throughout the country, not in ghettos. Settlement pattern affects the development of religious organizations. One can trace several stages of growth beyond the home influenced by the length of residence of the South Asians in a given location and by the size of the community there.

Cultural and religious organizations came into existence when children of the early immigrants reached an age to be socialized outside the home, and parents looked for help in raising their children. The first organizations created were national in character, gathering Asian Indians (and even Pakistanis) into social and cultural organizations such as India cultural centers. Because Hindus constituted a large majority of the members, the religious ethos of many of these organizations was Hindu: the organizations observed Hindu holidays and welcomed Hindu religious leaders as guests. Out of these organizations developed the Hindu temple societies, which raised funds and built Hindu temples in most major American cities. These are as elaborate as the Meenakshi Temple near Houston or the Rama Temple near Chicago and as modest as a residential house converted for use as a temple. Ecumenical Hindu temples attempt to serve Hindus from all regions of India. Images of many deities are placed in shrines in a single ecumenical temple, although some of these deities would not be found in the same temple in India. In the larger metropolitan areas, Gujarati, Tamil, Telugu, Hindi, and other regional groups establish separate organizations and temples where the language, ethos, form of deity, rituals, cuisine, and leaders from a particular region of India are prominent. Another constellation of groups comprises devotees of gurus, living or dead, and the hierarchy of religious leaders who preserve and transmit their teachings. As in India, the Hindu organizations in any major American metropolitan area create a complex network of organizations, temples, leaders, calendars, and rituals on a grid of national, ecumenical, regional-linguistic, and sectarian identity markers. These are the forms shaping the Hindu community at the end of the century and that provide the ingredients for an American Hinduism for the new century.

Jains

In India, Jains form a very small minority closely allied with Hindus, and they are renegotiating that relationship in the United States. Initially, Jains met regularly with Hindus at India cultural centers and observed special Jain festivals and rituals at home. They joined in building some ecumenical Hindu temples and established small Jain shrines in the temples, as, for example, in the Hindu temple in Monroeville, Pennsylvania. A majority of Jains in the United States have family origins in Gujarat, even though many of them migrated from Bombay or other cities of India. The Jain community is so small in the United States that only more recently and in large cities have they amassed sufficient resources, both human and financial, to establish separate Jain temples like the one in Bartlett, a suburb of Chicago.

Jains share with other Asian Indian religious groups the striking characteristic that they are organized and led by lay people who were part of the brain drain because, with the exception of the Christians, South Asian religious specialists were not among the first group of South Asian immigrants. Traditional rules for Jain monks and nuns prohibited them from traveling abroad, so fewer Jain religious specialists have been available in the United States to assist in the establishment of institutions. Two Jain monks did travel to the United States. One of them, Chitrabanu Muni, came in 1971, first to lecture as a visiting scholar at Harvard. Sushil Kumar Muni came to establish a series of teaching centers, the most important of which is Siddhachalam in the Pocono Mountains of Pennsylvania. Siddhachalam has become an important center for retreats and national conferences. Jains created two national organizations: the Jain Study Circle, which publishes a magazine that contains essays explaining Jain doctrine and practice, especially nonviolence and vegetarianism; and the Jain Association in North America, which engages in activities for the affiliated organizations, including a biennial convention. (Note that it is common for South Asian organizations and annual meetings to include membership from both Canada and the United States.)

Sikhs

Sikhs have roots in the Punjab region of India and occupy a space—both geographic and religious—between Hindus and Muslims, and they maintain an intricate amalgam of Sikh religious practice and Punjabi ethos. Sikhs established themselves in the United States earlier than other South Asian groups, having migrated from British Columbia into California to escape the 1907 anti-Oriental riots. They soon became isolated by restrictive immigration laws that prevented them from bringing brides or relatives from the Punjab to join them. Nevertheless, they pursued their traditional occupation as farmers and established a prosperous Sikh farming community and the first Sikh institutions. They were joined after 1965 by young professionals and their families, coming directly from the Punjab and the cities of India and representing different class, regional, and religious characteristics. The newer immigrants quickly established organizations and gurdwaras throughout the country. Gurdwaras are centers of instruction in the Sikh religion and Punjabi language and culture. There are 30 gurdwaras in California alone and approximately 80 in the United States overall.

The negotiations between the older and newer Sikh immigrant communities and the development of Sikh institutions were rudely interrupted by conflict between Sikhs and the Indian government over demands for an independent Sikh state in the Punjab to be called Khalistan. The complex issues of the dispute, involving preservation of Punjabi cultural and political identity and Sikh religious rights, deteriorated into an Indian army exercise in 1984, called Blue Star, in which the army occupied the most sacred Sikh shrine at Amritsar, which Sikhs often refer to as their Vatican. The conflict in India both galvanized and divided the Sikh community in the United States. The emotion was strong because threats to Punjabi identity and the Sikh religion in India are mirrored by less visible threats to both in America. Annual elections of officers for Sikh organizations became occasions for conflict and division, and fund drives were for a period more often directed to support for Khalistan independence than for establishing gurdwaras and other Sikh institutions in America. As political turmoil has subsided in the Punjab, American Sikhs have learned that their influence has diminished in India and are therefore free to return to negotiations between themselves and with other South Asian religious groups regarding the distinct Sikh identity they will create in the United States.

Muslims

Pakistan was created as an independent Muslim state in 1947, at the same time that India was also granted independence by the British. Subsequently, in a civil war, Pakistan divided into two Muslim countries: Pakistan and Bangladesh. Over 80 million Muslims are Indian citizens, however, so Muslims in the three countries of the Indian subcontinent constitute one of the largest concentrations of Muslims in the world. South Asian Muslims migrate from all three countries to join Muslims from over 60 nations who are now establishing themselves in the United States. Islam claims to establish one brotherhood of people from all national and ethnic groups, and nowhere outside of Mecca during the hajj pilgrimage would one find more national and ethnic groups exhibiting that brotherhood than in a mosque in an American metropolitan area. Muslims are a minority in India, although they hold significant political power there, and they form large majorities in Pakistan and Bangladesh; in the United States, South Asian Muslims form a minority within a minority.

Muslims share with others the tension between universality and particularity. Mosques must be open to all Muslims, and some are inclusive by necessity, as in communities with small immigrant populations, or by design, as in Houston, where decentralization from an inclusive central mosque led to the establishment of inclusive mosques throughout the area. In some metropolitan areas, such as Chicago, however, mosques serve distinct national or ethnic groups and are known as Asian, African, European, or Arab. The regional identity of the mosque is revealed by the native place of the governing boards, the training of the imams, the language of instruction and social intercourse, the modes of dress, and the cuisine at mosque functions. Over 1250 mosques and Islamic centers serve a growing American Islam that includes a significant Asian Indian and Pakistani component. National organizations like the Muslim Student Association and the Islamic Society of North America direct a wide array of educational, religious, and social welfare activities. New Muslim immigrants continue to arrive from all 60 countries, so Muslims from the Indian subcontinent are negotiating within a multicultural and multigenerational Islam what the shape of American Islam will be.

Christians

Christians come from where they are very small minorities among Hindus in India and Muslims in Pakistan to a context where they become part of a putative majority-Christian population. Christianity has a long history in India, claiming a tradition about the arrival of the Apostle Thomas as a missionary in A.D. 52 and another tradition about the coming of a different Thomas with a group of Syrian Christians in the fourth century. Although the accuracy of these traditions is questioned, Indian Christianity contains several strands reaching back to the earliest centuries: (1) St. Thomas Christians (also called Syrian Christians) preserve ancient oriental rites of Syrian Orthodox Christianity; (2) St. Xavier, the most important of the Roman Catholic missionaries in the sixteenth century, converted Christians from the lower castes and attempted to bring St. Thomas Christians into communion with Rome, thereby eventually creating Indian Christianity in three rites (Syro-Malabar, Syro-Malankara, and Latin); (3) Protestant missionaries established denominational churches and institutions throughout the Indian subcontinent during British colonial rule; (4) Pentecostal missionaries and indigenous leaders encourage a lively evangelistic effort; and (5) the Church of South India (1947) and the Church of North India (1970) united several denominations following Indian independence.

All these streams of Indian Christianity are now flowing into American Christianity with the immigrants and are expanding in most major metropolitan areas. Christian immigrants from India are unique in two ways. First, they immigrated on the shoulders of the women because Christian families and institutions in India produced a surplus of nurses who were admitted under interpretations of immigration regulations as part of the brain drain. The nurses were needed in inner-city American hospitals in the 1970s. The second difference is that they brought their priests and pastors with them, many of whom were spouses or siblings of nurses.

Indian Christian immigrants have followed several adaptive strategies. Many joined churches that are in communion with their churches in India. Although the bishops of the Mar Thoma church and the Church of South India at first actively discouraged the establishment of Indian churches in America, the attraction of Indian languages, rituals, and customs was enormously strong. Immigrants gathered in congregations where they could sing the songs of Zion, first in English in all-India Christian fellowships and then in Malayalam, Gujarati, Tamil, Telugu, Hindi, or one of the other regional languages. During the late 1980s and the 1990s, congregations and parishes established their own American dioceses, synods, judicatories, and national fellowship groups and affiliated with churches in India: the Mar Thoma church, the Malankara Syrian Orthodox church, various Pentecostal groups, the Brethren Assemblies, Syro-Malabar and Syro-Malankara Catholics, the Knanaya parishes (an endogamous castelike association), the Church of South India, and the Southern Asia Caucus of the United Methodist Church.

The highlights of church life for many Indian Christians are the annual family conferences that many of these churches hold over summer weekends, some of which attract several thousand Indian Christians. Some Indian pastors affiliate with American denominations, especially the Methodist, Episcopalian, and Catholic denominations, and serve as pastors of parishes or chaplains in hospitals. As individuals and congregations, these Christians are finding their place in American Christianity, and the process is fraught with complexity, disappointment, misunderstanding, hope, and potential. They add new ingredients to Christian pluralism in America.

Parsis

Parsis are a small and diminishing group in India, primarily centered in Bombay, who come to America to be reunited with fellow Zoroastrians who fled from persecution in Iran following the revolution under Ayatollah Khomeini. Parsis are descendants of migrants escaping Muslim persecution in Persia in the tenth century who found safe landing in Gujarat and then prosperity in Bombay. Now approximately 6500 Zoroastrians and Parsis from India and Iran reunite two strands of the religion in American cities, already with four Zoroastrian buildings: one each in Chicago and New York, and two in California. The Federation of Zoroastrian Associations of North America has a membership of 17 associations in the United States and 4 in Canada that sponsor publications, conferences, and youth activities. These immigrants from India and Iran speak different languages and preserve two distinct cultures and two interpretations of Zoroastrianism. Zoroastrians are unique among religious groups in rejecting converts not born into the religion; offspring of marriages of people outside the community are not eligible for membership. They often interpret their experience as immigrants to America as a second migration like that of their ancestors from Persia to India in the tenth century and say that American Zoroastrianism will constitute a vital and reformed form of the religion.

Their American cousins

Even before South Asian immigrants arrived, some Americans responded positively to their religions. The most notable example was the effects of the preaching of Swami Vivekenanda at the world's fair in Chicago in 1893. Indeed, immigrants arrived after 1965 to encounter people claiming to be converts to their religions, sometimes a form of religion very different from their own. Young members of the International Society of Krishna Consciousness (ISKCON), sometimes called the Hari Krishnas because of their devotion to Krishna and their public chanting of a Krishna mantra, were often dancing in the airport terminals when Hindu immigrants arrived, and their Krishna temples welcomed early immigrants. The Nation of Islam intrigued immigrants with a race-based interpretation of Islam and a set of rituals foreign to their experience of Islam. The white Sikhs were converts of Harbhajan Singh Puri, a teacher who linked Hatha yoga with religious aspects of Sikhism to attract a number of American converts.

The negotiations between these groups and their effects have been diverse. ISKCON attempted to attract the allegiance of Hindu immigrants, and for a brief period it appeared that ISKCON members, who had renounced the world, might become the primary religious specialists for Hindu immigrants, who were part of the brain drain engaged in gaining the world. However, the arrival of an array of religious specialists from India to serve institutions founded by immigrants and the turmoil and schisms within ISKCON have greatly reduced its size and influence. The so-called ghora ("white") Sikhs became almost irrelevant during the Khalistan controversies that racked the Sikh community. The Nation of Islam went through a metamorphosis to emerge as a much more orthodox form of Islam under the inspiration of Malcolm X and the subsequent leadership of Wallace Muhammad in the American Muslim Mission. Immigrant Muslims influenced this transformation by providing examples of traditional forms of Islam and by funding new, more orthodox initiatives. The interaction between these groups of Hindus, Muslims, and Sikhs regarding identity, activities, and new directions foreshadow the negotiations between these and other religions of immigrants regarding their place in American religion.

Recent immigration from most countries of the world is adding new religions and new forms of old religions to the complex tapestry woven by previous immigrants that is American religion. Immigrants from India and Pakistan add some of the most colorful and distinctive textures to the work—and some significant design challenges. The tapestry is still on the loom, so the work of weaving involves the many colors of the issues these immigrants share, the texture of their effect on American religions, and the shape of the reverse effects they have on the religions in the Indian subcontinent.

EXPERIENCES OF RECENT
IMMIGRANTS: THE POWER
OF RELIGION

In responses to questionnaires, immigrants commonly indicate that they are more religiously active in the United States than they were in India or Pakistan. The relative low level of involvement prior to migration is not so surprising because many of them came as young adults directly from university studies in the sciences, but the higher level of commitment in the United States is striking. It reflects the power inherent in religion to provide a transcendent foundation for personal and group identity in the midst of the enormous transitions that migration entails. The conjunction of that power with the special requirement that immigrants reformulate personal and group identities in new contexts helps to account for the fact that, as a country of immigrants, the United States is by many measures the most religious of the Western industrialized countries. Each new immigrant group, including new immigrants from India or Pakistan, turns to religion to shape and strengthen identity. Increasing secularization in the third quarter of the twentieth century may be the lingering result of the lull in immigration in the second quarter, and some revival of religion at the turn of the century, especially in conservative forms, may be due in part to the resurgence of immigration.

Plausibility structures

Migration results in threats to all sorts of plausibility structures that undergird individual and social knowledge and support civic order and personal health. A Christian from a small village of Kerala reported that the only familiar parts of the landscape when he arrived in New York were the church towers, and he took great comfort in their shadows. That is a symbol of the absence of many plausibility structures that had undergirded knowledge, morals, customs, leadership styles, and commitments. Immigrants gravitate to both religious and social organizations not in the first instance to keep themselves separate from the settled society but to gain a breathing space within recognized plausibility structures in order to establish new plausibility structures that will be effective for themselves and their children in their new homes. Even groups that form small minorities in India or Pakistan rely nonetheless on the structures that assign to them a place within a diverse society. Such social location is the result of long and intricate negotiations between social and religious groups that, to a large extent, are insecure in the United States. The new relation be-

tween various Asian Indian and Pakistani social and religious groups requires the introduction or revision of plausibility structures for both the immigrants and those in the receiving society that will support the new social reality. American religion is in the midst of such negotiations between religious groups and between them and other social groups.

Family and children

A marker for the establishment of immigrant religious organizations and buildings is the point at which children of the second generation reach the age when they are socialized outside the home. Parents are able to transmit whole cloth the plausibility structures that establish family identity and loyalty until that point. Thereupon, parents seek the assistance of other like-minded people in raising their children, often through the establishment of religious study groups and organizations. Sunday schools, summer camps, youth groups, and annual national conferences are adaptations to the American scene that help parents maintain some continuity of culture and religion with their children.

When asked what their major contribution to America might be, immigrants from India and Pakistan often reply, "Our close family ties." Family values are topics of many South Asian religious conferences and meetings. Immigrants from the Indian subcontinent have relatively few friends from the receiving society—in part because the primary channel for social intercourse in India and Pakistan is family, not friendship—so they are suspicious of American family life and fearful of bad influences from their children's peers. Many believe that American children do not care for their parents and will desert them in their old age and that American families fail to inculcate morals in the children. The greatest perceived threat to the integrity of the family is marriage to a person distant from the family by race, ethnic group, caste, religion, country of family origin, or social class. Parents' preferences for marriage partners reflect this list. Because arranged marriages are the traditional pattern in India and Pakistan, the American pattern of young people's searching for partners and even living together prior to marriage is very threatening to the immigrant families. Friendships and dating between boys and girls in a multicultural and multireligious society are occasions for great tension between parents and children. Religious groups often provide safe locations for intergenerational discussions of these issues and of the future of Asian Indian and Pakistani families. Religious leaders mediate such negotiations between the generations.

Strangers in a strange land

Immigrants find themselves to be strangers in a strange land. Even though most South Asian immigrants are fluent in English as a legacy of British influence in the Indian subcontinent, the use of their native languages is a powerful attraction for first-generation immigrants. As one immigrant remarked, "If I am going to sing the hymns of my childhood, I want to sing them in Malayalam" (and others would say "Gujarati" or "Tamil" or "Bengali"). Religious meetings are one of the few places where immigrants can feel at home outside their homes. There they can speak in their birth language; enjoy the ethos of their native place; participate in Indian or Pakistani music, drama, and other arts; taste traditional cuisine; and exercise leadership skills that involve oratory in the birth language and manipulation of other symbols. Religious organizations also provide the primary network connecting the immigrant with institutions and events in the Indian subcontinent.

A great sadness is that children of the second generation are losing love for and facility in the use of the family language and in the manipulation of other symbols. Indian languages are becoming sacred languages as they are used in temples, gurdwaras, and mosques. Sporadic attempts are made to hold language classes for the children, but many leaders realize that they are waging a losing battle and that the third generation will be alienated from their past. The older children often resist visits back to the family home and find themselves strangers in the strange land of the Indian subcontinent. How the religious organizations adapt to these realities is the most important challenge that they face. Have the parents gained the whole world but lost their children in the bargain? That is the awful question.

EFFECTS ON AMERICAN RELIGION AND SOCIETY: THE FUTURE OF THE JUDEO-CHRISTIAN SYNTHESIS

Recent immigrants witness the diminishing power of the Judeo-Christian synthesis in American civic, religious, and educational arenas. The Judeo-Christian tradition is a fairly recent creation resulting from the negotiations of nineteenth- and early-twentieth-century immigrants who developed the "Protestant-Catholic-Jew" ethos of mid-twentieth-century America. The political ethos of Enlightenment values provided a civic framework that both empowered the Judeo-Christian tradition and preserved the religious freedom cherished by many immigrants. The new social reality that involves the presence of many different religions and intellectual traditions that have no clear place in the earlier synthesis engenders a reformulation, a revision, or perhaps a negotiation of a new synthesis that some claim will be more adequate. A host of religions from many countries are involved in this negotiation, but Hindus, Muslims, and others from India and Pakistan are prominent participants.

Negotiations have begun regarding the integration of Islam into a new synthesis. Including Muslims is in some ways easier than involving Hindus, Jains, Sikhs, or Parsis because Islam is a part of the Abrahamic tradition, sharing some of the same religious syntax, stories, and heroes. It is also more difficult in some ways because of the suspicion of Islam and discrimination against Muslims common among Americans.

Regardless of the difficulties, the negotiation is essential because of the size and growth of the Muslim community. The recognition of that growth is shown by the inclusion of Muslim imams in the schedule of opening prayers for the U.S. Congress, provision of Muslim chaplains in prisons and other governmental institutions, and the invitations to Muslims to have the Id celebration in the White House. Muslims often claim that, sometime near the turn of the millennium, Islam will surpass Judaism to become the religion with the second-largest number of adherents in the United States. Internally, South Asian Muslims have been influential in moving African American Muslims toward more orthodox forms of Islam. That creates a four-way tension: between African American Muslims and immigrant Muslims, between African American Muslims and Jews, between African American Muslims and the black church, and between all these and the majority population. The results of the competition of black masjid and the black church for the lives and souls of African Americans may well be the most important development in American culture in the first decades of the new century. Externally, that has profound implications both for the relative levels of influence of American Jews and Muslims in U.S. foreign policy and for political negotiations in the Middle East and with other countries that have large Muslim populations.

Public negotiations with Hindus, Jains, or Sikhs often involve zoning codes and building regulations for religious structures or regulations about dress codes that conflict with religious sensibilities or rules. Mediating institutions, such as councils of churches or interfaith organizations, are now skeletons of their former selves and have been thus far ineffective in providing venues for effective negotiation. The promise of the open door of immigration to America is that the nation will be able to welcome, absorb, and protect the civil rights and freedoms of both new and old immigrants and their descendants. The reality in the new century could become levels of turmoil and conflict that characterized earlier periods of large immigration and threatened to destroy individual dreams and the civic order. Alternatively, *inshallah* ("if Allah wills"), as some new immigrants say, negotiations could result in the creation of a new synthesis that will provide a broad civic umbrella for the renewal and preservation of the American dream.

The United States as a missionary territory

Christian immigrants from many countries, including India and Pakistan, are disappointed when they reach the United States and discover that it is not "the shining city set on the hill." Indeed, many immigrants feel that America is in need of missionaries and a revival of religious and moral values cherished in their churches, mosques, gurdwaras, and temples. Although some elements of religions of the Indian subcontinent have gained allegiance of Americans in the past, the vitality of the new immigrant communities confronts Americans with new, permanent, self-renewing alternatives. Strong opposition to the proselytizing activities of some groups (ISKCON in the 1970s, for example) led some Hindu, Jain, and Sikh leaders to forswear any attempts to make converts. It was almost as if the terms of compromise between old and new immigrants was the agreement, "Don't touch our children, and we won't touch yours."

The primary outreach—beyond their own children—for most immigrant religious groups has been the unchurched, unmosqued, or unaffiliated compatriots. Strategies that have been used extend from a simple notice posted in South Asian grocery stores to elaborate advertising and public relations campaigns associated with religious festivals. Some Hindus, some Jains, and the Parsis think that conversion to their religions is impossible. South Asian Muslims have been active in establishing institutions that propagate Islam among immigrants, in the African American community, and in the wider society. Marriage with persons outside the religious group that involves the conversion of the partner is an early extension of immigrant religions into the receiving society. (Marriage to an American citizen is one of the easiest and quickest ways to gain permanent resident status.) Development of resident religious leaders, sophisticated communication networks, elaborate organizations, and impressive facilities attracts the interest and allegiance of people beyond the immigrant group. Hence, they provide new resources for the American marketplace of ideas and religious alternatives for seekers. The situation evolves quickly, but it is still too soon to determine how successful the newly introduced forms of religion will be either in preserving the allegiance of the second and third generations or in attracting converts.

Education for the new religious reality

The public educational system from kindergarten through university and religious education in the United States produced curricula and resources for incorporating people from many lands into a common civic and religious structure. Those curricula were based on the earlier synthesis. They were enshrined in the basic canons of the liberal arts and then summarized in various types of Western civilization courses.

Following World War II, revised thinking introduced forms of area studies to take account of the new global responsibilities assumed by the United States. Considerable turmoil in education and curriculum development results from responses to and attacks on the earlier canons and curricula under the banners of multiculturalism and postmodernism. The presence of vital immigrant communities and their customs, ideologies, and religions also fuels controversy about the adequacy of earlier models and current proposals for reform. In some instances, curricula that were intended to teach students about other parts of the world now function to teach students about their neighbors across the street. Indeed, college courses on the religions of India now enroll significant numbers of children of immigrants from India and Pakistan who are seeking to learn about their own ancestral religions. Colleges and universities are responding by hiring specialists who institute courses on Islam and other religions of the Indian subcontinent. South Asian immigrants are part of the brain drain who quickly established financial security for themselves, their families, and their communities. They have begun to raise money for endowed chairs and research centers in Indian studies, Sikh studies, and Jain studies in American universities. Hindus are establishing a Hindu university in Florida, and Muslims are developing a religious school network and an Islamic university. These educational initiatives will help shape American education into the new century.

Transnationalism

Migration from India and Pakistan takes place in a radically different context of rapid mobility and communication that brings profound changes to the experience of both the immigrants and other citizens. Asian Indian and Pakistani families maintain almost immediate contact with family members and institutions in several countries, including in East Africa, the gulf states, the United Kingdom, Canada, and the United States. It is a new transnational reality in which individuals and families occupy and are intimately influenced by social locations in two or more countries. In this transnational context, religions of the Indian subcontinent have become world religions in new ways that call into question rubrics of analyses developed in relation to earlier immigrant groups. "Ethnicity" and "nationality" are categories of social description that require some revision to account for the current transnational reality; it is not just that new ethnic groups can be added to any list but that the category of ethnicity could be misleading. Both the earlier immigration and the midcentury lull in immigration were accompanied by difficulties of communication so that immigrants had difficulty communicating with relatives and institutions in their homelands or in other countries and, in relative isolation, formed ethnic groups on American models. Now travel and communication are rapid so that immigrants are more directly shaped by contacts abroad. In this regard, computer-assisted communication on the Internet is significant. Religious groups increasingly use the Internet to transmit information and define their religions.

Transnational networks make it increasingly possible for the United States to receive religious leaders and religious messages from India and Pakistan. They also enhance the capability of the new immigrants in the United States to exercise influence and authority in the Indian subcontinent. The effects that new immigrants are having on American society and religion are becoming clearer, but the effects that immigrants have on religious and social institutions back home are often overlooked. The United States has become an important funding source for religious leaders and institutions there. Families remit funds to relatives, a portion of which are donated to religious causes. Hindu, Jain, Sikh, Muslim, and Christian religious specialists come from India and Pakistan each summer to visit disciples and followers and to collect gifts for their activities. Although remittances of nonresident Indians and Pakistanis are important sources of hard currency for those countries, it is impossible to trace or estimate how much is donated. The networks handle not just money but also ideas, modes of behavior, and styles of leadership that have enormous potential for shaping religion in India and Pakistan at the same time that immigrants are affecting American religion.

CONCLUSION

Few people recognized the profound effects that post-1965 immigration would have on American religion and society. Those effects are permanent, but the exact shape of future developments is dependent upon the vagaries of revisions in the immigration laws and changes in administrative regulations, the results of which are incalculable. Nevertheless, it seems safe to make a few predictions. Immigration from India and Pakistan will continue for the foreseeable future, primarily under the family-reunification provisions of the immigration law, which will constitute a constant transfusion for the nascent religious organizations. Asian Indians and Pakistanis will continue to establish religious organizations and to build temples, mosques, gurdwaras, and churches. Their religions will gain increasing visibility, and some will become more active in attracting participation and support from the society at large. If the analysis of the effects of the mid-century lull are close to accurate, it seems likely that portions of American society will become more religious as we move into the new century and people turn to a variety of forms of religion both new and old to create, preserve, and transmit elements of personal and group identity. The crystal ball does not reveal whether the result will ultimately be a breakdown in the civic order that provided the foundation for religious freedom and economic opportunity or a renewal in the American experiment, which is unique in human annals, in preserving freedom and democracy that has attracted immigrants and sheltered our common life. One best faces the nagging fear of the former with fervent prayers for the latter and all sorts of good work to enhance its likelihood.

References

U.S. Immigration and Naturalization Service (INS). 1982. *Statistical Yearbook of the Immigration and Naturalization Service*. Washington, DC: INS.

———. 1991. *Statistical Yearbook of the Immigration and Naturalization Service*. Washington, DC: INS.

———. 1995. *Statistical Yearbook of the Immigration and Naturalization Service*. Washington, DC: INS.

Postdenominational Christianity in the Twenty-First Century

By DONALD E. MILLER

ABSTRACT: Substantial changes in worship style and organizational structure are transforming the way Christianity will be experienced in the next millennium. The style of Christianity dominated by eighteenth-century hymns, a routinized liturgy, and bureaucratized layers of social organization is gradually dying. In its place are emerging hundreds of new-paradigm churches, which are appropriating stylistic and organizational elements from our postmodern culture. This reformation, unlike the one led by Martin Luther, is challenging not doctrine but the medium through which the message of Christianity is articulated. Appropriating contemporary cultural forms, these postdenominational churches are creating a new genre of worship music; they are restructuring the organization of institutional Christianity; and they are democratizing access to the sacred by radicalizing the Protestant principle of priesthood of all believers. This trend within American Christianity is illustrated by describing research on three religious movements—Calvary Chapel, Vineyard Christian Fellowship, and Hope Chapel—that have emerged since the mid-1960s and now number collectively more than a thousand organizations.

Donald E. Miller is Firestone Professor of Religion at the University of Southern California. In addition, he is the director of the university's Center for Religion and Civic Culture. His current research is on congregation-based community organizing in Los Angeles. In 1997 he published Reinventing American Protestantism: Christianity in the New Millennium, *which draws on extensive fieldwork related to three rapidly growing Christian movements.*

CHRISTIANITY is currently undergoing a structural transformation in the United States: the historical mainline denominations are declining, and a variety of independent churches, as well as informal networks of congregations and new Christian movements, are emerging. These new-paradigm churches are rewriting the way Christianity will look in the early part of the twenty-first century, absent the church steeples, stained glass windows, and clerical garb of clergy—all of which represent routinized Christianity. Increasing numbers of Christians will be meeting in school gymnasiums, public auditoriums, and theaters, and, as these groups become more established, in former grocery stores, converted warehouses, and utilitarian spaces that have been constructed or reconstructed to serve the needs of thousands of new converts who wish to distance themselves from establishment religion.

The revolution that is transforming the Protestant landscape does not have to do with the content of Christianity so much as it does with the envelope in which it is placed. The gospel being preached is biblical and rooted in the first century, but the medium of presentation is contemporary and postmodern. In the place of organs and choirs are bands and singers. The beloved eighteenth-century hymns of the mainline congregations have been replaced with melodies drawn from rock and roll, blues, jazz, and country-western. The hierarchical structures of decision making, including denominational polity and layers of internal congregational bureaucracy, have been radically simplified to encourage members to act in response to the leading of the Holy Spirit as they initiate new programs and projects, rather than conform to top-down management plans. This revolution in style and organizational structure is a rebirth of the Protestant principle of the priesthood of all believers.

It is too early to know if we are witnessing a second reformation, or whether this transformation might better be classified as another Great Awakening. If it is a second reformation, then we would expect a radical restructuring of how Christianity will be experienced in the twenty-first century. For example, the identity of Christians as Roman Catholic, Orthodox, or Protestant (including Baptist, Presbyterian, and Episcopal) will decline in importance because of the emergence of a new organizational model that eschews the relevance of these distinctions. Local congregations will be the primary organizational form instead. Denominational seminaries, transcongregational policies, and uniform educational materials will be viewed as anachronisms of an earlier age. Centralized and hierarchical organizational structures will be replaced by radical innovation within congregations that are attempting to meet the needs of people struggling for meaning in our postmodern society.

A less radical interpretation of the restructuring of American religion is that we are witnessing a brief interlude where dysfunctional denominational forms are being discarded and new denominations are being born. Theoretically, this latter interpretation draws on the well-established model of church-sect evolution, in which institutional Christianity is reformed by people who desire a more intense experience of religion and who appeal to the vision of the tradition's founding charismatic prophet (see Troeltsch 1960; Niebuhr 1963; Iannaccone 1986; Finke and Stark 1989). Sectarian movements challenge the ritual and organizational complexity that inevitably evolves during the course of an institution's history. According to church-sect theory, reform is a cyclical process that occurs whenever a religion has become too compromised with its culture, although the irony is that sects go through a process of routinization themselves, needing eventually to be reformed.

Whether one views the current restructuring of American religion as the death of denominational Christianity or the birth of a new organizational form, there is little question but that the script of American Christianity is being rewritten. The fastest-growing churches in America are independent congregations that typically share the following characteristics: they were started after the mid-1960s; the majority of congregational members were born after 1945; seminary training of clergy is optional; worship is contemporary; lay leadership is highly valued; the churches have extensive small-group ministries; clergy and congregants dress informally; tolerance of different personal styles is prized; pastors are understated, humble, and self-revealing; bodily, rather than merely cognitive, participation in worship is the norm; the gifts of the Holy Spirit are affirmed; and Bible-centered teaching predominates over topical sermonizing. In contrast, mainline Christianity often represents the opposite of these characteristics, being filled with graying heads, highly educated clergy, liturgical worship, and rationalized beliefs. In contrast to the growing new-paradigm churches, mainline denominations are missing an entire generation of young people who are not attracted to establishment religion (see Hoge, Johnson, and Luidens 1994).

METHODOLOGY, DEFINITIONS, HISTORY

My research on new-paradigm Christianity has focused on three movements—Calvary Chapel, Vineyard Christian Fellowship, and Hope Chapel—that emerged after the mid-1960s and are responses to cultural revolutions that occurred in the last third of this century. The development of these three movements is described in some detail in my book *Reinventing American Protestantism: Christianity in the New Millennium* (1997), so I will not retell the history of these groups in this article. However, I do see them as representative of new-paradigm Christianity, and, on occasion, I will cite statistics from the surveys with clergy and members that were done for this study.[1] Calvary, Vineyard, and Hope, while currently numbering about 1000 congregations collectively, are but the tip of the iceberg of an emerging trend in American Christianity. Many of the largest mega-churches in America are independent or, alternatively, de-emphasize their denominational affiliation, acting like independent churches.

The actual number of churches that one might count as part of the postdenominational phenomenon is difficult to estimate,[2] because many sociologists still operate with an earlier set of denominational categories. However, a vocabulary is beginning to emerge that includes such terms as "seeker-sensitive" congregations, recognizing that church done in the old way is not attracting the baby-boom generation and their children. Furthermore, constraining oneself to theological categories such as fundamentalist, evangelical, and Pentecostal is not particularly useful in describing new-paradigm churches because these terms tend to focus on the message rather than the medium in which it is expressed. Hence, while it is accurate to say that conservative churches are growing while liberal churches tend to be declining (Kelley 1972), this generalization fails to capture the unique characteristics of postdenominational growth. New-paradigm churches are not trying simply to reform denominational Christianity; they are reinventing it—a much more radical activity—by founding new congregations that are not constrained by layers of bureaucracy, existing institutional forms, and people who say that "it can't be done that way."

The origins of new-paradigm Christianity reach back to the Jesus movement of the American counterculture (see Ellwood 1994). Long-haired youths who had traded in their hashish pipes for a Bible failed to find acceptance in established churches and consequently were meeting in parks, led by charismatic pastors—themselves recent converts—who were modeling Christianity after the first-century church. These individuals, who could more easily imagine Jesus playing a guitar than a pipe organ, set to work writing and singing songs that reflected their experience of a changed life. Many of the leaders of new-paradigm megachurches had conversion experiences during this era, but their institutional genius led them to evolve with the culture. Consequently, the youths currently joining these movements today are rapping for Jesus rather than strumming chords reminiscent of the melodic tones of the singing group Peter, Paul, and Mary. The sermons, small groups, and programs of these churches are addressing issues of the late 1990s, not the rebellions against authority of the 1960s. Indeed, members of new-paradigm churches are struggling to rediscover the meaning of authority and accountability as they try to rebuild families, community, and an ethic of personal responsibility, which is why the social issues being debated in the national conventions of many of the mainline churches (most of which stress so-called liberation themes of one variety or another) are not compelling to this generation. New-paradigm converts are trying to reconstruct their lives after divorce, they are seeking a wholesome and safe place to raise their children, and they are committing their resources to the church as a way of countering the fragmentation of personal life in a postmodern culture. Members of new-paradigm churches are not fundamentalists seeking to repudiate the theological errors of liberal Protestantism; rather, they are involved in a task of personal and cultural reconstruction, scarcely caring what is occurring in other venues of Christendom.

With this brief sketch as background, what are the specific elements of new-paradigm Christianity, and why is it growing? In an attempt to answer these two interrelated questions, I will generalize in the following pages from my research on Calvary Chapel, Vineyard Christian Fellowship, and Hope Chapel by making some summary statements related to their music, worship, theology, social organization, and growth and the franchising of new-paradigm churches. My assumption is that these three movements symbolize a much broader trend of restructuring in American religion and hence provide a window into what Christianity may look like in the twenty-first century.

MUSIC

Just as new-paradigm churches seldom have steeples—with members frequently meeting in public auditoriums and refurbished industrial buildings—the music of new-paradigm churches has an equally populist character. It comes from the people and reflects their religious experience set to melodies and instrumentation that are similar to what members would listen to on their car radios. According to Chuck Fromm, founder of Maranatha Music, the most powerful songs in the early Jesus movement were written by truckers, former strippers, and house-

wives who wanted to share their love of God and the personal transformation they had undergone. Early leaders in the Jesus movement, such as Chuck Smith, were wise enough to allow this music into the church, often sung by people who had just converted and who went straight from entertaining in the local bar to writing songs and performing them at church-sponsored concerts and evening church services.

According to historian Nathan Hatch, the same pattern had occurred during the Second Great Awakening (1800-1830). States Hatch (1989, 146), "At the turn of the nineteenth century a groundswell of self-made tunesmiths, indifferent to authorized hymnody, created their own simple verses and set them to rousing popular tunes." He says that the music for these songs was borrowed indiscriminately from "a wide variety of secular tunes of love, war, homesickness, piracy, robbery, and murder." The established churches of the time—such as the Episcopalians, Presbyterians, and Congregationalists—viewed these religious "ditties" as vulgar street songs, unfit for respectable religion. But this musical innovation was a protest against the dreary and theologically laden prose of the establishment hymns, which failed to express the vital religious experience of members of the rapidly growing dissident churches of the period.

Although the Second Great Awakening represented a powerful flowering of religious folk music, it is by no means unique in Christian history. Martin Luther is often quoted as saying that, if music is the handmaiden of theology, why should the devil have all the good tunes?[3] Indeed, many of Luther's hymns were written in the vernacular and set to barroom melodies. At the time of the Reformation, these songs represented a decided break with churchly musical convention, but, sung today, they represent establishment religion, just as do the hymns of Charles Wesley. Likewise, the music of new-paradigm churches sounds offensive to the educated musical ear of a person used to listening to Bach, Mozart, and Beethoven. Lyrics, which are often illuminated on a wall by an overhead projector, are sung by band members (typically several guitarists, a keyboard player, drummer, and assorted vocalists). On most songs, the audience joins the band in praising God. The goal is worship, not performance (except when played in concert settings).

The musical idiom varies with the congregation, the worship leader, and the particular venue. The mark of a successful new-paradigm church is that it has a unique sound, which reflects the worship of the congregation. Within a church, there may also be variation from one group to another, so that the worship of the youths typically has a harder, rock-and-roll sound than the worship music of the adults. In addition, morning worship may be mellower than Sunday evening worship, when people, on occasion, even dance to the music being played. What is distinctive about new-paradigm churches is that worship leaders and members are constantly writing new music. This practice, obviously, keeps the music culturally current and the lyrics reflective of the congregation's experi-

ence. Furthermore, people are undoubtedly attracted to different churches based on the music that is played. Hence, one church may reflect a black gospel tonality, another church a New Age style of arrangement, and still another church the imprint of a particular artist who has influenced the worship leader.

Perhaps not surprisingly, some of the new-paradigm pastors whom I interviewed worried that the music they were playing had become too professional and too ingrown, thus losing the cutting-edge quality that it had possessed only a few years ago. Other clergy acknowledged that the music that they liked personally (for example, 1960s rock and roll) was irrelevant to many of their high-school-aged youths, and hence they were attempting to create a context for musical innovation among the youths. Thus, rather than fearing whether music 200 years old might feel dated (a source of angst among progressive choirmasters in mainline churches), these pastors were concerned about the culture gap created over several decades.

WORSHIP

The worship style varies from one new-paradigm congregation to another, but it often is relatively simple, providing an opportunity for people to access the sacred in deep and personal ways. A typical Vineyard Fellowship service, for example, opens with a brief prayer, inviting the audience to enter into the presence of God. Then for the next 30-40 minutes, a band leads the people in singing worship songs. The lyrics are projected onto a screen or wall where all can see them. There are no hymnals or prayer books. It is not unusual to see tears in an attender's eyes, and the music typically has a very intimate quality, as if one is talking directly to God, praising him, loving him. Then, as the band leaves the stage, ushers silently pass offering baskets, without fanfare and often without any announcement. Sometimes there is simply a box at the back of the church where one can leave a contribution. For the next half hour or so, the pastor shares his reflections on a passage of Scripture, often drawing on his own personal experiences as a way of relating to the concerns of the audience.[4] The style is informal, not oratorical.

In Vineyard services, the period of teaching ends with an invitation to individuals who desire prayer to come forward. This is the third and last element of the service. A lay member of the church who is part of the ministry team joins each individual who has come for prayer. Quietly, this lay minister inquires about the person's need and then often places his or her hand on the other's shoulder. In a large church, dozens of these paired groupings may occur, beginning with those who come to the front of the meeting space and then growing in clusters around the church, as more and more people pray for each other. There is something very gentle and caring about ministry time in the Vineyard.

The ministry time of the Vineyard is reserved for small-group home Bible studies or a midweek service. In seeker-sensitive churches such as Vineyard churches, the ambience of the Sunday morning worship service is directed to people who are unchurched, and an effort is made to bridge the culture gap between the profane world of everyday life and the lifestyle and beliefs appropriate to a Christian. The Sunday morning service includes upbeat praise music, a sermon that speaks to personal concerns shared by large numbers of people living in a postmodern society, and perhaps a skit or brief dramatic presentation that portrays a dilemma associated with child rearing, business relations, or lifestyle choice. This is a service to which one can invite nonchurchgoing friends, knowing that they will feel comfortable and yet will be introduced to the values associated with Christianity.

In my interviews with members of new-paradigm churches, I was frequently told that the minute they walked into one of these churches, they felt at home, especially compared to their experience in more traditional churches. They were searching for answers to problems in their lives, and here was a place that these issues were being addressed but in an ambience where they could feel comfortable. People, including the clergy, were dressed casually. The music had a value-laden content but was culturally current. There was a spirit of warmth and acceptance, including an acknowledgment that everyone has personal problems and that these problems are appropriately expressed within the context of a caring community of people. There was an upbeat, joyful atmosphere. People seemed to be present out of choice rather than obligation. Furthermore, in my interviews, people reported being touched emotionally by the worship service, encountering feelings that secular culture provided little context for accessing. It was as if they could lower their guard, admit their failures, and acknowledge their dependence. Feelings of hope, the possibility of forgiveness, and the option of being part of a nurturing community led them to consider the teachings that framed what they were experiencing.

THEOLOGY

New-paradigm Christians represent something of a paradox: on the one hand, they appropriate the technology and cultural idiom of postmodern culture, and, yet, on the other hand, their teaching is rooted in first-century biblical narratives about Jesus and the early Christian church. This apparent contradiction is resolved when one examines their epistemology. They refuse to privilege an Enlightenment worldview that precludes the supernatural. Indeed, they have taken a page out of the manual of science and root their conclusions in experience. More specifically, taking the teachings of Jesus as their point of reference, they pray for the sick and expect miracles, they cast out demons and anticipate mental healing, and they seek encounters with God through visions, dreams, and prophetic utterance by members of the community. In short, they are radical empiricists, generalizing from their experience of God rather than starting deductively with various propositions about God's nature.

While new-paradigm Christians may appropriately be classified as being theologically conservative, they tend to be relatively uninterested in doctrine. Doctrine is something that evolves over time and represents a high-culture tradition of reconciling philosophical theories with religious convictions. In contrast, new-paradigm Christians are doctrinal minimalists. Their focus is on retelling the narratives of the Bible and seeking analogues to the experience of their members. So long as one subscribes to the basic teachings of Jesus and the practice of the early Christians, there is room for debate on the details of interpretation. The goal is for members to have a relationship with Jesus, not to pledge allegiance to a particular catechism or doctrinal statement. The theological method is inductive (starting with one's experience) rather than deductive (ascribing to a set of beliefs). The form of belief is self-consciously primitivist (modeling practice after the Christians of the first century) rather than dogmatic and philosophical. In fact, seldom will one encounter apologetic defenses of the faith that draw on rational argumentation. Instead the focus is on "inviting Jesus into your heart" and witnessing his transforming love.

New-paradigm Christians have taken a step beyond their liberal counterparts in that they seek a unity between mind and body rather than subjugating all knowledge to the realm of cognition. Noncognitive experiences, such as those encountered in worship and moments of religious experience (for example, visions, speaking in tongues, prophetic utterance, and other ecstatic states) are also viewed as legitimate ways of knowing. These Christians are pioneering a new epistemology, one that seeks to move beyond the limitations of the Enlightenment-based understanding of religion that informs most modern critics of religion (such as Hume, Freud, and Marx) and makes room for realities that do not nicely fit within the parameters of a materialistic worldview. Detached reason, they contend, is not the only guide to things ultimate.

I see members of these churches as cultural innovators rather than backward-looking fundamentalists. Far from being premodern, they are challenging the limitations of a purely materialistic worldview. Unlike many within the liberal church tradition who seek truth by demythologizing the Bible, new-paradigm Christians are discovering dimensions of human experience that have been precluded by modern epistemological assumptions. As postmodern primitivists—if such an oxymoron may be used—new-paradigm Christians are involved in a project of resacralizing their world, breaking down the barriers between the sacred and the profane that Enlightenment scholars have imposed. For those caught in a critical, "modern consciousness" (that is, many liberal, mainline Protestants), God and the supernatural are part of one realm, with humans in another and the two seldom interpenetrating. In contrast, new-paradigm Christians are decidedly postmodern in refusing to absolutize the last 200 years of science-dominated thinking. For them, the sacred is active in everyday life. Verification is personal; one need not rely on expert opinion. Indeed, it is liberals who sound defensive when talking about the sacred, constantly relegating God to the realm of the inexplicable. New-paradigm Christians are quite comfortable with an epistemology that breaks with critical thought and interjects God into everyday experience, denying the sacred-profane split.

SOCIAL
ORGANIZATION

One place where the sacred-profane dichotomy has been challenged is in the distinction between lay and professional ministry. As religious movements routinize and become more established, there is a tendency for functions that were previously performed by ordinary members to be assumed by specially certified professionals. In new-paradigm churches, the senior pastor is typically a very strong visionary and may even be somewhat autocratic in exercising veto power, but, simultaneously, many aspects of ministry are entrusted to lay members. In fact, it is the laity who oftentimes suggest new ministries that should be started. Moreover, rather than having this ministry assigned for development to a member of the clergy, a lay member is encouraged to conceptualize the program and then implement it with assistance of other lay members. Clergy members are available for consultation, advice, and support, but the ministry is put in the hands of the people.

In the typical mainline church, not only would the clergy be central to implementing a new ministry but dozens of committee meetings would be required to conceptualize the program and several levels of approval would be necessary before the project could actually be started. By the time the idea would finally be implemented, the need may have changed and the commitment of the person who originally suggested the new ministry may have moderated because of the diffusion of responsibility. Hence, instead of forming committees, new-paradigm churches try to honor lay initiative, take risks with people who have a vision, and offer these individuals clerical support as needed, without overregulating and thereby denting enthusiasm for a project.

The core experience of community in new-paradigm churches is not participation in committee meetings but commitment to a small group meeting—variously called a home fellowship, care group, kinship, mini-church—that convenes in a member's home. Typically there are 10-15 people in one of these groups. They meet weekly, and the focus is usually Bible study or performing a particular ministry in the church. One of the startling things about these groups is the degree of physical interaction between the members. The warmth of human contact that characterized extended family relations of yesteryear is being rediscovered in the mutual care experienced in home fellowships. Men hug each other, and prayer partners touch those who are in pain. One person whom I interviewed said that "Mini-Church is the family that I never had." Indeed, these individuals do what extended families have done for centuries: they share each other's burdens, comfort one another, rejoice in each other's

victories, and acknowledge their dependency by reaching out to grasp one another, dissolving the separation on which autonomous, self-sufficient modern urbanites so pride themselves. They also hold each other accountable to shared standards of behavior.

This focus on intimacy and avoiding centralized bureaucracy is mirrored in the way that churches relate to each other within these movements. Clergy education, to the extent that it exists, is done at the local church level rather than centralizing training in a seminary with professors of theology. The larger megachurches will oftentimes have a pastor training program, but much of the education is done through mentoring, and typically students are simultaneously holding down full-time jobs. Also, there is little attempt to standardize curricula across a movement. While curriculum standardization may have been necessary prior to desktop publishing, now the local church can produce educational materials that are targeted to their specific audience and that reflect the views and values of the people carrying out the instruction.

In addition, there is minimal oversight of local churches by a centralized bureaucracy such as a denominational headquarters or a regional diocesan office. Accountability is informal and typically is to the senior pastor of the mother church from which the daughter church group was spawned. New-paradigm churches have boards of elders, but they are often self-perpetuating and consist of people who have been selected because they support the senior pastor's vision.

Furthermore, appointment is based on maturity in the faith rather than one's professional accomplishments or the size of one's annual donation to the church.

When staff are added to new-paradigm churches, they usually are added by means of internal appointments rather than national searches. Lay people are elevated to full-time clergy because of the fruits of their ministry: for example, they have demonstrated leadership through leading a Bible study in their home that continually needed to be split due to growth, or they were heading a Sunday education program for youths with dozens of lay volunteers. External appointments are eschewed because outsiders lack the genetic code of the community. Each of these new-paradigm churches is unique, and professional skills are not demanded so much as commitment to a vision that is held by the senior pastor. One of the favorite statements of the founder of Calvary Chapel, Chuck Smith, is that "God qualifies the called; he does not call the qualified." Thus, professional degrees are not so important as someone who has demonstrated his or her sensitivity to the leading of the Holy Spirit.

GROWTH OF NEW-PARADIGM CHURCHES

A simple generalization about the viability of any organization is that it needs a marketing strategy for soliciting new members. New-paradigm churches pursue this agenda in a variety of culturally current ways that attract people who otherwise might never enter the door of a church. For example, many people first encountered one of these churches at a church-sponsored athletic event such as a softball game or a concert where Christian music was performed in an idiom to which they could relate. Furthermore, these events were typically held in stadiums, auditoriums, or outdoor venues that were not associated with establishment religion. In addition, the other people who attended these programs were individuals like themselves, in terms of background, age, and appearance.

Prospective members were typically invited to church-related events by someone they respected in their neighborhood or at work. At the event, one or more individuals may have given a short testimony in which they explained how their life had been changed by an encounter with Jesus (or such a testimony may have been given in a personal conversation at a later time with the individual who invited them). Specific issues were identified in these talks or conversations that spoke to some need in the testimony giver's life, and the solution was then posed: a relationship with Jesus. On occasion, the decision to "accept Jesus as Savior and Lord" of the person's life was followed by dramatic changes (for example, throwing away drugs to which he or she was addicted), and at other times, it was the presence of a supportive community (for example, in helping him or her to cope with a failing marriage) that enabled incremental changes in the person's life.

In my congregational surveys, 37 percent of the respondents said that they had had a conversion experience while attending a Calvary, Vineyard, or Hope Chapel church. Interestingly, over a quarter of the individuals I surveyed had grown up in Roman Catholic backgrounds, 10 percent in liberal Protestant homes, and 13 percent without a church affiliation. Furthermore, many of the individuals who joined these new-paradigm churches were, prior to conversion, engaged in lifestyles that were at odds with the values of the churches they eventually joined. For example, a quarter of the respondents said that they had frequently used marijuana or drugs in the past. An equal proportion said that they had often abused alcohol. Over a third said that they had engaged in a pattern of premarital sex. Perhaps surprisingly, the pastors of new-paradigm churches reported such preconversion behavior even more frequently than their members. Hence, joining a new-paradigm church, and the conversion experience associated with it, represented a substantial alternative to the life members had been living. From a market standpoint, one way in which new-paradigm churches are growing is by attracting people who otherwise might not be attending church, or, even if they were attending a church, it was not one that offered them the same type of transformative religious experience that they now are having.

FRANCHISING NEW GROUPS

Churches in these new-paradigm movements typically start in one of several ways. First, an individual has a conversion experience. He is mentored in the faith by someone who is senior in Christian experience. The individual participates in a Bible study and then eventually starts leading a group of his own. It grows and splits because of too many members, and this pattern continues to repeat itself. At some point, this individual responds to a call by the Holy Spirit to start a church. Once again, people respond to the teaching of this individual, only this time he continues his shepherding role over the various Bible studies that have emerged and at some point the people, demanding more of his time, tell him that they will take care of his financial needs if he will quit his secular job. He does, and a church is born, which first meets in rented space; often it moves from place to place as it expands. Eventually the members purchase a piece of commercial real estate.

An alternative pattern is that a church expands and expands and at some point the senior pastor decides to give away 50-100 members of his congregation who live in proximity to each other and are commuting to the church. In addition, he offers his most talented staff member the opportunity to lead this group, aware that not only will he lose financial support for his church but, in addition, he is going to create a leadership vacuum that will need to be filled. While this practice of giving away members and staff may seem like a self-defeating strategy for the mother church, the typical result is that new leadership is developed within the congregation to assume the role of the departing pastor, thus maintaining a dynamic organization that involves new people and new ideas. In addition, very often new people will join the church within a period of a few months, replenishing the ranks but forestalling the need to build additional space to accommodate this growing congregation.

Lest this pattern of new church plants seem too simple, it should be noted that it is also true that many people feel led to start a church but the Bible study they lead never grows beyond a few dozen people. The leaders of the movements I interviewed take a pragmatic view of these failures, indicating that one must look at the fruits of an individual's work in judging whether they are called to ministry or not. In the meantime, however, church planting is happening across the United States and in dozens of countries overseas as people respond to their perception of the Holy Spirit's call. While there is an emerging science of demographic analysis to indicate what constitutes good soil for church planting, perhaps one would not be surprised that some of the most vigorous movements do not rely on social science research but instead depend solely on their vision of God's claim on their lives. Indeed, when churches start hiring demographers to plot their spiritual course, then, most surely, one is witnessing the evolution of a movement into a more routinized stage of its existence.

CONCLUSION

The current growth of new-paradigm churches should not be surprising for several reasons: (1) they have eliminated many of the inefficiencies of bureaucratized religion by an appeal to the first-century model of Christianity; (2) this purged form of religion corresponds to the countercultural worldview of baby boomers, who reject institutionalized religion; (3) with their bureaucratically lean, lay-oriented organizational structure, new-paradigm churches develop programs sensitive to the needs of their constituency; (4) new-paradigm churches offer a style of worship that is attractive to people alienated from establishment religion because it is in their own idiom; (5) this worship and the corresponding message provide direct access to an experience of the sacred, which has the potential of transforming people's lives by addressing their deepest personal needs.

Stated theoretically, upstart sects are always more likely than mainline, established religion to be experiencing growth when measured in percentage terms (see Finke and Stark 1992). Sects are reform movements that appeal to people for whom established religion is no longer meeting their needs, primarily because it has become too routinized, too this-worldly, and too accommodated to the secular culture. What is distinctive about new-paradigm churches is that they are sectarian but not in the stereotypical way of withdrawing from the world. Rather, they embrace modern technology, they intentionally make their boundaries permeable in ways that attract unchurched people, and they blur the sacred-profane dichotomy in their emphasis on the priesthood of all believers.

These postmodern primitivists may be pioneering a new sociological category, where reforming the tradition is not the focus so much as reinventing it in ways that connect the historical message to a medium of expression that has cultural resonance. Hence, members of these postmodern sects are not simply recovering the power of the primitive message; they are changing the way in which their message is expressed (in worship and in organizational form), which is at least as important. Message and medium are much more dynamic and interdependent than the fathers of church-sect theory ever imagined. The problem is not simply that the church type has accommodated to prevailing secular values; the reason denominational Christianity is declining is that it expresses its message in culturally archaic forms. New-paradigm churches, in contrast, appropriate contemporary cultural forms while simultaneously rejecting societal values that they perceive to be corrupt.

Hence, one reason that conservative churches are growing while liberal churches are declining (Kelley 1972) is the following: liberals modernized the message of Christianity, but they left relatively untouched the medium through which the message was being communicated (including both worship forms and organizational structures). In contrast, conservatives—and particularly the new-paradigm churches I have been discussing—modernized (and continue to reinvent on a weekly basis) the medium, but they have refused to tinker with the supernaturalism inherent in the New Testament narratives. Consequently, many mainline churches are preaching a message that is widely available elsewhere in the secular culture, while continuing to worship and organize themselves in ways that lack cultural resonance. This is a deadly formula for institutional existence, and it is why I expect Christianity to look rather different in the next century as members of mainline churches age and die without attracting a new generation of youths to fill their pews. In contrast, new-paradigm churches understand the need to constantly update the envelope in which the message is placed while simultaneously recognizing that life-changing experiences of the sacred are what define a healthy religion.

During my research on new-paradigm churches, I kept rereading William James's classic *Varieties of Religious Experience* (1961), in which he argues that encounters with the divine that restructure human life are the essence of religion. Although James was hostile to organized religion, I believe that churches (as well as synagogues and mosques) that provide access to the sacred at a deep level are more likely to grow and expand in membership, while those that do not offer life-changing, affective religious experience tend, over time, to decline and eventually die. According to this formulation, ritually oriented churches, including those that are part of the mainline denominations, will grow if congregants within these churches are encountering the sacred in profound ways. On the other hand, if ritual has become removed from religious experience, functioning in James's terms as mere secondary accretion, then decline is inevitable.

Notes

1. I wish to acknowledge the support of the Lilly Endowment in funding this research, as well as the contribution of my two principal research assistants, Brenda Brasher and Paul Kennedy.

2. The first attempt to convene religious leaders representing this movement was the National Symposium on the Postdenominational Church, 21-23 May 1996, in Pasadena, California, called by C. Peter Wagner, professor of missions at Fuller Theological Seminary.

3. This quotation is also attributed to John and Charles Wesley and William Booth, although the best-documented attribution is to a biography written by E. W. Broome of a nineteenth-century English preacher, the Reverend Rowland Hill: "He did not see any reason why the devil should have all the good tunes."

4. I am intentionally using the male pronoun in this and other descriptions since almost all of the pastors of new-paradigm churches are male.

References

Ellwood, Robert S. 1994. *The Sixties Spiritual Awakening: American Religion Moving from Modern to Postmodern*. New Brunswick, NJ: Rutgers University Press.

Finke, Roger and Rodney Stark. 1989. How the Upstart Sects Won America: 1776-1850. *Journal for the Scientific Study of Religion* 28:27-44.

———. 1992. *The Churching of America, 1776-1990: Winners and Losers in Our Religious Economy*. New Brunswick, NJ: Rutgers University Press.

Hatch, Nathan. 1989. *The Democratization of American Christianity*. New Haven, CT: Yale University Press.

Hoge, Dean R., Benton Johnson, and Donald A. Luidens. 1994. *Vanishing Boundaries: The Religion of Mainline Protestant Baby Boomers*. Louisville, KY: Westminster, Knox Press.

Iannaccone, Laurence R. 1986. A Formal Model of Church and Sect. *American Journal of Sociology* 94(supp.):241-68.

James, William. 1961. *The Varieties of Religious Experience: A Study in Human Nature*. New York: Collier Books.

Kelley, Dean. 1972. *Why Conservative Churches Are Growing*. San Francisco: Harper & Row.

Miller, Donald E. 1997. *Reinventing American Protestantism: Christianity in the New Millennium*. Berkeley: University of California Press.

Niebuhr, H. Richard. 1963. *The Social Sources of Denominationalism*. Cleveland, OH: Meridian Books.

Troeltsch, Ernst. 1960. *The Social Teaching of the Christian Churches*. 2 vols. New York: Harper & Row.

ANNALS, *AAPSS*, **558**, July 1998

Modernity, the Religious, and the Spiritual

By WADE CLARK ROOF

ABSTRACT: Research on the post–World War II generations offers the opportunity to examine significant trends in American religion that will shape the early decades of the next century. A reclaiming of the spiritual, the more experiential aspects of religion, is at the very heart of these changes for younger cohorts of Americans. The crucial question is, Will religious institutions adapt to these experiential quests and provide the symbolic resources needed to sustain them? Drawing from insights from Ernst Troeltsch, several possible scenarios are described as we move into the new century.

Wade Clark Roof is the J. F. Rowny Professor of Religion and Society at the University of California at Santa Barbara. He is the author, most recently, of A Generation of Seekers *and the past president of the Society for the Scientific Study of Religion. Currently, he is conducting research on generational patterns in religion and culture in the United States.*

RECENTLY, while checking in at a motel in Fresno, California, I happened to notice a stack of brochures describing a seminar on spiritual formation. Had I been in Santa Barbara or Berkeley, I would not have been at all surprised, but this was Fresno, well on the other side of the mountains, far removed from the New Age centers of coastal California. What kind of spiritual seminar would attract the citizens of this more traditional, churchgoing community? I read further in the brochure about the seminar leader, about whom it was written, "In her ministry, she weaves Native American spirituality, Quaker and feminist spirituality into her Hispanic roots with their traditions." Reading further, I discovered that the seminar leader was, lo and behold, a United Methodist pastor from Texas!

All of this is not that surprising, of course, when one thinks about California (or Texas) and its mix of cultures and religions, but for me it provided a moment of reflection on just how far, and perhaps how deep, the spiritual quests of our time now reach. What was most striking was the blatant mixing of spiritual themes in a framework of self-reflexivity and self-discovery. Patchwork spirituality and the metaphor of weaving as a practical religious ideal were being promulgated by a pastor within a mainline Protestant denomination. That I would find this surprising is itself interesting, indicative of something much more subtle, that, as a middle-class white male, I remained bound up within my own Euro-American tradition as if this still naturally set the normative standards for the country.

In this article, I explore two issues related to the current interest in spirituality: the styles of spirituality now emerging among young Americans, and the relation of this spirituality to organized religion. Both bear upon the redrawing of religious boundaries in the late twentieth century. I draw heavily from my own research on the post–World War II baby-boom generation, the lead cohort in American society responsible for so many changes in cultural values and lifestyles. My approach is sociological, concerned more with describing the patterns as they are now developing than with making a normative judgment about them. Ernst Troeltsch's earlier work on church, sect, and mysticism and more recent cultural and religious interpretation provide a theoretical framework for my reflections.

TROELTSCH ON MYSTICISM

We begin with Troeltsch since he gave us categories that have shaped the modern sociology of religion and the study of Christianity in Western culture in particular. Our purpose is not just to lift up his insights about religious forms but also to see how his perspective and categories shed light on the contemporary spiritual scene. I believe they do, and in ways that are crucial to our understanding of organized religion and its future in the years to come.

For Troeltsch, writing early in this century, Christianity could assume any of three basic social forms: the church, the sect, and mysticism. He sought to describe the social expression of fundamental religious impulses. To this end, Christianity's basic social forms were defined as follows: the church embraces the society, or is distinguished by its accommodation to the world; the sect rejects the society and tries to transform the world in keeping with its religious ideals; the mystic is indifferent to the world and to transforming it and is concerned with inward spirituality (Troeltsch 1931). All three forms were regarded by Troeltsch as authentically Christian, each having roots in the New Testament; each also had strengths as well as weaknesses. The three were understood by Troeltsch to exist in tension with one another and never as isolated forms independent from their environments.

It is his third type, mysticism, that most concerns us here. By mysticism, Troeltsch had in mind a "direct, inward, and present religious experience," that is, as commentator Garrett E. Paul (1993, 677) says, something "more internal than external, more individual than institutional, more experiential than scriptural." The church emphasizes the sacraments as mediated through an institution; the sect insists upon personal conversion and strict commitment; but the mystic, who may or may not be linked to a particular religious body, is concerned with inner experience. This type of inward spirituality was attractive to Troeltsch partly because he very much disliked dogmatism and authoritarianism and also, as Paul points out, because Troeltsch

had a profound appreciation for the historical relativity of all social forms of religion.

Though less attention has been given to this inward form of religion than to the other two types, Troeltsch saw mysticism, ironically, as having a distinctive affinity with the emerging modern world of the twentieth century. For one thing, mysticism favors a monistic conception of reality that meshes well with a scientific and rational outlook. A unified worldview arising out of the mystical experience is not burdened with the dualisms, such as mind versus body, that are so frequently associated with the religious establishments. Mysticism emphasizes as well a universal religious consciousness, or a relative stance toward religious truth, and thus a polymorphic conception, or notion that truth may be found in many ways and in many traditions. Mystics transcend conventional religious boundaries and, in so doing, develop a broadened outlook on the meaning of the religious. Affinity with the modern world lies with the trends toward greater individualism and personal autonomy. Modernity has brought with it the breakdown of much tradition and social ascription, thereby freeing the individual to pursue his or her own religious concerns. As the authority of religious institutions declined, Troeltsch foresaw a growing emphasis on inner freedom and personal experience especially among the more literate social classes. In time, this free-reigning subjectivity would lead to what today in our highly subjective culture we refer to as self-development and self-actualization.

Already in his own time, he spoke of mysticism as "the secret religion of the educated classes" (Campbell 1978).

Careful analysis of Troeltsch's work reveals that he spoke of mysticism in a double sense. He saw it as having, as psychologist Ralph W. Hood, Jr., says, a "Janus-faced nature," which helps explain why religious institutions have had ambivalent, mixed responses to the mystical impulse. Commenting further on this point, he writes:

In one sense, mysticism is simply a profound, primary religious awareness of transcendent reality that serves as a human experiential basis for religious institutions and dogmas. Such a mysticism is compatible with almost any dogma or structure and is simply the existential foundation that religion molds into its various social forms. As such it has no unique sociological importance.

He then goes on to say:

In another sense, mysticism as a separate form emerges historically as a deliberate cultivated act of transcendence, often rising in opposition to established religious institutions, if not independently of them. As such, it is an independent religious form, distinct from both church and sect. (Hood 1985, 287)

Mysticism in the first sense, then, is interpreted within a tradition and has the capacity of revitalizing that tradition, whereas in the second sense, mysticism is not contained by institutional boundaries and is looked upon as something that is humanly cultivated. The first is supportive of existing structures; the second breaks away from the establishment.

In the language of contemporary social scientists, there are two crucial variables for describing mysticism: whether it is "religiously interpreted," and whether it reflects an orientation toward transcendence that is more "deliberately cultivated," independently of traditional dogma and sacraments.

Not only do we find both types of mysticism in Troeltsch's thinking—indeed, there is tension between the one and the other, between those religious impulses that devote energy to inward piety, yet within religious structures, and those that break away and create new structures. There is a related tension as well between the individual and subjectivity, on the one hand, and community, history, and tradition, on the other hand. In his own work, this tension is never fully resolved. He saw the rise of a more individualistic, mystical consciousness, yet was suspicious of a "frivolous subjectivity" cut off from symbol, myth, and community. Greater individualism and subjectivity seemed to be inevitable and, in some ways, spiritually promising, yet he questioned whether this was a sustainable religious expression. Thus his theology and sociology are somewhat at odds, in the sense that he envisioned, or perhaps feared, a future that potentially threatened his own Christian vision.

Obviously, Troeltsch had remarkable foresight. He captured something of the religious predicament that is unfolding as we approach the turn of a new century. Perhaps more so than other classical theorists, even Max Weber or Emile Durkheim, he grasped the forces that were reshaping twentieth-century religion and society. To quote Garrett E. Paul again:

Troeltsch, at the beginning of the century, was keenly aware of many trends that became apparent to most observers only at its end: the collapse of Eurocentrism; the perceived relativity of all historical events and knowledge (including scientific knowledge); an awareness that Christianity is relative to its Western, largely European history and environment; the emergence of a profound global pluralism; the central role of practice in theology; the growing impact of the social sciences on our view of the world and of ourselves; and dramatic changes in the role of religious institutions and religious thought. (Paul 1993, 676)

These are themes often associated with late-modern or postmodern thinking.[1] As this century moves to its close, we are faced with a situation in which global cultures and religions are transplanted into our own backyards, in which people are exposed to religious diversity as never before. We are confronted with a pluralism of values, beliefs, and lifestyles, widely celebrated as multiculturalism, calling into question what used to pass as core American values. We are increasingly aware of the fragmentation of life and the lack of overarching, or triumphalist, narratives, myths, or frameworks of knowledge. Even for someone as hesitant as I am to think of myself as postmodernist, it would be difficult not to conclude that Troeltsch anticipated many of the epistemological and foundational issues that have emerged as central to the modernist-

postmodernist debates in recent times.

THE CONTEMPORARY SPIRITUAL SCENE

Turning to the contemporary spiritual scene, the question, simply put, becomes, What do we make of spirituality, its patterns, and its sensibilities today, in light of Troeltsch's views on mysticism and the evolution of the twentieth century? Admittedly, the question calls for careful analysis and sober reflection and judgment. Considering the vast array of phenomena that today are described as spiritual—the rediscovery of Eastern traditions; the Pentecostal, charismatic, and born-again evangelical movements; and, more recently, the many forms of New Age spirituality, Goddess Worship, neopaganism, ecospirituality, and even the latest craze of all-night Generation X raves—we must of necessity paint a picture in broad strokes. William James's "varieties of religious experience" could not be more fitting as a description of the religious landscape in any era than it is today.

What is meant by "spirituality"? It is not an easy word to define, but my preference is in keeping with that of philosopher Peter H. Van Ness, who, in his recent exploration of the term and its meanings, focuses upon a concern for the wholeness of life. To cite Van Ness:

The spiritual aspect of human existence is here hypothesized to have an outer and inner complexion. Facing outward, human existence is spiritual insofar as it intentionally engages reality as a maximally inclusive whole and makes the cosmos an intentional object of thought and feeling. Facing inward, life has a spiritual dimension to the extent that it is experienced as the project of one's most vital and enduring self, and it is structured by experiences of sudden transformation and subsequent slow development. An integration of these inner and outer characteristics is achieved by equating the spiritual dimension with the existential task of discovering one's truest self in the context of reality and cosmic totality. (Van Ness 1992, 13-14)

Based upon the research for my book, *A Generation of Seekers: The Spiritual Journeys of the Baby Boom Generation* (Roof 1993), I conclude that this quest for wholeness is broadly based in contemporary society. More than any other, it was the theme that came through in the hundreds of interviews that we conducted with a random sample of young Americans largely in their thirties and forties. While members of this generation vary greatly in their concerns, the theme is found among Christians as well as non-Christians, among Protestant mainliners and Protestant evangelicals, among New Age adherents, at one end of the spiritual spectrum, and fundamentalists, at the other end. Although these different groups express it differently, what they seem to search for is a sense of wholeness as defined from within their own theological or metaphysical perspectives.

But what kind of wholeness? And is such wholeness possible in the world as we know it today? The wholeness that is sought involves far more, in my judgment, than what popular self-help manuals provide on how to feel good, on finding the inner child, or on women running with wolves. As usual, the popular media simplify heavy existential concerns and turn them into packages of rules and procedures. I believe, however, that this quest involves nothing less than a radical protest against the values and outlook implicit in modernity—the post-Enlightenment, highly rational and scientific worldview of the past several hundred years that has privileged mind over body, technology over nature, innovation over tradition, knowledge over experience, mastery over mystery. Perhaps we fail to realize just how much the parameters of life have changed since the Enlightenment. Modernity involves great risks, far greater than in previous eras, such as nuclear destruction and environmental damage. Modernity creates great insecurities, in part because of the uncertainties of, and lack of control over, contemporary life, in realms ranging from international relations to intimate relations. Modernity alienates, as when people feel cut off from their natural environments, or when the medical establishment concerns itself only with the body and not with the mind and body, or when human life loses its connections with animal life and Earth's ecosystems more generally. Fragmented knowledge and highly specialized institutional sectors lie at the very heart of today's spiritual malaise.

The impact of modernity is far from all negative, of course, even with respect to the wholeness of life. Modernity generates its own counter-responses, not the least of which is a revival of moral and religious orthodoxies. But the quest for wholeness manifests itself in other ways, too, namely, in new modes of consciousness associated with the rediscovery of spiritual roots. "Roots, being underground energies," Matthew Fox writes, "can easily be covered over and covered up" (1981, 2). This means, as Fox himself points out, that spiritual roots are often forgotten, if not violently repressed. Many rich spiritual themes that have long been overlooked because Christian tradition was subjected to the political, economic, and sexual dominance of Western religious structures, are now reappearing. Recognition of the powers of creativity, justice, and compassion, the importance of a new and living cosmology, and a deepening of our imageries of God are, for Fox, such themes. In keeping with his outlook, Western spirituality is of two basic types: one that starts with the experience of sin and espouses a spiritual motif of fall and redemption, and another that looks upon life as a blessing and celebrates a creation-centered spirituality. It is the latter that, in his judgment, has been neglected and that is so desperately needed today: the reaffirmation of a tradition emphasizing humanity's potential and not just its fallenness.

In the American context, too, there is a spiritual dualism embodied in the religious culture the elements of which have long served as checks on one another, but which today is weakening. I refer to the historical tension between mastery and control as a dominant Protestant spiritual theme and letting go, or the spiritual freeing of oneself from all that is beyond one's own power to control and conforming one's mind and heart to the larger flow of powers in the universe. Draw-

ing from Ralph Waldo Emerson and others, this latter influence has emphasized a strong positive conception of the spiritual self as an entity in the process of becoming. Both offer a type of harmony, with mastery and control, in the first instance, leading to collective discipline and the building of a kingdom of God, and letting go, in the second, leading to a vision of infinite possibilities and powers resident within each individual and recognized as one with the powers of the universe, the divine soul. Both express well the "supply-side spirituality" that is deeply rooted in the American experience, as Roland A. Delattre (1990) points out, but it is the second of these, he notes, that has been rediscovered in our time. Because mastery and control have become closely aligned with a culture of consumption in the late twentieth century, letting go offers resources and guidance for recovery in a context in which abundance and acquisition so often lead to pathological results.

Regarding the Western world generally, sociologist Anthony Giddens (1991a) is correct, I think, when he says that modernity forces a "return of the repressed," that is, it arouses the existential concerns of an increasingly reflexive self concerned with the moral meaning of existence. To speak of a reflexive self is to acknowledge that we are not what tradition or family or even our ascriptive social characteristics simply tell us we are but what we make of ourselves in interaction with our cultural heritage. Whether out of choice or because of concerns forced upon us, we make ourselves into people with passions and causes, armed with agendas for social action and resolve for personal change. The peace movement, ecological consciousness, holistic health, feminist movements, animal rights, family values, male bonding, and concern for children are all good examples. Giddens's term for these is "life politics," which clearly has a holistic, or spiritual, meaning. "Reflexive spirituality" is the term I propose, emphasizing a spirituality that is engaging, probing, ever trying to respond appropriately to the challenges unfolding in a changing world.

As a visit to any large bookstore will demonstrate, interest in spirituality in both the sense of life politics and self-reflexivity is pervasive today. If, as Martin E. Marty (1967) says, spirituality as a topic was abandoned in public discourse back in the secular 1960s, then clearly it has returned with a vengeance. On the shelves are found creation spirituality, eucharistic spirituality, Native American spirituality, twelve-step spirituality, Eastern spirituality, feminist spirituality, Earth-based spirituality, women's spirituality, men's spirituality, in addition, of course, to medieval mysticism and any number of Jewish and Christian spiritual traditions. Journey is a major metaphor, second only to recovery, suggesting the crucial importance of spiritual growth as an ideal. Running through much of this literature, and in the non-Christian materials especially, one finds an expanded vocabulary of wholeness, conveyed by such words as "connectedness," "unity," "harmony," "peace," "centeredness." Relationships extend well beyond the human to include the animal kingdom, the ecosystem, and all forms of creation. Wholeness extends to the body, in the sense of both awareness of the body and its needs—such as fitness, diet, and exercise—and awareness of an embodied self that feels, hears, sees, touches, smells, experiences. In the body-centered context, the focus shifts away from dogma and creeds and toward a more personal, more experiential mode of expression. Wholeness is expressed in the more balanced perspective on letting go versus mastery and control, in part a response to so much emphasis upon the latter historically in American culture.

Survey statistics paint a portrait of this contemporary spiritual culture. About a fourth of the young Americans, and even more among the better-educated, whom I surveyed report believing in reincarnation. Sixty percent say one ought to explore differing religious teachings and not stick to a single faith. Equal numbers agreed and disagreed with the statement "All the great religions of the world are equally true and good." A recent study by Hoge, Johnson, and Luiden (1994) of what happened to young people confirmed within the United Presbyterian Church (U.S.A.) back in the 1960s finds, even within this well-established Protestant denomination, high levels of individualism, moral and theological relativism, and willingness to consider other religions. Fifty-five percent of those confirmed agreed that "all the different religions are equally good ways of helping a person find ultimate truth." The title of the study in which these statistics are reported—appropriately enough, *Vanishing Boundaries*—

aptly sums up the situation for a new generation of mainline Protestants.

THE UNANSWERED QUESTION

Now let us return to Troeltsch and to the question arising from his view of mysticism. Recall his observation that there are two types of mysticism, that which is religiously interpreted arising from a religious tradition and that which is deliberately cultivated and not contained within a tradition. This is a crucial distinction, bearing directly upon the issues before us. Put simply, Is religious language as found, say, within mainline Protestantism sufficiently resourceful to provide an encompassing, inspiring worldview for these younger generations of spiritual questers?

The question is not easily answered. Perhaps the best answer is, "It depends." It clearly depends on the continuity and quality of experience within organized religion. Using the language developed by Robert Bellah and his associates in *Habits of the Heart* (Bellah et al. 1985), much depends on whether religion functions as a "community of memory" and thus as a source of familiar language, symbol, and myth. For the loyalists in my study, people who have continued from childhood to the present with some sort of connection with a religious tradition, by and large, religion functions in this way. Roughly a third of the boomer generation continue in some ongoing, engaging way to draw upon traditional religious language for an understanding of themselves and others. These are people who, relatively speaking, know something about the Bible, about Christianity, and about religious history. Compared with many others of their generation, they were far less touched by the moral and lifestyle changes emanating from the 1960s and are more inclined to accept religious authority as vested within an existing institution.

It is from this constituency that many religiously based spiritual movements attract followers—groups like Cursillo, the Navigators, Marriage Encounter, Women Aglow, and Renew. Because these are very traditional groups supplementing Christian teachings, and having to do largely with marriage and family, they are generally regarded as coexisting with, but not substituting for, the churches. They make great use of the mastery and control language and generally regard it as authentically religious. Their appeal lies in the focused attention they bring to a particular sphere of the Christian life. While these groups do on occasion provoke theological and ideological disagreement on such matters especially as abortion and lifestyle freedom, they seem not to raise serious problems of ecclesiology. In addition, many evangelical churches have been quite successful in creating small groups—including a twelve-step counterpart—that cater to journey and recovery spiritual themes. Here they have been able to draw on the post-1960s' quest for self-fulfillment, including overtures to feminist values, and on the more recent cultures of addiction and victimization yet for the most part are able to contain these impulses within the religious institution. The evangelical movement engages spiritual issues through specialized niche ministries to people of varying life circumstances and offers an experiential faith bearing upon, though distinct in emphasis from, the larger self-obsessed culture of which it is a part. By comparison with the more old-line denominations, the evangelical and charismatic churches have largely cornered the market on spirituality.

But when we turn to other boomers, the ties with religion become much more tenuous. A large number of them, and perhaps an even larger number of so-called busters, or Generation Xers, have had little contact with religious institutions since childhood or early youth. Some of them are returnees, who were once religiously active, then dropped out, but are now exploring a traditional religious home; others are seekers, whose quests take them on far-reaching spiritual journeys. The two types are quite different and must be looked at separately.

Returnees often bring with them an open spiritual attitude when they reconnect with churches or synagogues. They are more open to spiritual exploration than are the loyalists, more likely to admit that they find it not at all difficult to combine, say, a belief in reincarnation or the practice of yoga with Christian or Jewish doctrines. Even within the more evangelical Christian community, there appears to be a movement away from orthodox doctrines, toward what James Davison Hunter (1985) describes as a more "copacetic" style of religion (160) or what George Barna (quoted in Dart 1994) de-

scribes as a "big trend toward a diverse and inclusive spirituality." Returnees, both evangelical and non-evangelical, are attracted to small groups within churches where they can, as Robert Wuthnow (1994) says, "share the journey." Many are drawn to voluntary organizations that provide opportunities for specific, hands-on activities, such as Habitat for Humanity, Prison Visitation, and other social service or social justice groups. Some are returning to old-line congregations and finding within their liturgies and traditions spiritual nourishment.

But it is the seekers who are at the cutting edge of the contemporary spiritual quest. Typically, they find religious language to be distant from, and out of touch with, their everyday lives and are more likely to think of themselves as spiritual than as religious. In terms of social profile,

— they are among the more highly educated and often belong to the so-called knowledge classes, which look upon symbols, beliefs, and values as humanly constructed;
— they are highly individualistic and consumption oriented, inclined to select for themselves what they will believe or practice;
— they are mentally mobile in the sense that they can imagine themselves in many settings and circumstances, but often they are not rooted deeply in any, in keeping with what Peter Berger and associates (Berger, Berger, and Kellner 1973) once called "a metaphysical loss of 'home'" (82);

— they frequently subscribe to a multilayered or pastiche-style spirituality that mixes and matches elements from a variety of religious traditions, chosen more for their experiential than their objective-truth value and for their ability to help one to grow as a person; and

— they often move from one spiritual exploration to another, giving the impression of being more interested in the journey than in the destination.

Institutional commitment does not easily follow for many of these people; if they find a voluntary activity that fits their needs, often the commitment is to that particular organization or activity and often only for a short period of time. Generally, my research underscores a widespread fluidity, people's beginning and ending religious activities and affiliation with organizations at a relatively fast pace.

From this we get a picture of contemporary spirituality that fits rather strikingly the late-modern or postmodern conception: loss of the grand narrative; fragmented and relative conception of truth; pessimism about progress; science and rational explanation; and search for truth from many sources. This type of spirituality is driven not just by the failure of the established religions to nurture a meaningful and fulfilling inner life but also by conditions endemic to modernity itself.

Peter Van Ness (1992), whose definition of spirituality as wholeness was already quoted, suggests that interest today in the spiritual, and in spiritual discipline in particular, may well be a response to the diversion and decadence of a consumerist culture. People turn to spirituality perhaps as an act of political resistance, to reclaim their own lives and to bolster their sense of self over against the addictive patterns of consumption on which so much of our corporate capitalist economy rests. Spirituality as a political act is calculated and evaluated, something deliberately cultivated and highly subjective—features, of course, which look a lot like Troeltsch's second type of mysticism. If this is true, then it would appear that there is a substantial—and perhaps growing—constituency for whom the language of organized religion is not especially sustaining spiritually yet who are deeply spiritual or mystical in their own way.

IMPLICATIONS FOR RELIGIOUS INSTITUTIONS

What does all this mean for religious institutions as we enter a new century? One possibility is that contemporary spirituality movements may be a source of renewal for churches, synagogues, mosques, and temples. Such movements can help these communities reclaim their spiritual roots and help restore what Rabbi Abraham Heschel (1966) once called "depth theology" (119). "Depth" implies the weight of tradition, reaching back to the premodern, beyond dogma and particular expressions of faith and institutional form that have come to be taken as normative in more recent times. "Depth" also suggests something collective and not merely personal, that is, common nourishing, a community of memory. "Depth" implies an embracing of the whole person, body and all. To the extent that spiritual roots are reclaimed, religious communities will break out of their cultural captivities and rediscover how much spiritual diversity there is within their own histories. Traditions embodying spirituality in many modes—feminine, ecological, creation, justice, nonviolence—all have roots within Western history. Hence today's spiritual ferment may be less a forging of the new than a reclaiming of the old. Viewed in this way, the challenge for the established faiths is to redefine boundaries so as to encompass and reclaim modes of spirituality that are a legitimate part of their heritages.

A second possibility is that the reclaiming of the spiritual may help in redefining the religious. This is no small feat considering that what is defined as religious has been greatly conditioned by the values, outlook, and transformations of life in the modern period. To cite perhaps the most obvious example, many mainstream Protestant churches have so accommodated modernity by emphasizing creed and doctrine that they have lost the depth and experiential dimensions—emotion, feelings, soul. This loss is compounded by a serious disjuncture between the private and public realms of experience within the more liberal theological traditions, thereby eroding their ability to engage the culture and to sustain a vision of wholeness. Indeed, the revolt against organized religion by many young Americans since the 1960s might be viewed as essentially a reaction to this loss of unity and inwardness. Anything that helps to reclaim these dimensions of a living faith are of crucial significance in transforming the religious institutions.

Yet another possibility is that, with spiritual renewal, there might follow a redrawing of the boundaries of the religious within the culture. Already there are some signs that this is happening. Those religious groups most successful today in reaching out to the boomer and buster generations are the so-called seeker churches—congregations that do not just cater to journey and recovery themes but also engage both personal and cultural issues that touch upon the human spirit. The boundaries of the religious are expanding, being redrawn to include the quests of women, of minorities, of varying lifestyle constituencies, and the wisdom, the languages, and the experiences they bring with them. At one level, this development might appear as simply a marketing strategy, nothing more than the playing out of the latest techniques of the church-growth entrepreneurs. Yet looking at it through Troeltschean lenses, we can postulate a more fundamental shift in religious formation in keeping with the notion of a late-modern or postmodern sensibility, namely, the shift from religion as rooted in a self-contained tradition to religion as linked to individual biographies and drawing from symbols, beliefs, and practices that are reflexively cultivated. Troeltsch's vision of the future seems to have been prophetic: once tradition, or collective memory, erodes, as it has for many people, they experience themselves as individual seekers looking for meaning in connections wherever they can find them, and often in the fragmented experiences people have in the late twentieth century.

My comments are not meant to imply, as some radical postmodernists suggest, that religious tradition has lost all claims on truth in the emerging, new world. Signs, here and there, point to a reclaiming of tradition. But my comments are to suggest that religious institutions must posture themselves differently in the world now emerging. We know about the churchlike pattern of accommodation and of the sectlike pattern of rejecting the culture, but we know far less about how religious institutions should posture themselves in a time of radical mysticism when historical, institutionalized modes of religious interpretation have lost much of their coherence. Today, some commentators suggest that religious communities should declare themselves as aliens in a strange world and intensify the boundaries separating them from the surrounding culture. My own view is otherwise: faith communities should celebrate the life shared by their respective members yet keep the outer boundaries permeable; they should remember their pasts but engage the culture around them and listen always to the spiritual cries of the world; they should claim their heritage but not blind themselves to the wisdom of other traditions. In so doing, these communities may discover—perhaps to their own surprise—that fresh, unanticipated insights may yet come their way.

Note

1. Here is not the place for a lengthy discussion of postmodernist thinking. The French social theorists readily come to mind: Jean-François Lyotard, Michel Foucault, Pierre Bourdieu, and others. For a recent exposition of postmodernist thinking as it applies to American religion, see Ellwood (1994). The term "late modern," as opposed to "postmodern," for describing the current period is used by Giddens (1991b).

References

Bellah, Robert N., Richard Madsen, William M. Sullivan, Ann Swidler, and Steven M. Tipton. 1985. *Habits of the Heart: Individualism and Commitment in American Life*. Berkeley: University of California Press.

Berger, Peter, Brigitte Berger, and Hansfried Kellner. 1973. *The Homeless Mind*. New York: Vintage.

Campbell, Colin. 1978. The Secret Religion of the Educated Classes. *Sociological Analysis* 39:146-56.

Dart, John. 1994. Survey Finds Drop in Evangelicals' Ranks for 2nd Year. *Los Angeles Times*, 13 Aug.

Delattre, Roland A. 1990. Supply-Side Spirituality: A Case Study in the Cultural Interpretation of Religious Ethics in America. In *Religion and the Life of the Nation*, ed. Rowland A. Sherrill. Urbana: University of Illinois Press.

Ellwood, Robert S. 1994. *The Sixties Spiritual Awakening: American Religion Moving from Modern to Postmodern*. New Brunswick, NJ: Rutgers University Press.

Fox, Matthew. 1981. *Western Spirituality: Historical Roots, Ecumenical Routes*. Santa Fe, NM: Bear.

Giddens, Anthony. 1991a. *The Consequences of Modernity*. Stanford, CA: Stanford University Press.

———. 1991b. *Modernity and Self-Identity: Self and Society in the Late Modern*

Age. Stanford, CA: Stanford University Press.

Heschel, Abraham. 1966. *The Insecurity of Freedom*. New York: Farrar, Straus, & Giroux.

Hoge, Dean R., Benton Johnson, and Donald A. Luiden. 1994. *Vanishing Boundaries: The Religion of Mainline Protestant Baby Boomers*. Louisville, KY: Westminster/John Knox Press.

Hood, Ralph W., Jr. 1985. Mysticism. In *The Sacred in a Secular Age*, ed. Phillip E. Hammond. Berkeley: University of California Press.

Hunter, James Davison. 1985. Conservative Protestantism. In *The Sacred in a Secular Age*, ed. Phillip E. Hammond. Berkeley: University of California Press.

Marty, Martin E. 1967. The Spirit's Holy Errand: The Search for a Spiritual Style in Secular America. *Daedalus* 96(1):99-115.

Paul, Garrett E. 1993. Why Troeltsch? Why Today? Theology for the 21st Century. *Christian Century* 110:676-77.

Roof, Wade Clark. 1993. *A Generation of Seekers: The Spiritual Journeys of the Baby Boom Generation*. San Francisco: Harper San Francisco.

Troeltsch, Ernst. 1931. *The Social Teaching of the Christian Churches*. Trans. Olive Wyon. London: George Allen & Unwin.

Van Ness, Peter H. 1992. *Spirituality, Diversion, and Decadence: The Contemporary Predicament*. Albany: State University of New York Press.

Wuthnow, Robert. 1994. *Sharing the Journey*. New York: Free Press.

Book Department

INTERNATIONAL RELATIONS AND POLITICS

BILL, JAMES A. 1997. *George Ball: Behind the Scenes in U.S. Foreign Policy.* Pp. xvii, 274. New Haven, CT: Yale University Press. $30.00.

Former secretary of state Dean Acheson paid 52-year-old statesman George Ball the ultimate compliment in 1971. "Keep on making sense," Acheson wrote. "You've got the field all to yourself." Acheson was serious in his estimation. As presidential adviser, undersecretary of state, and ambassador to the United Nations during the Kennedy and Johnson administrations, the caustic Ball had emerged as a foreign policy sage, a crusty and capable "wise man," a shrewd Illinois lawyer known to have the most envied Rolodex in Washington. Without ever holding an elective office or cabinet post, Ball profoundly affected U.S. Cold War policymaking for the better. Echoing Acheson, Senator William Fulbright noted in 1979 that Ball was "the living American who had been most effective in changing things for the better."

A native-born pragmatist, Ball's calling card was his unflinching candor, a trait that he unleashed on such world leaders as Charles DeGaulle, Jean Monnet, Konrad Adenauer, Abba Eban, and Edward Heath. They all treasured his diplomatic acumen. As James A. Bill, professor of government at William and Mary College, makes clear in *George Ball: Behind the Scenes in U.S. Foreign Policy,* a finely crafted and incisive biography, these accolades were well deserved. Perhaps more than any other statesman of his era, Ball was right on the big issues of the day such as urging President Lyndon Johnson to limit U.S. involvement in Vietnam, working to establish European unity, and trying to reconstruct America's policy toward Israel. He brilliantly managed crises in Cuba, Cyprus, and the Congo. "He was able to link ideals to realities and maintain his focus on the public good," Bill writes. "Those who look to the future of statecraft will do well to understand George Ball's model."

Deviating from traditional biography, Bill devotes chapters to analyzing the essence of Ball's statecraft, including his ability to spot talented second-tier lawyers operating in the bowels of the federal bureaucracy. Often he would promote these unknowns to government positions of responsibility. Meanwhile, Bill's balanced comparison of Henry Kissinger's realpolitik and George Ball's *Phronesis* should be of great interest to all students of international affairs.

Bill had special access to Ball's personal archive and interviewed his subject, and dozens of his associates, many times. The result is a scrupulously researched book, brimming with fresh anecdotes, which is essential reading for anyone interested in the last 40 years of U.S. foreign policymaking.

DOUGLAS BRINKLEY

University of New Orleans
Louisiana

HOLSTI, OLE R. 1997. *Public Opinion and American Foreign Policy.* Pp. x, 257. Ann Arbor: University of Michigan Press. $44.50. Paperbound, $19.95.

Despite continuing evidence of the low level of public information on specific aspects of foreign affairs, Ole Holsti shows that many opinion experts are more likely now than earlier to view public beliefs on American foreign policy as stable, rational, and structured. Employing data on the Soviet Union and Russia, military interventions such as the 1991 gulf war, and trade-related issues, Holsti indicates that public opinion may become a more important factor in forming American foreign policy in the future.

He attributes the new, more liberal outlook on public opinion to a series of systematic studies initiated after the Vietnam war, when the American leadership recognized that both it and the general public were more divided than before on foreign policy issues. In a very readable, systematic, and thoughtful way, Holsti describes this new research. Some of the results are quite surprising.

The evidence shows that differences of opinion between leaders and between members of the general public are structured along similar dimensions. Holsti accepts two of these dimensions: one is militant internationalism (militarism-nonmilitarism); the other is cooperative internationalism (multilateralism-unilateralism). Although leaders and the public share identical positions on some issues associated with these dimensions, they take very different positions on other issues. Leaders are much more willing than the public to use American

troops abroad, to support foreign aid, and to embrace free trade.

The differences between individuals in American society on these dimensions are best explained by partisanship and ideology. Of these two factors, political ideology is more salient than partisanship. Conservatives are much more likely than liberals to support militant internationalism and oppose cooperative internationalism, whereas liberals are much more likely than conservatives to support cooperative internationalism and oppose militant internationalism. These ideological and partisan differences are much more useful in accounting for the differences in opinion on foreign policy than other sociodemographic factors such as generation, age, gender, region, education, and race. The results with regard to these other factors are both weaker and more mixed than the results involving partisanship and ideology.

Holsti acknowledges that "the most notable failure" of ideology and partisanship to explain differences between individuals occurs in issues related to trade. I believe that the failure of the academic community to explain differences of opinion on these economic questions arises because we have not yet developed adequate questions to measure a third dimension that I have called internationalism-isolationism.

WILLIAM O. CHITTICK

University of Georgia
Athens

JEFFREYS-JONES, RHODRI. 1997. *Changing Differences: Women and the Shaping of American Foreign Policy, 1917-94.* Pp. ix, 262. New Brunswick, NJ: Rutgers University Press. Paperbound, $17.95.

Henry Kissinger recently welcomed Madeleine Albright to a Council on Foreign Relations dinner by saying, "We are a fraternity of Secretaries of State." Albright responded, "Henry, I hate to tell you, it's not a fraternity anymore." In this book, Rhodri Jeffreys-Jones shows how women reached the top echelons of power.

In the 1920s, women lobbied for consumer issues like tariff reform and free trade. They were often pacifists like Congresswoman Jeannette Rankin, who voted against entry into both world wars. Jeffreys-Jones examines the stereotypical critique of women: either "iron doves," too gentle to press the nuclear button, or "iron ladies," overcompensating with toughness. Women were vulnerable to the Red smear or sexual innuendo, but the end of the Cold War has undercut the rationale for at least the "parlor pink" charge.

Jeffreys-Jones neatly contrasts Margaret Chase Smith and Bella Abzug. Smith suffered from "breakthrough syndrome," which led her to abandon moderation and call for the use of nuclear weapons in Korea, expanded defense spending, and the Vietnam draft. Defense spending benefited her home state of Maine, but her constituents later rejected her aggressive stance on Vietnam. Jeffreys-Jones views Smith's early hawkishness as political opportunism, but that fails to explain why she held to the hard line until it ended her career.

Bella Abzug emerges as a principled congresswoman, rough-hewn and profane. Her opposition to Vietnam and her commitment to arms reduction led her to call for defense cuts in favor of education and social welfare programs. This emerges as her rational response to the escalating Reagan-era defense budget.

The comparative international focus on women as leaders might have been expanded to consider them as parliamentarians. Jeffreys-Jones finds that American women have been slow to win their share of seats in Congress, but that has recently improved.

One wishes the author had dealt in more detail with women as diplomats. She describes Alison Palmer's efforts to overturn biased State Department rules without explaining how they forced women out of the Foreign Service if they married.

Jeffreys-Jones concludes that the iron doves and iron ladies have dissolved in the mainstream, but there remains a narrowing gap in the way women and men view foreign affairs. The old fraternity can anticipate a slightly different viewpoint from women, but nothing so strange that they should have been excluded from the club for so long.

TERESA A. THOMAS

Fitchburg State College
Massachusetts

AFRICA, ASIA, AND LATIN AMERICA

DUMPER, MICHAEL. 1997. *The Politics of Jerusalem Since 1967.* Pp. iv, 365. New York: Columbia University Press. $29.50.

Michael Dumper has provided a useful addition to the fast-growing literature on the political future of Jerusalem. With both restraint and wisdom, he has devoted most of his work to an explication of the political approaches to the city and their practical implications, rather than to a prescription for what should happen to the city in the course of the unfolding peace process. Drawing upon a range of secondary sources and his own research, Dumper constructs an argument that cogently challenges the status quo. He articulates the need to address the complex lives of the city's inhabitants, along with the vested and evolving interests of Israeli and Palestinian nationalism, Jewish, Christian, and Muslim religious sensibilities, and the broader political forces that are brought to bear on the fate of the city.

Dumper pursues this aim in nine roughly chronological chapters that run the gamut from historical underpinnings to garbage collection and up through international involvement in the peace process. It is appropriate that he does so, inasmuch as the mundane features of everyday life in Jerusalem rest on historical patterns and infrastructures and, in turn, affect the range of policy and practical options open to politicians. He collects the various threads running through these issues into four themes, described in his concluding chapter. The first is that international interest in Jerusalem cannot be ignored. Next is that the religious status of the city imposes limits on sovereign action within and concerning it. The third argument is that Israeli efforts to consolidate control of the city in practical terms have created new problems for governing Jerusalem. The final argument, which is really the book's raison d'être, is that resolution of the issues relating to Jerusalem requires recognition of the Palestinian role in the city.

Dumper's case for the first of these four points has its flaws but is fundamentally reasonable. His final point seems obvious but bears repeating, particularly in light of his third argument, which highlights changes in the city under Israeli rule and the way that they may direct future negotiations. Herein Dumper's sympathies are both useful and problematic. In challenging Israeli policy toward Jerusalem and its tangible expression, Dumper tends to downplay the inherent difficulties in governing a divided and relatively poor city, while at the same time negating some of the self-imposed Israeli limits, and efforts to provide for the welfare of the city as a whole. Despite this, and certain errors or questionable constructions, Dumper is to be commended for his reasoned and even tone. In the third ar-

gument, he draws attention to growth and infrastructure issues (driven primarily by Israelis but by Palestinians as well) that are often ignored but that are being played out with real political consequences and to the detriment of the city itself. For that reason, its readability, and its lack of vitriol, *The Politics of Jerusalem Since 1967* is worthy of attention.

SHAUL COHEN

University of Oregon
Eugene

EUROPE

HANHIMAKI, JUSSI M. 1997. *Containing Coexistence: America, Russia, and the "Finnish Solution," 1945-1956.* Pp. xx, 279. Kent, OH: Kent State University Press. $39.00.

Finnish diplomacy confronted two clusters of problems during the Cold War. One was a function of geography. Finland faced on its eastern flank the immensity of Soviet power. Proximity obligated Finland's leaders to craft a cautious policy to avoid provoking Soviet ire. It could, if aroused, have triggered a decisive Soviet intervention. Whether achieved by military force or subtler means of subversion, an intervention would have destroyed the democratic vitality of the Finnish polity—which in fact flourished throughout the Cold War despite injunctions by Finnish officialdom that the press and pundits not belabor Soviet defects. Intervention by the USSR would also have reduced Finland to subservient status, indistinguishable from that of the Warsaw Pact satellite states.

The second cluster of concerns stemmed from Western, particularly American, ambivalence toward Finland. On the one hand, Western security planners appreciated the geopolitical facts of life that limited Finland's diplomatic maneuverability. Moreover, Western policy-makers did not attribute undue significance to the 1948 Soviet-Finnish treaty of friendship but saw it for what it was: a codified expression of reassurance that so allayed Soviet suspicions that the USSR did not inflict upon Finland severe penalty—in contrast with Czechoslovakia in 1948. In addition, Washington strategists thought initially that the Finnish policy of accommodation provided unhappy Eastern Europe with a more plausible model of future life in the Soviet neighborhood than did contemporaneous Yugoslav defiance.

On the other hand, as the Cold War continued and the division of Europe hardened into two rival camps, U.S. policymakers increasingly faulted Finnish statecraft. It was scored for being overly solicitous of the Soviet Union, of hobbling the cause of rollback. Indeed, Finnish professions of neutrality came to be viewed in Washington with considerable unease. Eventually, the Finnish example of adjustment to Soviet power was read as a harbinger of Western Europe's dark future should the cohesion or determination of the North Atlantic Treaty Organization weaken. An important objective of U.S. policy was therefore to thwart the gravitational pull of Soviet power on irresolute West Europeans—to save them from "Finlandization."

Successive governments in Helsinki had to deflect these criticisms and retain enough American goodwill to deter the USSR from interfering massively in Finnish affairs. This balancing act, played for the highest stakes of national integrity, was managed by the Finns with skill, as described in Hanhimaki's excellent book. He has drawn on a wealth of recently declassified documents of Soviet, Finnish, and U.S. origin to analyze one of the more harrowing struggles for sustainable independence waged by a small country. His portraits of Finnish leaders—notably Paasikivi, Kekkonen,

Fagerholm—are well drawn and give life to some impressive figures only vaguely known to American audiences. Finally, Hanhimaki makes broader and useful points about the nature of Soviet external policy (primarily driven by security logic rather than Marxist ideological commitments), thereby adding interpretive value to his work and contributing handsomely to ongoing debates on early Cold War history.

DAVID MAYERS

Boston University
Massachusetts

UNITED STATES

GILBERT, NEIL. 1997. *Welfare Justice: Restoring Social Equity.* Pp. xii, 216. New Haven, CT: Yale University Press. $25.00. Paperbound, $14.00.

Recent welfare reform legislation has, ironically, stimulated a more serious debate about the nature and scope of social provision in the United States than occurred in the years preceding its passage. In this collection of six essays, Neil Gilbert contributes to this debate by analyzing the "social trends and public policies that fostered inequities in the American welfare state and how these inequities might be addressed." He examines such issues as fairness (particularly in regard to gender and family issues), the expansion of social rights, the growing emphasis on social obligations, the rise of advocacy research, and the privatization of welfare. His concluding essay projects current developments into the next century and articulates a vision of what he terms the "enabling state."

In three essays, Gilbert attempts to define a middle ground in today's often contentious policy debates. (The three other essays are largely arenas for Gilbert to joust with long-standing opponents among feminists and "advocacy researchers," particularly around issues of sexual assault and homelessness. It is not clear how they relate to the book's central theme; moreover, their arguments are often based on a selective and somewhat spurious use of sources.)

Gilbert argues that the U.S. welfare system has strayed from its original purposes as a result of sweeping social developments (changes in the role of women and the nature of family life), the growing emphasis on entitlements, the push for gender equality, and the unforeseen consequences of welfare policies themselves (the rise of single-parent families, adolescent pregnancies). At times, his analysis is both ahistorical and decontextualized. Gilbert repeatedly defines socioeconomic issues, such as economic inequality and poverty and their consequences, in behavioral or cultural terms. He assumes that welfare recipients are not just poorer than the rest of us, but that they are different, too. The key to "restoring social equity," in Gilbert's view, is to shift the nation's philosophy of social protection "from emphasizing rights to clarifying responsibilities." Although he expresses far more compassion for the recipients of services (particularly children) than do most of today's neoconservative social scientists, Gilbert is clearly influenced by Lawrence Mead, Amitai Etzioni, and Charles Murray, whose ideas Gilbert claims "have achieved the status of conventional wisdom in the field."

What is perhaps most striking in a book that seeks "a fairer balance between the right to welfare and the responsibility for self-sufficiency" are its omissions. Despite Gilbert's focus on the centrality of marketplace solutions in the emerging enabling state, he scarcely mentions the effects of economic globalization on wages or job opportunities for U.S. workers. Although he frequently comments on the behaviors of welfare recipients, Gilbert writes nothing about the effects of institutional racism on the structure of the U.S. welfare system and public attitudes about welfare. Gilbert's conception of equity similarly ignores the inequities that currently exist in the nation's tax laws and distribution of government subsidies and that are reflected by the growing inequality of income and wealth. Given the distinctions that Gilbert makes between "taxpayers" and "beneficiaries," his narrow definition of who is "dependent" on government resources, and his acceptance of social control mechanisms as effective instruments of social policy, it is not clear who or what will be enabled in the social welfare system he proposes. Given these omissions, it is unlikely that Gilbert's proposed solutions would be either just or equitable.

MICHAEL REISCH

University of Pennsylvania
Philadelphia

HAMILTON, DONA COOPER and CHARLES V. HAMILTON. 1997. *The Dual Agenda: Race and Social Welfare Policies of Civil Rights Organizations.* Pp. xii, 335. New York: Columbia University Press.

Historically, policymakers in the United States have fought over how to improve the life chances of disadvantaged populations. In *The Dual Agenda*, Dona Cooper Hamilton and Charles V. Hamilton document how mainstream civil rights organizations like the National Urban League (NUL) and the National Association for the Advancement of Colored People (NAACP) were founded on the dual agenda of eliminating racial exclusion and domination (civil rights) and advancing universal social welfare for all disadvantaged populations (social welfare). The authors argue that civil rights organizations accomplished this task by emphasizing social policies such as universal social welfare, full employment, and federal hegemony over all social welfare programs.

According to the authors, by opposing the two-tier system, established by the landmark 1935 Social Security Act, the civil rights organizations anticipated the conflict and controversy surrounding second-tier public assistance. For the 60 years following this act, civil rights organizations fought for the universal social welfare that did not distinguish between social insurance and public assistance. The civil rights organizations fought to universalize social welfare by merging the two tiers of the original act.

Jobs have historically been the "linchpin of the civil rights groups' social welfare agenda." Fair and full employment have been key issues among civil rights organizations since the end of World War II. Several examples clearly suggest a need to revise the view of the agenda of civil rights organizations. During World War II, civil rights organizations fought for African American inclusion in defense industry jobs and related job training. In 1963, Whitney M. Young, the head of the NUL, called for a "Domestic Marshall Plan." In 1978, civil rights organizations supported passage of the Full Employment and Balanced Growth Act, although it "had little resemblance to Hawkins's original bill." In 1991, the NUL proposed a "new Marshall Plan for America" similar to the Domestic Marshall Plan introduced in 1963. Civil rights organizations have repeatedly fought against the race-based efforts to characterize full employment as some form of "racial preferential treatment."

During the 1992 presidential campaign, Bill Clinton presented several proposals that contained various elements of the NUL Marshall Plan for America. The strategy behind the NUL's Marshall Plan and Clinton's various proposals was the "hidden agenda" suggested by Professor William J. Wilson. However, the weight of history rendered the "hidden agenda" strategy problematic. The authors of *The Dual Agenda* note that "efforts to improve the economic well-being of those most in need by emphasizing programs for those already better off . . . became easier said than done."

In this comprehensive treatment of the NUL and NAACP policies, *The Dual Agenda* corrects mistaken perceptions regarding civil rights organizations as race-based advocates and presents the civil rights agenda as a universal agenda for social welfare. Dona Cooper Hamilton and Charles V. Hamilton know more than anyone else about race and social welfare policies in the United States. This important book replaces much fantasy and ideology with fact and historical analysis, demonstrating the consequences of race-based opposition to civil rights and social welfare and its impact on the quality of life for the entire nation. Those who are concerned about the future of American social welfare policy must read *The Dual Agenda* and come to grips with the six-decade struggle of the civil rights movement to establish "more equitable social welfare policies for all the poor in our society."

ANTONIO McDANIEL

University of Pennsylvania
Philadelphia

HYMAN, HAROLD M. 1997. *The Reconstruction Justice of Salmon P. Chase: In Re Turner and Texas v. White.* Pp. xii, 186. Lawrence: University Press of Kansas. $25.00. Paperbound, $12.95.

Until recently, historians have not given Salmon P. Chase a high rating. Dismissed by some as an opportunistic trimmer bent on becoming president, others have viewed his role as chief justice during Reconstruction as one in which the Court was dominated and even intimidated by Congress. Recent biographers have done much to rehabilitate Chase's reputation as a dedicated, antislavery statesman, and the publication of his papers by the Kent State University Press has made him more accessible to scholars and the general public alike. Now, Harold Hyman has effectively challenged the view that Chase's Reconstruction Court years were ineffective and portrays the chief justice as an activist in behalf of former slaves and the permanency of the Union over the states.

In analyzing two key Reconstruction decisions, Hyman has effectively placed them in the context of Chase's whole life. The cases raised the questions of the rights of the former slaves and the status of the Confederate states and as such focused on issues Chase had been concerned with since the 1830s—the legal rights of those held in bondage and the supremacy of the federal government over the states. Elizabeth Turner, a young black woman and former slave, sought her release from an apprenticeship contract, which Chase ruled in a Maryland circuit court decision violated the Thirteenth Amendment because it amounted to a continuation of slavery. In the better-known Texas case, Chase extended protection to bondholders deprived of their property by a state claiming to have seceded from the Union with this memorable opinion: "The Constitution in all its provisions, looks to an indestructible Union, composed of indestructible states." Hyman convincingly ties the two cases together and shows how they brought a climax to Chase's career, even though a Court retreat on these issues, with the chief justice in dissent, began even before Chase's death in 1873.

The book does have its shortcomings. Chase was governor of Ohio for four years: from 1856 to 1859, not from 1855 to 1861. Chase did not serve as senator from 1859 to 1861. He was elected in 1860 but never assumed his seat because of his appointment to be secretary of the Treas-

ury. The author is given to long and cumbersome sentences, and he produces a book that, although designed for the college student, is a difficult read and comprehensible only to those well versed in constitutional law and history. Most important, the study is repetitive, extends well beyond the length necessary, and would have been more appropriate as a journal article. Still, Hyman has produced an important evaluation and appreciation of Chase's significance in post–Civil War issues.

FREDERICK J. BLUE

Youngstown State University
Ohio

WILLIAMS, ROBERT A., JR. 1997. *Linking Arms Together: American Indian Treaty Visions of Law and Peace, 1600-1800*. Pp. viii, 192. New York: Oxford University Press. $29.95.

Some years ago, Robert Williams, a professor of law at the University of Arizona, set out to examine the intellectual foundations of Indian-white relations. The result was *The American Indian in Western Legal Thought* (Oxford University Press, 1990), a rich, meticulous analysis of how Europeans conceptualized and justified their seizure of a continent and their subordination of its peoples.

As he notes in the volume reviewed here, however, Williams had uncovered only the European side of the intellectual encounter. What about the Indians? After all, until the late eighteenth century, Indian power severely limited European action. The Creeks, Iroquois, and others were forces to be reckoned with, controlling hinterland resources, tipping the balance of power among the Europeans through their own choices of alliance, and playing a crucial role in the fur trade economy on which much of colonial prosperity depended. The treaties they made with Europeans were the result of genuine negotiations. What understandings did they bring to the table? This question is the subject of *Linking Arms Together*.

Examining the statements and ritual practices that Indian diplomats introduced into treaty making and other interactions with their European counterparts, Williams detects a number of key themes. Indians conceived treaties as establishing relationships of trust, mutual obligation, and convergent interest between the parties. Indian diplomats often addressed Europeans in kinship terms. This was more than metaphor or courtesy; it underscored the nature of the relationship Indians believed they were entering. They used rituals—often dismissed by Europeans—to sanctify both treaty making and its results. Some of these Indian understandings, argues Williams, such as the notion of trust, have become centerpieces of federal Indian law; the legal heritage of Indian-white relations is partly indigenous.

One of the major achievements of this book is its reconstruction of treaty making as both creative and genuinely bilateral. The more accustomed view sees it as a process in which European power forced reluctant tribes to give up land, authority, and freedom. But until late in the eighteenth century at least, a number of Indian nations used treaty making not only to solve immediate problems but as a tool in forging the cooperative, multicultural, international order they envisioned as a possible and desirable product of the European presence. Of course, European power eventually prevailed. As that power grew, the Indian vision was overwhelmed by the less inclusive notions of the invaders.

Linking Arms Together is neither as detailed nor as rich as Williams's first book, but it remains impressive: an ambitious and deeply suggestive effort to illuminate indigenous thought at the

time of the European encounter and put it back in the history of Indian-white relations and federal Indian law—where it belongs.

STEPHEN CORNELL

University of California
San Diego

SOCIOLOGY

WEGAR, KATARINA. 1997. *Adoption, Identity, and Kinship: The Debate over Sealed Birth Records*. Pp. xv, 167. New Haven, CT: Yale University Press. $22.50.

Often the best way to understand something is to step outside of it. Think of how many of our words for understanding and ways of thinking reflect that: insight, perspective, vision, distance.

To have some new insight, perspective, vision, and distance with respect to the family as an institution, take a look at it from over here in the world of adoption. It is not that adoption itself is not more than worthy of our time and attention, and it is not that we do not have an awful lot to learn about adoption per se, but adoption takes its meaning from family. What is the meaning of family? One way to learn that is to look at family through the lens of adoption.

This is what Katarina Wegar does for us. By taking the relatively esoteric issue of the debate over sealed birth records as her focus, she gives us a view of family, kinship, and identity that is not available from any other stance.

Adoption is an "as if" situation: our children by adoption are ours "as if" born to us. It is a legal fiction, right down to legally faked birth certificates. I have one child by adoption and so possess a legal document placing me somewhere I never was, doing something I know I did not do. "Sealing the records" means that an adoptee has no access to the original birth certificate, the one that names the woman who really did give birth, and that birth mothers have no access to the records of adoption. It is "as if" that child were never born to that woman.

Yet it is not truly "as if." A woman who bears a baby is changed forevermore. And people continue to speak about adoption in ways that they would never speak of birth. A colleague, a seemingly perfectly sensible, educated anthropologist, recently asked me, "How's your adopted daughter working out?" as if she was perhaps a car or a new computer and not a child I had been raising for eight years, since she was eight days old, "as if" she were mine.

Adoption makes us confront "mine" as relationship, "mine" as identity, and "mine" as politics. Rather, to be more accurate and give credit as due, Wegar's reading of the debate around sealed records in adoption makes us confront these issues.

Wegar begins the book by introducing the "difference dilemma," as it is known in adoption, the tension between "as if" and "not really." She shows that in this as in so many public debates, it is the dialogue itself, rather than either side, that expresses the larger social concerns. We believe that kinship is defined by blood or genes, and we believe that kinship transcends body. Adoption plays along that fault line, challenging both understandings of kinship.

Wegar then offers a solid and blessedly brief history of adoption and the sealed-records controversy; a discussion of the role of adoption in the development of social work; and the challenge to professional understandings offered by the search movement. The heart of the book is chapter 4, in which Wegar states, "The debate over adoption reform serves as a symbolic background for conflicting perceptions of the nature of kinship, identity and attachment."

Wegar argues persuasively in this book that while the need to know one's genetic heritage is surely a socially constructed need, that makes it no less real to those denied such information. Equally persuasively, she argues that kinship, relatedness, and attachment are complex and do not lend themselves to simple formulas or simplistic theories.

BARBARA KATZ ROTHMAN

Baruch College and
    the Graduate School
    of the City University
    of New York

ECONOMICS

HEEKS, RICHARD. 1996. *India's Software Industry: State Policy, Liberalisation and Industrial Development.* Pp. 428. New Delhi: Sage. $39.95.

The intellectual ascendance of neoliberalism in the 1970s led to calls for a significantly reduced role for the state in economic development compared to the role prevalent under the structuralist model that had hitherto influenced policymaking in the Third World. Following years of autarkic economic policies, India, too, began liberalizing in the 1980s, a process that accelerated after 1991. As this was also the period when India emerged as the Third World's leading software exporter, Heeks assesses the impact of liberalization on the development of the Indian software industry to draw policy lessons for the effective promotion of the industry. Though his conclusions only reinforce the now widely accepted idea that the state has a crucial role to play in promoting industry through selective intervention to support certain market outcomes, this book will prove valuable to anyone interested in the Indian software industry as it provides the best-researched and most thorough portrait of the industry to date.

Heeks begins by providing an overview of the policies that have enabled software production, especially for export, to grow rapidly. He argues, however, that the quantitative expansion in exports not only masks the likelihood that India was probably a net importer of software until the mid-1990s, but it also belies the limited qualitative transformation in the industry. India remains a supplier of relatively low-paid, labor-intensive programming skills for custom software. While a shortage of experienced personnel prevents the industry from taking on more skilled tasks such as analysis and design, financial constraints prevent it from elbowing its way into the lucrative market for packaged software. Production for export dwarfs production for the domestic market, as the latter is small and dominated by imported packaged software.

For India to go beyond being a mere low-skilled software production base, Heeks calls for policy interventions by the state. On the demand side, the state should encourage the development of the domestic market through greater procurement and by regulating the access that foreign firms have. Besides providing a platform for more competitive exports, a larger domestic market also ensures a wider application of software to improve the efficiency of various economic sectors. On the supply side, the state should encourage the upgrading of local technological capability by supporting research projects; expand training to overcome skill constraints; provide a secure legal environment by enforcing copyright laws strictly; develop new mechanisms to finance the industry; and make appropriate infrastructural investments as in telecommunications.

BALAJI PARTHASARATHY

University of California
Berkeley

VOGELSANG, INGO and BRIDGER MITCHELL. 1997. *Telecommunications Competition: The Last Ten Miles.* Pp. xvi, 364. Cambridge: MIT Press; Washington, DC: American Enterprise Institute Press. $35.00.

This book, part of the American Enterprise Institute's series Studies in Telecommunications Deregulation, provides a comprehensive overview of the current status of local telecommunications competition, the final frontier for the industry, and the likely developments for the future. Vogelsang and Mitchell focus mainly on developments in the United States but also include a useful comparative chapter on events in the United Kingdom that provides several lessons for American policymakers.

The book's strength is in covering well the technological, regulatory, and market economic changes that affect local telecommunications. While there is little new material that will surprise experts, the book does provide telecommunications specialists with a fully comprehensive picture of local competition. Vogelsang and Mitchell give nonspecialists a clear sense of the critical issues, nicely balancing the views of different interested parties without taking sides, and including enough basic material as well as an extensive glossary of telecommunications terms and acronyms.

The authors believe that local competition is likely to succeed within a decade. They explain emerging technologies and how both wholesale and retail forms of competition will work, and they focus on the critical interconnection issue. They note that competition will grow in three overlapping waves of market entry, one moving progressively from long distance to local calling, one from dense urban areas to more rural areas, and the third moving from large to small business customers and later to residential consumers.

The book is timely, as many analysts have questioned why the February 1996 Telecommunications Act has not yet led to much real local competition for most consumers. The authors include an analysis of key Federal Communications Commission decisions made in late 1996 to implement the act. Vogelsang and Mitchell have analyzed these issues for decades, and their wide range of experience and knowledge shows well throughout. Their footnotes often refer to unpublished analyses that provide more detailed estimates of contemporary issues than published sources can.

Given such clear writing and broad scope, only a few criticisms can be raised. While the authors clarify complex congressional, Federal Communications Commission, and state jurisdictional issues and policies, they do not shed much light on telecommunications politics, except as a constraint to achieving optimal economic policies. They also run the risk of having much of what they have outlined here become irrelevant or outmoded in this most rapidly moving industry, where recent mega-mergers and surprise technological shifts can alter the landscape within months. As of 1997, however, their analysis is state-of-the-art.

PAUL TESKE

State University of New York
Stony Brook

OTHER BOOKS

AHLUWALIA, D. PAL and PAUL NURSEY-BRAY, eds. 1997. *The Post-Colonial Condition: Contemporary Politics in Africa*. Pp. xi, 252. Commack, NY: Nova Science. No price.

————, eds. 1997. *Post-Colonialism: Culture and Identity in Africa*. Pp. viii, 242. Commack, NY: Nova Science. No price.

ALDRICH, JOHN H. 1995. *Why Parties? The Origin and Transformation of Party Politics in America*. Pp. xi, 349. Chicago: University of Chicago Press. $48.00. Paperbound, $16.95.

ALLINSON, GARY D. 1997. *Japan's Postwar History*. Pp. xiv, 208. Ithaca, NY: Cornell University Press. $39.95. Paperbound, $14.95.

ASHWORTH, JOHN. 1996. *Slavery, Capitalism, and Politics in the Antebellum Republic*. Vol. 1, *Commerce and Compromise, 1820-1850*. Pp. xii, 520. New York: Cambridge University Press. $64.95. Paperbound, $19.95.

AXINN, GEORGE H. and NANCY W. AXINN. 1997. *Collaboration in International Rural Development*. Pp. 334. New Delhi: Sage. $39.95. Paperbound, $18.95.

AZIZ, ABDUL and SUDHIR KRISHNA, eds. 1996. *Land Reforms in India: Karnataka Promises Kept and Missed*. Vol. 4. Pp. 302. New Delhi: Sage. $32.00.

BARNES, WILLIAM R. and LARRY C. LEDEBUR. 1997. *The New Regional Economies: The United States Common Market and the Global Economy*. Pp. xvi, 189. Thousand Oaks, CA: Sage. $42.00. Paperbound, $19.95.

BENDER, THOMAS. 1997. *Intellect and Public Life: Essays on the Social History of Academic Intellectuals in the United States*. Pp. xix, 179. Baltimore, MD: Johns Hopkins University Press. Paperbound, $14.95.

BENHABIB, SEYLA. 1996. *The Reluctant Modernism of Hannah Arendt*. Pp. xxxviii, 247. Thousand Oaks, CA: Sage. $42.00. Paperbound, $18.95.

BOUCHER, DAVID, ed. 1997. *The British Idealists*. Pp. xlvi, 304. New York: Cambridge University Press. No price.

BRILMAYER, LEA. 1996. *American Hegemony: Political Morality in a One-Superpower World*. Pp. xi, 263. New Haven, CT: Yale University Press. $35.00. Paperbound, $17.00.

BURGOYNE, JOHN and MICHAEL REYNOLDS, eds. 1998. *Management Learning: Integrating Perspectives in Theory and Practice*. Pp. viii, 342. Thousand Oaks, CA: Sage. $85.00. Paperbound, $35.00.

BURMAN, ERICA, ed. 1997. *Feminists and Psychological Practice*. Pp. x, 198. Thousand Oaks, CA: Sage. $75.00. Paperbound, $27.95.

BURNER, DAVID. 1996. *Making Peace with the 60s*. Pp. 295. Princeton, NJ: Princeton University Press. No price.

CASKEY, LARRY. 1997. *Rim of the Wheel*. Pp. 326. Raleigh, NC: Pentland Press. $24.95.

CASTELLS, MANUEL. 1998. *End of Millennium*. Vol. 2. Pp. xiv, 418. Cambridge, MA: Basil Blackwell. Paperbound, $26.95.

CELOZA, ALBERT F. 1997. *Ferdinand Marcos and the Philippines: The Political Economy of Authoritarianism*. Pp. vii, 144. Westport, CT: Praeger. $55.00.

CHALOFSKY, BARRY. 1997. *The Home and Land Buyer's Guide to the Environment*. Pp. ix, 131. New Brunswick, NJ: CUPR Press. Paperbound, $16.95.

COBB, ROGER W. and MARC HOWARD ROSS, eds. 1997. *Cultural Strategies of Agenda Denial: Avoidance, Attack, and Redefinition*. Pp. xiii, 230. Lawrence: University Press of Kansas. $35.00. Paperbound, $16.95.

COHEN, STEPHEN D., JOEL R. PAUL, and ROBERT A. BLECKER. 1996. *Fundamentals of United States Foreign Trade Policy: Economics, Politics,*

Laws, and Issues. Pp. xvi, 311. Boulder, CO: Westview Press. $65.00. Paperbound, $22.95.

COKER, CHRISTOPHER. 1998. *Twilight of the West.* Pp. x, 203. Boulder, CO: Westview Press. $28.00.

COOKE, PAUL D. 1996. *Hobbes and Christianity: Reassessing the Bible in Leviathan.* Pp. xv, 282. Lanham, MD: Rowman & Littlefield. $62.50. Paperbound, $23.95.

CORTRIGHT, DAVID, ed. 1997. *The Price of Peace: Incentives and International Conflict Prevention.* Pp. xiv, 347. Lanham, MD: Rowman & Littlefield. $65.00. Paperbound, $24.95.

COSSA, RALPH A., ed. 1997. *Restructuring the United States–Japan Alliance: Toward a More Equal Partnership.* Pp. xiv, 153. Washington, DC: Center for Strategic and International Studies. Paperbound, $18.95.

CREWE, IVOR and ANTHONY KING. 1996. *SDP: The Birth, Life and Death of the Social Democratic Party.* Pp. xxiv, 611. New York: Oxford University Press. $47.00.

CROUCH, ANTHONY. 1997. *Inside Counselling: Becoming and Being a Professional Counsellor.* Pp. xiii, 184. Thousand Oaks, CA: Sage. $55.00. Paperbound, $19.95.

DORIAN, GARO. 1997. *The Russian Way.* Pp. v, 268. Pittsburgh, PA: Dorrance. $22.00.

DOUGLAS, MARY and BARON ISHERWOOD. 1997. *The World of Goods: Towards an Anthropology of Consumption.* Pp. xxvii, 169. New York: Routledge. $59.95. Paperbound, $17.95.

DREU, CARSTEN DE and EVERT VAN DE VLIERT, eds. 1997. *Using Conflict in Organizations.* Pp. x, 229. Thousand Oaks, CA: Sage. $75.00. Paperbound, $26.95.

ENTELIS, JOHN P., ed. 1997. *Islam, Democracy, and the State in North Africa.* Pp. xxv, 228. Bloomington: Indiana University Press. Paperbound, no price.

EUROMEDIA RESEARCH GROUP. 1997. *The Media in Western Europe: The Euromedia Handbook.* Pp. xi, 265. Thousand Oaks, CA: Sage. $69.95. Paperbound, $22.95.

FALK, PASI and COLIN CAMPBELL, eds. 1997. *The Shopping Experience.* Pp. viii, 212. Thousand Oaks, CA: Sage. $79.95. Paperbound, $29.95.

FEODOROFF, NICHOLAS V., ed. 1997. *Forced Repatriation.* Pp. vii, 217. Commack, NY: Nova Science. $34.00.

FOLEY, MICHAEL and JOHN E. OWENS. 1996. *Congress and the Presidency: Institutional Politics in a Separated System.* Pp. xiv, 432. New York: Manchester University Press. Distributed by St. Martin's Press, New York. $74.95. Paperbound, $24.95.

FRIEDENBERG, ROBERT V., ed. 1997. *Rhetorical Studies of National Political Debates: 1996.* Pp. xiv, 102. Westport, CT: Praeger. Paperbound, $17.95.

GALLHOFER, IRMTRAUD N. and WILLEM E. SARIS. 1997. *Collective Choice Processes: A Qualitative and Quantitative Analysis of Foreign Policy Decision-Making.* Pp. xi, 212. Westport, CT: Praeger. $59.95.

GARG, PULIN K. and INDIRA J. PARIKH. 1995. *Crossroads of Culture: A Study in the Culture of Transience.* Pp. 222. New Delhi: Sage. $23.95.

GLASBERG, DAVITA SILFEN and DAN SKIDMORE. 1997. *Corporate Welfare Policy and the Welfare State: Bank Deregulation and the Savings and Loan Bailout.* Pp. vii, 172. Hawthorne, NY: Aldine de Gruyter. Paperbound, no price.

GOODCHILD, PHILIP. 1996. *Deleuze and Guattari: An Introduction to the Politics of Desire.* Pp. ix, 226. Thousand Oaks, CA: Sage. $69.95. Paperbound, $22.95.

GRANT, ALAN. 1997. *The American Political Process.* 6th ed. Pp. vii, 379. Brookfield, VT: Ashgate. $64.95.

GRAUWE, PAUL DE. 1997. *The Economics of Monetary Integration.* 3d ed. Pp. xiv, 228. New York: Oxford University Press. $78.00. Paperbound, $24.95.

GREEN, CHARLES, ed. 1997. *Globalization and Survival in the Black Diaspora: The New Urban Challenge.* Pp. xiv, 396. Albany: State University of New York Press. Paperbound, $21.95.

HALL, JOHN R., ed. 1997. *Reworking Class.* Pp. xiii, 408. Ithaca, NY: Cornell University Press. $52.50. Paperbound, $19.95.

HECKSCHER, CHARLES C. 1996. *The New Unionism: Employee Involvement in the Changing Corporation.* Pp. xxxiv, 302. Ithaca, NY: Cornell University Press. Paperbound, $16.95.

HEFNER, ROBERT W., ed. 1998. *Market Cultures: Society and Morality in the New Asian Capitalisms.* Pp. vii, 328. Boulder, CO: Westview Press. $76.00. Paperbound, $22.00.

HERRING, GEORGE C. 1996. *LBJ and Vietnam: A Different Kind of War.* Pp. xiv, 228. Austin: University of Texas Press. Paperbound, $14.95.

HETHERINGTON, KEVIN. 1998. *The Badlands of Modernity: Heterotopia and Social Ordering.* Pp. x, 164. New York: Routledge. $75.00. Paperbound, $22.99.

HIBBARD, SCOTT W. and DAVID LITTLE. 1997. *Islamic Activism and United States Foreign Policy.* Pp. xxvii, 137. Washington, DC: United States Institute of Peace Press. Paperbound, $8.95.

HOMBS, MARY ELLEN. 1996. *Welfare Reform.* Pp. xv, 165. Santa Barbara, CA: ABC-CLIO. $39.50.

HORTON, IAN, ed. 1997. *The Needs of Counsellors and Psychotherapists: Emotional, Social, Physical, Professional.* Pp. x, 243. Thousand Oaks, CA: Sage. $65.00. Paperbound, $23.95.

HUMPHREY, CAROL SUE. 1996. *The Press of the Young Republic, 1783-1833.* Pp. xiv, 182. Westport, CT: Greenwood Press. $59.95.

JAMES, HAROLD. 1996. *International Monetary Cooperation Since Bretton Woods.* Pp. xvi, 742. New York: Oxford University Press. $45.00.

JELEN, TED G. and CLYDE WILCOX. 1995. *Public Attitudes Toward Church and State.* Pp. xvii, 189. Armonk, NY: M. E. Sharpe. $50.00. Paperbound, $19.95.

JENKINS, PETER. 1997. *Counselling, Psychotherapy and the Law.* Pp. xii, 340. Thousand Oaks, CA: Sage. $65.00. Paperbound, $25.95.

JENNINGS, JEREMY and ANTHONY KEMP-WELCH, eds. 1997. *Intellectuals in Politics: From the Dreyfus Affair to Salman Rushdie* Pp. viii, 304. New York: Routledge. $69.95. Paperbound, $18.95.

JOFFE, E.G.H., M. J. HACHEMI, and E. W. WATKINS, eds. 1997. *Yemen Today: Crisis and Solutions.* Pp. 284. London: Caravel Press. Paperbound, $24.99.

JOHNSTON, BARBARA ROSE, ed. 1997. *Life and Death Matters: Human Rights and the Environment at the End of the Millennium.* Pp. 350. Walnut Creek, CA: Altamira Press. Paperbound, $23.95.

KAPUR, MALAVIKA. 1995. *Mental Health of Indian Children.* Pp. 348. New Delhi: Sage. $26.95.

KEITH, NELSON W. 1997. *Reframing International Development: Globalism, Postmodernity, and Difference.* Pp. xi, 311. Thousand Oaks, CA: Sage. $56.00. Paperbound, $25.95.

KHAZANOV, ANATOLY M. 1996. *After the USSR: Ethnicity, Nationalism, and Politics in the Commonwealth of Independent States.* Pp. xxi, 311. Madison: University of Wisconsin Press. $24.95.

KLEINE-AHLBRANDT, WILLIAM LAIRD. 1995. *The Burden of Victory: France, Britain and the Enforcement of the Versailles Peace, 1919-1925.* Pp. xiii, 342. Lanham, MD: University Press of America. $66.00. Paperbound, $41.00.

LANGSTON, THOMAS S. 1995. *With Reverence and Contempt: How Americans Think About Their President.* Pp. xv, 180. Baltimore, MD: Johns Hopkins University Press. No price.

LARSEN, HANNE HARTVIG, ed. 1998. *Cases in Marketing.* Pp. xi, 205. Thousand Oaks, CA: Sage. $79.95. Paperbound, $35.00.

LEBEDEV, IGOR. 1997. *Aviation Lend-Lease to Russia: Historical Observations.* Pp. x, 244. Commack, NY: Nova Science. No price.

LEFEVER, ERNEST W. 1998. *The Irony of Virtue: Ethics and American Power.* Pp. xi, 254. Boulder, CO: Westview Press. $26.00.

LICHBACH, MARK IRVING and ALAN S. ZUCKERMAN, eds. 1997. *Comparative Politics.* Pp. xiii, 321. New York: Cambridge University Press. $54.95. Paperbound, $17.95.

LILLY, TERI ANN, MARCIE PITT-CAT-SOUPHES, and BRADLEY K. GOOGINS, comps. 1997. *Work-Family Research: An Annotated Bibliography.* Pp. xviii, 315. Westport, CT: Greenwood Press. $69.50.

LIPSET, SEYMOUR MARTIN. 1996. *American Exceptionalism: A Double-Edged Sword.* Pp. 352. New York: Norton. $27.50.

MACESICH, GEORGE. 1997. *World Economy at the Crossroads.* Pp. x, 138. Westport, CT: Praeger. $49.95.

MACIONIS, JOHN J. and VINCENT N. PARRILLO. 1998. *Cities and Urban Life.* Pp. xxiii, 432. Upper Saddle River, NJ: Prentice Hall. No price.

MACKEWN, JENNIFER. 1997. *Developing Gestalt Counseling.* Pp. ix, 262. Thousand Oaks, CA: Sage. $35.00. Paperbound, $16.95.

MALIK, K. N. 1997. *India and the United Kingdom: Change and Continuity in the 1980s.* Pp. 320. New Delhi: Sage. $36.00.

MARION, DAVID E. 1997. *The Jurisprudence of Justice William J. Brennan, Jr.: The Law and Politics of "Libertarian Dignity."* Pp. x, 177. Lanham, MD: Rowman & Littlefield. $52.50. Paperbound, $21.95.

MAYFIELD, JAMES B. 1997. *One Can Make a Difference: The Challenges and Opportunities of Dealing with World Poverty.* Pp. 508. Lanham, MD: University Press of America. Paperbound, no price.

McDOWELL, GARY L. and SHARON L. NOBLE, eds. 1997. *Reason and Republicanism: Thomas Jefferson's Legacy of Liberty.* Pp. ix, 325. Lanham, MD: Rowman & Littlefield. $67.50. Paperbound, $24.95.

MEARNS, DAVE. 1997. *Person-Centered Counselling Training.* Pp. xvii, 227. Thousand Oaks, CA: Sage. $59.95. Paperbound, $24.50.

MEINECKE, FRIEDRICH. 1998. *Machiavellism: The Doctrine of Raison D'Etat and Its Place in Modern History.* Pp. xlvi, 438. New Brunswick, NJ: Transaction. Paperbound, $27.95.

MELLOR, PHILIP A. and CHRIS SHILLING. 1997. *Re-Forming the Body: Religion, Community and Modernity.* Pp. vi, 234. Thousand Oaks, CA: Sage. $75.00. Paperbound, $26.95.

MISCIAGNO, PATRICIA S. 1997. *Rethinking Feminist Identification: The Case for De Facto Feminism.* Pp. xxiv, 127. Westport, CT: Praeger. $49.95.

MONTGOMERY, JOHN D., ed. 1997. *Values in Education: Social Capital Formation in Asia and the Pacific.* Pp. x, 199. Hollis, NH: Hollis. No price.

MOON, MARILYN. 1993. *Medicare Now and in the Future.* Pp. xvi, 263. Washington, DC: Urban Institute Press. $57.00. Paperbound, $24.00.

MORONE, JAMES A. 1998. *The Democratic Wish: Popular Participation and the Limits of American Government.*

Pp. xiii, 402. New Haven, CT: Yale University Press. Paperbound, $18.00.

MULHALL, STEPHEN and ADAM SWIFT. 1996. *Liberals and Communitarians.* 2d ed. Pp. xxii, 363. Cambridge, MA: Basil Blackwell. Paperbound, $21.95.

OTTOSEN, GARRY K. and DOUGLAS N. THOMPSON. 1996. *Reducing Unemployment: A Case for Government Deregulation.* Pp. 171. Westport, CT: Praeger. $49.95.

PANWAR, J. S. 1997. *Marketing in the New Era: Combating Competition in a Globalizing Economy.* Pp. 277. New Delhi: Sage. $36.00.

PEREIRA, ANTHONY W. 1997. *The End of the Peasantry: The Rural Labor Movement in Northeast Brazil, 1961-1988.* Pp. xxi, 232. Pittsburgh, PA: University of Pittsburgh Press. $45.00. Paperbound, $19.95.

PETERSON, PAUL E. 1995. *The Price of Federalism.* Pp. xix, 239. Washington, DC: Brookings Institution. Paperbound, no price.

PILGRIM, DAVID. 1997. *Psychotherapy and Society.* Pp. xii, 170. Thousand Oaks, CA: Sage. $69.95. Paperbound, $23.95.

PRESTON, P. W. 1997. *Political/Cultural Identity: Citizens and Nations in a Global Era.* Pp. viii, 198. Thousand Oaks, CA: Sage. Paperbound, $26.95.

REEHER, GRANT and JOSEPH CAMMARANO, eds. 1997. *Education for Citizenship: Ideas and Innovations in Political Learning.* Pp. xv, 248. Lanham, MD: Rowman & Littlefield. $65.00. Paperbound, $24.95.

SARAT, AUSTIN and STUART SCHEINGOLD, eds. 1998. *Cause Lawyering: Political Commitments and Professional Responsibilities.* Pp. viii, 560. New York: Oxford University Press. No price.

SAREWITZ, DANIEL. 1996. *Frontiers of Illusion: Science, Technology, and the Politics of Progress.* Pp. xi, 235. Philadelphia: Temple University Press. Paperbound, no price.

SARMA, ATUL, GERRIT FABER, and PRADEP KUMAR MEHTA. 1997. *Meeting the Challenges of the European Union: Prospects of Indian Exports.* Pp. 346. New Delhi: Sage. $38.00.

TESTER, KEITH. 1997. *Moral Culture.* Pp. vii, 164. Thousand Oaks, CA: Sage. $69.95. Paperbound, $23.95.

THOMPSON, KENNETH, ed. 1997. *Media and Cultural Regulation.* Pp. 248. Thousand Oaks, CA: Sage. $75.00. Paperbound, $26.95.

WALTON, HANES, JR. 1997. *African-American Power and Politics: The Political Context Variable.* Pp. xxxvii, 475. New York: Columbia University Press. $45.00. Paperbound, $21.50.

WATSON, JAMES L., ed. 1998. *Golden Arches East: McDonald's in East Asia.* Pp. xvi, 256. Stanford, CA: Stanford University Press. $45.00. Paperbound, $16.95.

INDEX

Travel without good planning, and you're bound *to get lost.*

However far you wander, you need an insurance plan that stays in place. Pick one up from AAPSS and you're covered wherever you go. As long as you're a member, we'll help you find your way to the best of plans, and always at the most competi- *tive rates. If you're less than enchanted with your current insurance carrier, call us at 800 424-9883, or in Washington, DC at 202 457-6820. We promise you'll never get a crumby deal. And you'll never have to go into the woods alone.*

Term Life
Catastrophe Major Medical
Member Assistance
High Limit Accident
Medicare Supplement

INSURANCE FOR AAPSS MEMBERS

This plan is administered by Seabury & Smith, a Marsh & McLennan Company.
The term life plan is underwritten by the New York Life Insurance Company,
51 Madison Avenue, New York, NY 10010, on Policy Form GMR.

RELIGION IN THE NEWS
Faith and Journalism in American Public Discourse
by STEWART M. HOOVER,
Center for Mass Media Research, University of Colorado, Boulder

Since the 1970s, more and more religious stories have made their way to headline news—the Islamic Revolution in Iran, televangelism and its scandals, and the rise of the Evangelical New Right and its role in politics, to name but a few. Media treatment of religion can be seen as a kind of indicator of the broader role and status of religion on the contemporary scene. To better understand the relationship between religion and the news media, both in everyday practice and in the larger context of American public discourse, author Stewart M. Hoover gives a cultural-historical analysis in his book, **Religion in the News.** The resulting insights provide important clues as to the place of religion in American life, the role of the media in cultural discourse, and the prospects of institutional religion in the media age.

This volume is highly recommended to media professionals, journalists, people in the religious community, and for classroom use in religious studies and media studies programs.

**1998 (September) / 224 pages (tent.) / $48.00 (h) (0-7619-1677-6)
/ $22.95 (p) (0-7619-1678-4)**

SAGE PUBLICATIONS, INC. · 2455 Teller Road, Thousand Oaks, CA 91320 · (805) 499-0721 · Fax (805) 499-0871
SAGE PUBLICATIONS, LTD. · 6 Bonhill Street, London EC2A 4PU, England
SAGE PUBLICATIONS INDIA PVT. LTD. · M-32 Greater Kailash Market—I, New Delhi 110 048, India

A8596

RELIGION IN AGING AND HEALTH
Theoretical Foundations and Methodological Frontiers

edited by JEFFREY S. LEVIN,
Department of Family and Community Medicine,
Eastern Virginia Medical School, Norfolk
Foreword by Martin E. Marty

"There is an extensive literature documenting the salutary effect of religion on human health and well-being. Yet, this literature is largely ignored in mainstream medicine and social science. The essays in this book take stock of the empirical studies, reflect on the reasons why they have had such little impact, and provide direction for future reflection and research."
—Journal of Nervous and Mental Disease

"Jeffrey S. Levin's book lives up to its subtitle. It is a solid castigation of researchers who have long ignored the role of religion in late life mental health. . . . Anyone doing quantitative research on religion or health or aging can benefit from this book's suggestions. . . . Author and subject indexes finish off this well-edited book."
—Clinical Gerontologist

How does religion influence one's aging and health? **Religion in Aging and Health** brings together key scholars and scientists from several fields to advance epidemiologic and gerontological research into the role of religion in physical and mental health, psychological well-being, and other psychosocial and health outcomes. The first part of the volume contains four chapters that provide a theoretical context for this field, and addresses such issues as hope, forgiveness, the psychodynamics of faith and belief, and coping. The second part seeks to advance the methodological sophistication of research in this area and emphasizes measurement and design issues and the study of religion, aging, and health among African Americans.

With contributions from such distinguished people as Harold G. Koenig, David B. Larson, Robert Joseph Taylor, and Dan G. Blazer, **Religion in Aging and Health** is essential reading for all those interested in gerontology, psychology, sociology, nursing and health, and social work.

Sage Focus Editions, Volume 166
1993 / 256 pages / $63.50 (h) (54387) / $27.50 (p) (54395)

SAGE PUBLICATIONS, INC. · 2455 Teller Road, Thousand Oaks, CA 91320 · (805) 499-0721 · Fax (805) 499-0871
SAGE PUBLICATIONS, LTD. · 6 Bonhill Street, London EC2A 4PU, England
SAGE PUBLICATIONS INDIA PVT. LTD. · M-32 Greater Kailash Market—I, New Delhi 110 048, India